LIFE AND LIMB

LIFE AND LIMB

A True Story of Tragedy and Survival Against the Odds

JAMIE ANDREW

PORTRAIT

Visit the Portrait website!

· ·

PORTRAIT Piatkus publishes a wide range of non-fiction, including biography, history, science, music, popular culture and sport.

If you want to:
- read descriptions of our popular titles
- buy our books over the internet
- take advantage of our special offers
- enter our monthly competition
- learn more about your favourite Piatkus authors

VISIT OUR WEBSITE AT: www.portraitbooks.com

Copyright © 2003 by Jamie Andrew

First published in 2003 by **Portrait**
an imprint of Judy Piatkus Limited
5 Windmill Street
London W1T 2JA
e-mail: info@piatkus.co.uk

Reprinted 2004

The moral right of the author has been asserted

A catalogue record for this book is available from the British Library

ISBN 0–7499–5007–2

This book has been printed on paper manufactured with respect for the environment using wood from managed sustainable resources

Text design by Paul Saunders

Typeset by Phoenix Photosetting, Chatham, Kent
Printed and bound in Great Britain by
Mackays Ltd, Chatham

To Anna

In fond memory of Jamie Fisher, 1971–1999

Acknowledgements

I am indebted to so many people that I hardly know where to begin. So I'll begin, like this book, with a snowboarding trip to Chamonix. Peter, Inge, Rodney, Jacqui, Jim, Gordon, Jo, Mullion, Francois, Ned, Rowena, Simon, Sam, Gav, Iain, Martin and Alastair, thank you all for helping Anna through hard times and my profound apologies for ruining your holiday. I wish I could have been with you. The same thanks also to Miles Bright and Jules Cartwright. In the PGHM thank you to Blaise Agresti, Gilles Trousselier, Alain Place, Daniel Poujol, Christian Bare-Guillet, Philippe Debernardi, Philippe Pouts, Alain Iglesis and everyone else who played a part, no matter how small, in my rescue. You saved my life guys and I will be forever grateful. Likewise to Pascal Brun and Corrado Truchet at CMBH. Thank you for going the extra mile. In Chamonix Hospital I would like to thank Dr Bernard Marsigny, Rik Verhellen, Guy Allamel, Dr Jérôme Moracchioli, Dr Francois Lecoq, Dr Manu Cauchy and all the other doctors and medical staff involved in my treatment. Once again, you saved my life. I only wish you could have saved your excellent hospital from the meddlings of French bureaucrats.

The nurses, auxiliaries and other staff, all of whom were wonderful to me throughout my stay in Chamonix, are too numerous to mention and many I never knew by name, but I would especially like to thank Pascale Milliet, Dominique Folio and Francine Arrigoni, all of whom remain good friends. Also in the valley I would like to thank Anne Sauvy and John Wilkinson for being so generous with their hospitality. The same goes to Manu and Cécile Cauchy and their kids Alix and Pierrot, and to Sophie and Jérôme Moracchioli, who have all made Anna and me very welcome in their homes. Manu, Alain, Philippe, Jérôme, Francine, Bernard Fontanile, Nicolas Charre, Sophie: it has been a pleasure spending time with all of you in the mountains. Among the staff of the PMR Hospital in Edinburgh, although the PMR itself is no more, my special gratitude goes to Colin Howie, Roddy MacDonald, Helen Scott, Doreen Falls, Joy, the nursing staff of Ward 6, and everyone else who helped make my stay in the PMR as pleasant and as short as possible. At RES thanks to David Gow, Morag Marks, Malcolm Griffiths, Rob Farley, Bill Douglas and everyone else for having the technology to rebuild me. John de Courcy and team, and Peter Arnott and team, thanks for licking me into shape. Geoff Allan and Jamie Gillespie, thanks for being there over the long miles. Gordon Bisset and Alan Forrest, thanks for the job.

My parents, Howard and Catherine, and Anna's parents, Geoff and Sinikka, have all been wonderfully supportive, as have my sister Louise and Anna's brother Thomas. My friends, without exception, have been fantastic over the past few years and I truly know now what friends are for. It would be unfair of me to make an incomplete list but I would like to single out Chris Pasteur for being 'the best'. I am very grateful to Neil Cocker, John Irving, Euan Thorneycroft and Alan Brooke for their help and comments on the text. I would like to offer my most sincere thanks to all of the Fisher family and to Alice Brockington for being so kind to me and for showing me how to have the strength to carry on. Thanks also to Betty Winder for the Kendal mint cake. Finally, my heartfelt gratitude to my wife Anna who is the light of my life and without whom I simply don't know how I would manage.

Climbing Terms

adze(s) – the wedge-shaped rear end of the axe head. The pointed front end is called the pick

arête – a sharp snow or rock ridge

belay – to secure a climber to the mountain by tying the rope off round a rock spike, piton, nut, etc., or by holding the rope through a friction brake (belay device) which is a rock spike, piton, nut, etc. to which climbers secure themselves.

bivvy bag – a waterproof and windproof bag used as a temporary or emergency shelter

brèche – a break or gap in a ridge

chossy – a skiers' term for snow that is broken-up/blocky/crumbly

couloir – a steep chute, which may have snow or ice.

flake(s) – a thin, partially detached piece of rock

'frique/téléférique – a mountain cable car

groove line(s) – a shallow fissure in a rock face

karabiner(s) – a sprung metal clip used to attach a rope to an anchor

météo – French for weather forecast

pitch – a section of a route, up to a rope length in extent

securiste – French for rescuer

séracs – unstable ice pinnacles

stance – a small ledge or foothold where a belay is taken

Contents

Contents

Prologue

The Cosmiques Arête, Aiguille du Midi in the French Alps

THE SNOW SLOPE sweeps up ahead of us, gently at first, then more steeply where it passes between rocky outcrops. Above, our route joins the crest of the ridge and disappears from view, hidden by the projecting rocks.

On all sides the vast mountain chains of the European Alps fill the horizon – range upon range of jagged snowy peaks receding in lines into the distance. Closer at hand, all around us, rise the incredible icy spires of the Chamonix Aiguilles, fairy-tale peaks that are every mountaineer's dream.

'OK,' says Julio. 'You ready? We go,' and he sets off up the slope, vigorously kicking steps in the snow with each swing of his cramponed boots. As soon as the length of rope that joins us comes tight I follow on, placing my feet carefully in the steps he has made. Third on the rope, Manu climbs behind me, patient and controlled.

Before long I'm getting hot and I start to sweat. The sun, which has been hiding behind thick clouds for the past few days, now burns fiercely in the sky and I feel its dazzling rays beating on me from all directions, reflected in the pristine snow. Julio, who does everything with a manner of urgency, sets a fast pace and I'm soon struggling to keep up. The sweat trickles down my brow and into my eyes and my breathing becomes laboured, my lungs heavy in the thin air. I know that we've got all day and there's no particular hurry so I allow the rope to come tight and shout out, 'Lentement! Plus lentement! Slow down!'

For a while Julio relents, but it isn't long before he is straining at the leash again.

Manu laughs. 'Julio, he loves the mountains. When he sees a mountain, he is like a dog that sees a rabbit. You can't stop him.'

So I resign myself to a day of being pulled along in Julio's wake.

The ridge we are climbing is called the Cosmiques Arête, a 1,000-foot-long knife-edge of snowy rocks and ice perched dizzyingly high above the French mountain resort town of Chamonix. The difficulties aren't great but the situation is superb and the interest is sustained throughout the length of the climb. The route finishes on the 3,842m summit of the Aiguille du Midi, a peak accessible by cable car, which adds to the climb's popularity. But today we have the arête to ourselves.

The climbing soon becomes more intricate and I have to use my axe to pull myself up over short bulges and steep sections of ice. On the crest of the arête we weave round massive perched blocks of granite, *gendarmes* guarding the narrow ridge. The drop on either side is breathtaking.

At one point the way ahead is blocked by a deep cleft slicing through the ridge. We make an abseil down into the frozen depths of the cleft, then begin the climb back out the other side. I'm finding the climbing quite awkward now and have to use my feet with care and precision. I jam the pick of my axe into a thin rock crack and torque for purchase, holding my breath as I pull. When I swing the axe into a patch of hard ice the pick slams in to the hilt with a satisfying 'Thock'.

Eventually we come to a wide, level section of ridge, and take the opportunity to have a rest and a bite to eat. I swing my rucksack off my back, push it into the snow and sit down on it. This is a good chance to dry off my legs. The sweat is getting quite uncomfortable.

'Manu,' I ask, 'could you give me a hand here, please?'

Manu unzips the lower part of my overtrousers and pushes them back to reveal the carbon fibre and titanium of my artificial legs.

Prologue

With a click of the release button the left leg comes free and Manu pulls it off and plants it beside me in the snow. He does the same with the right leg, then he helps me peel back the inner socks and silicone liners until my bare stumps are exposed, flushed with heat and dripping with sweat. The relief is enormous and I stretch out and enjoy the feeling of cool air circulating round my hot stumps.

Normally I would take my legs off myself – I like to be as independent as possible – but my right arm, round-ended and handless, is firmly strapped into the socket of my specially modified ice axe. My left arm, like the other three limbs, is also a truncated stump and is gloved up to the elbow so right now I am more or less helpless, reliant on the assistance of Julio and Manu.

I don't mind though. In the two and a half years since I became a quadruple amputee I have come to accept that I can't do everything for myself all the time. I'm just thankful for all the things I can still do. Constantly being indebted to people isn't such a bad thing either. It brings you closer, builds bonds.

I look up and my gaze travels across the distant mountains, rows of pointed white peaks, like teeth, lining the horizon. Instinctively my eyes find my mountain, Les Droites. I scan its serrated summit ridge, settling on the slight dip of the Brèche des Droites, an almost insignificant break in the ridge that will always remain a place of utmost importance in my mind.

In a flash I am back there, clinging to that tiny ledge hewn from ice, hard as granite, the Siberian wind rifling through, piercing the many layers of clothing to my very heart. Jamie is beside me, battling with the driving snow that falls in blankets, digging with all his might.

And Julio is there too, forcing hot tea between my cracked lips, cutting my rope with his sharp knife, signalling to the helicopter which pitches and rolls like a small boat in high seas.

Then my eyes travel down from the *brèche*, trace out the thin ribbon of ice that marks the descent route, a relatively easy descent, down to the glacier below. The descent we never made.

I will always be there, stranded at that terrible *brèche*, with the ice and the wind and the snow. With Julio. With Jamie, the other Jamie – Jamie Fisher – who is gone now for ever.

How did this happen to me? Why? What strange twists of fate have taken me from being the bold, independent, carefree climber I was then to become the bizarre individual I am now, without hands, without feet, intent on proving to myself and to the world that I can go on as before? Could things have turned out any different? Questions I have asked myself a thousand times, ask myself a thousand times a day. Now, back in the mountains that so nearly cost me my life, I am searching for answers.

Today the *brèche* smiles at me serenely in the sunshine. On a day like this it's hard to imagine those desperate scenes of two and a half years ago. Manu laughs as he helps me put my legs back on. Julio scuttles off along the ridge, stamping out a broad track as he goes, till the rope comes tight again.

I stand up, wobble slightly as my stumps settle into the prosthetic legs, and we climb on.

PART ONE

The Edge of the Knife

CHAPTER ONE

Beau Temps

IT WAS SATURDAY, 23 January 1999, and as our bus pulled into the bustling French resort of Chamonix all eyes turned to the mountains. High above us, far above the steeply wooded walls of the Arve Valley, rose the impossible lofty spikes of the Chamonix Aiguilles, glowing white in their winter garb, each one a diamond, shining in an infinite blue sky.

We lugged our cumbersome bags off the coach and onto a waiting shuttle-bus. As the bus wound its way slowly up the valley our group talked excitedly about the snow conditions, what lifts would be open, and the off-piste possibilities. But I stared up at the mountains with a different thought in mind.

We were a large and fluid group of friends, mainly from Edinburgh or with links to Edinburgh, who had taken advantage of a budget airline's last-minute deal to snatch a week's snowboarding and skiing here in the French Alps. Our man on the scene, Miles Bright, had reported back good snow conditions and a week of perfect weather, and those that could get the time off work had grabbed the opportunity to fly out for a short holiday. There were over twenty of us, coming and going at different times during the week, staying in a chalet and a couple of apartments up in Argentière, a satellite resort to Chamonix a few miles further up the valley.

The seven of us arriving now were the vanguard of the group. We were actually supposed to be eight: myself, my girlfriend Anna Wyatt, Jamie Fisher, and five others, but Jamie had unfortunately been left behind at Liverpool Airport.

We were all booked on the 6.00 a.m. flight from Liverpool to Geneva except Jamie who had left it too late and had had to get a ticket for the 6.00 p.m. flight. Nevertheless he joined us on the overnight drive to Liverpool, adamant that there was bound to be a cancellation on the earlier flight.

As it turned out there were quite a few passengers who didn't show up for the flight, so Jamie advanced to the check-in desk to claim his place, but the laconic girl behind the desk was not helpful. Yes, it did appear that there were some free seats, but she couldn't reallocate seats until boarding was closed in case passengers arrived at the last minute. Once boarding was closed she would know if there were any free seats. However, once boarding was closed it would be too late to check in. It wasn't possible. No sir, a manager wasn't available. No sir, there was nothing she could do.

Exasperated, blowing steam out of his ears, Jamie was condemned to pass the day at Liverpool Airport. This would mean arriving in Geneva well after the last bus to Chamonix, but with typical stoicism he assured the rest of us he'd somehow catch us up and graciously waved us goodbye as we filed through to the departure lounge.

That afternoon, the remaining seven of us checked into the chalet, hired snowboards, bought food and met up with several later arrivals from our group, including Stu Fisher, Jamie's dad, who had also come out for a week's skiing. In high spirits we rounded off the day by cooking up a big meal in the chalet and cracking open more than a few bottles of wine to celebrate the beginning of the holiday.

Sunday the 24th dawned another clear and sparkling day. A buzz of excitement charged round the chalet ensuring that nobody lay in bed too long and we were all soon munching baguettes and jam and slurping bowlfuls of tea and coffee. I was beginning to wonder if perhaps Jamie hadn't made it to Chamonix the previous night but suddenly there was a crash of falling skis from the vestibule, the

4

inner door banged open, and there he stood, in a typically dishevelled state, rucksack on his back, trademark grin splitting his face from ear to ear.

As usual with Jamie, there was some story to tell of misadventure and unlikely fortune, much embellished probably, since we'd left him at Liverpool Airport, the details of which I don't recall. He told his tale with relish and took his time for proper effect, but each time he looked up and glanced out of the window I could see a light in his eyes that betrayed his impatience to get up into the mountains.

We dispensed with breakfast and, while the others prepared for a day on the slopes, Jamie and I talked about going climbing.

'It's too good a chance to miss!' extolled Jamie. 'The conditions look perfect and this high pressure is settled in for at least three more days. I'll bet Jules is already up there, on the Croz or the Frêney.'

Julian Cartwright was a friend of ours who was also over in Chamonix at the time.

'I should be able to hook up with him if you want to go snowboarding,' he added as an afterthought. Jamie would never pressurise anybody into doing anything. It always had to be your own choice. I didn't need much persuading though. He was right – it was too good a chance to miss.

'What if we do something that's quite quick?' I said. 'A day or two. Then we can spend the rest of the week boarding.'

'OK, what about the Droites North Face?'

Perhaps a little more than I'd intended, but attractive nevertheless. We'd discussed the North Face of Les Droites in the past and I knew that it was high on Jamie's hit list. I had certainly wanted to do it for ages.

'How long will it take?' I asked.

'If we take the last *'frique* up to the Grands Montets this afternoon we can bivvy in the *'frique* station. It's less than a two-hour walk to the foot of the Droites and we should manage the route in a day and a half.'

'And what about the descent?'

'Quite easy. Down the south side of the mountain to the Couvercle Hut. We should get back to the valley by Wednesday lunchtime. Thursday at the latest.'

I considered Jamie's proposal for a moment. I was very tempted by the thought of taking a plum route like the North Face of Les Droites and Jamie's optimism was convincing.

'OK, yeah, let's do it,' I said. 'The Droites. Excellent. That gives us all day to get ready. I think the last *'frique* goes about four.'

Jamie volunteered to sort the climbing gear out, buy fuel for the stove and food from town, and get a final weather forecast. I wanted to spend the morning snowboarding with Anna, knowing that she would be worried about us going up into the mountains, and I wanted to have some time with her before leaving.

I gave Jamie my climbing gear then Anna and I got our things together, grabbed our snowboards, and with a few of the others headed for the pistes.

Argentière bustled with brightly coloured people, clumping up and down the snowy streets, each person with skis or a snowboard slung over their shoulder. Against the backdrop of picturesque, snow-laden chalets and icy peaks, tanned faces all around smiled from behind mirrored sunglasses, sometimes reflecting the mountains in their lenses. Snatches of conversations in German, French and Italian filled the air and I couldn't imagine a place more the antithesis of Edinburgh in dreary January. This kind of winter break was just what I needed to lift myself out of the seasonal dumps that so often herald the beginning of a new year in Scotland – an injection of action and sunshine to kick-start the season.

However, I was unable to relax that morning and as we rode a shuttle-bus up to the little village of Le Tour, and caught a cable car high up into the fields of snow at the head of the valley, a knot of tension was growing in my stomach. It wasn't that I was particularly worried about the difficulty of the route – it was well within our capabilities. Nor was I unduly concerned about the hazards we would encounter en route, or about the thought of the cold and discomfort we would have to endure during the climb. This feeling was a fusion of all the small niggling doubts and worries that ran through my mind – a general feeling of unease and anticipation. It was as if an electric charge of apprehension was building inside me, like my gut was a capacitor, storing up anxiety. I knew the feeling well for I suffered it before every major route I attempted and knew that it wouldn't go away until the moment I first swung my ice axe at the foot of the climb. Then the electricity would discharge and all that nervous energy would flow out and drive me up the mountain. Until then, however, I would be stuck with this growing sense of angst.

I hoped to point out the peak of Les Droites to Anna from the cable car, but it is a retiring peak and remained hidden behind the massive bulk of L'Aiguille Verte, and the closer Aiguille du Chardonnet. However, we could see the summit of the Grands Montets Téléférique where Jamie and I planned to spend the coming night. We could also see the ugly snout of the Argentière Glacier, spewing its vast jumble of *séracs* and blocks of ice out into the Arve Valley. It would be higher up this glacier, from its calmer upper reaches, that we would begin our climb tomorrow.

Anna turned away from this panorama to face the more amenable ski slopes below us, not relishing the prospect of my imminent departure. The cable car pulled into the station with a clank of metal on metal and we stepped out onto the sunlit piste.

The next couple of hours were spent enjoying some excellent snowboarding. The lovely long runs gave us ample opportunity to practise our technique, carving our turns through beautiful powdery snow. Neither of us were particularly experienced snowboarders but nor were most of our friends and we all had great fun racing down the slopes, sometimes in control, often not, wiping-out regularly in the soft snow, and laughing at each other as we struggled to extricate ourselves from snowdrifts.

Not for the first time in my life, I found myself wishing that I didn't feel so driven to go and climb the mountains. I wished that it was enough to simply be among them, admiring their beauty from the safety of the piste. It would be very pleasant to forget about the climb and spend the week swooping through the snow in the daytime and partying with my friends in the bars and cafés in the evenings. However, there was a hunger inside me that just wouldn't be satisfied with such sanitised entertainment. I felt I had to experience the raw grandeur of the mountains close up, to be involved personally. By their very existence the mountains seemed to be throwing down a gauntlet and I was compelled to take up that gauntlet, to pit myself against nature's wildest invention. In taking up that challenge I somehow found fulfilment. I felt more real. I needed to climb in order to feel alive.

The time came to go. In front of the cable car station Anna and I made our goodbyes.

'Will you be careful?' she pleaded.

'Don't you worry,' I reassured her, 'I'll be back before you know it.'

'Will you wear your sunglasses?'

'Yes.'

'And watch out for avalanches?'

'Yes.'

'And will you remember to drink lots of water?'

I knew that she was worried about me and was trying somehow to help me stay safe by warning me of all the dangers she could think of.

'Don't worry. Everything will be fine.'

'Do you promise?'

'I promise. I'll see you soon, OK?'

'OK. See you soon. Love you.'

'I love you too.'

We kissed, then I hopped into a cable car and waved from the window as it carried me off down the hill.

Back in the valley I found Jamie at the chalet, busying himself with the lightweight petrol stove, sending jets of sooty yellow flame licking towards the kitchen ceiling.

'All right, Fish-face?' I greeted him. 'Are you sure it's a good idea, playing with that in here?'

'I'm just making sure it works all right,' he protested. 'It'd be a disaster if we got up there and found that our stove wasn't working.'

'I suppose so, but perhaps now you know it works you could put it away before you burn the place down.'

Jamie put the stove away, then we had a hurried lunch before getting on with the packing. We agreed that it would be wise to go on the heavy side. Alpine climbers often cut down on weight to the bare minimum in order to be able to travel fast. By sacrificing items like sleeping bags, spare clothes and stove, one can climb super light and super fast, accomplishing one's objective in a day and avoiding a night spent on the mountain. This approach is all very well in the summer but we estimated that due to the length of our intended route, with the short amount of daylight available, and the very low temperature, we would be unlikely to complete the climb and make the descent in a day. We would therefore need gear to survive the Alpine winter night. You don't take chances in the Alps in winter.

Apart from all our climbing equipment, ropes, slings, karabiners, ice screws, ice axes and crampons, we each packed a sleeping bag, a bivvy bag, a sleeping mat, a mug, a water bottle and a spoon. We also took the stove and one pan, Jamie's penknife and food for three days.

I wanted to be sure that I wasn't going to get cold so I took plenty of clothes. I wore one pair of socks, thermal long johns, fleece trousers, two thermal tops, a fleece pullover, a fleece jacket and my mountaineering boots. I packed my down jacket, Goretex overtrousers and jacket, mittens, spare mittens and a balaclava. Jamie took a similar amount of clothing. No chances.

'Did you get the forecast?' I asked as we packed.

'Yeah, it's pretty good. High pressure's settled. Clear again tomorrow and on Tuesday morning. Possibly some snow on Tuesday afternoon, then clear again on Wednesday.'

'Sounds good. Not much snow on Tuesday, I hope?'

'No, just a light band. We should be on the way down by then anyway.'

Time was catching up with us and we were soon rushing about madly to get everything together before the last *téléférique* at a quarter past four. I'd hoped to spend some time sharpening the ice tools but instead threw the file into my sack to do it later on. Hastily I scribbled a note to Anna on a scrap of paper. I drew a picture of a smiling stick man brandishing axes and crampons and below it wrote, 'See you soon xxxx'. I left the note on her pillow.

We left the chalet, pulling the door behind us, and tore up the road to the Grands Montets Téléférique station. Fortunately it was only a few hundred yards from where we were staying and we arrived there breathless with a couple of minutes to spare.

Soon we were being lifted gracefully skyward in a large glass-walled cabin, empty apart from ourselves. The silent motion of this giant elevator was eerie as the snow-covered buildings below us sank out of sight. Jamie gazed quietly out of the cabin window and I turned my mind to the climb ahead of us.

The North Face of Les Droites. At exactly 4,000 metres Les Droites is not one of the highest mountains in the great massif of the Haute Savoie. Nor, when viewed from the south, is it one of the more impressive. On that side Les Droites presents a short and undistinguished face, rising from above the Mer de Glace, and the higher Talèfre Glacier, to a lofty serrated summit blade. It is on its north side, however, that the mountain comes into its own. A great chain of mountains – L'Aiguille Verte, L'Aiguille du Jardin, Les Droites, Les Courtes, L'Aiguille du Triolet and Mont Dolent – form a vast barrier of rock and ice, 10 kilometres long and 1,000 metres high, which walls in the enormous snaking Argentière Glacier on its south side. Each mountain has an impressive and forbidding north face, dropping sheer from the airy ridge to the banked edge of the glacier, but none is more impressive or more difficult to climb than the North Face of Les Droites.

By 1952, the face had been climbed by flanking lines on both sides, but the great challenge of the North Face remained. The face was finally conquered in September 1955 by Philippe Corneau and Maurice Davaille, who took six days to produce one of the best and most difficult mixed routes in the Alps. Modern techniques and improved equipment have reduced the normal time for an ascent to two days. The first true winter ascent of the climb was made in January 1975 by a British pair and this was the feat we hoped to emulate.

In actual fact the climb is well suited to a winter ascent. The mixed rock and ice climbing higher up the face is aided by the presence of a good build-up of winter ice, and during recent warm summers the lower ice field has often melted considerably, rendering the route unclimbable throughout the summer season.

Jamie and I were hoping that with plenty of well-consolidated snow and ice, and with a settled spell of fine weather, we would find the ideal conditions for an ascent of this famous climb.

* * *

Forests of ice-encrusted trees swept by beneath us, their branches twinkling in the afternoon sun. Then there were no more trees, only snow and rocks, and we came to the midway Lognan Station. We changed into another cabin and continued our ascent. Now there was only inhospitable terrain beneath us, jagged rocky ridges and icy gullies falling away out of sight down the mountainside. My ears were beginning to pop as we gained altitude and I swallowed several times to clear them.

We began to slow down as we approached a large tunnel in a rock buttress ahead of us – the site of the top station. The cabin swung gently as it eased into the station and came to a halt. The doors slid open and we got out.

The top station of the Grands Montets Téléférique, at an altitude of 3,250 metres, is almost entirely built into the mountain, on a little rock peak which projects from the great ridge that falls from L'Aiguille Verte down to the Arve Valley. We stepped out onto a large steel terrace and drank in the view.

Across to the north and east, towering over the northern side of the Argentière Glacier, stood the elegant peaks of L'Aiguille du Chardonnet, L'Aiguille d'Argentière, and standing sentry at the head of the glacier, the pyramid of Mont Dolent. The mighty Aiguille Verte, and its smaller monolithic partner Les Drus, swallowed up most of our view to the south, but across to the south-west we could see the greatest glacier in the area, the Mer de Glace. Rising above the Mer de Glace were the crazy, shattered pinnacles of the Aiguilles des Grands Charmoz and the Aiguille du Grépon. Behind them, the solitary spike of L'Aiguille du Midi, and far away in the distance was the bulky white dome of Mont Blanc. To the west and north-west, across on the other side of the Arve Valley, the smaller but jagged Aiguilles Rouges thrust their fingers skyward. All around us the most magnificent peaks of the French Alps glittered and shone in the lazy afternoon sunlight.

A few skiers were still lingering on the terrace before making the last run of the day and we watched them descending the steps from the terrace down to the snowy platform from where the run begins. One by one they clicked on their skis, adjusted their goggles, and schussed off, quickly disappearing out of sight. I imagined the wonderful, rushing pleasure of that descent, arcing down the wide Argentière Glacier, then through pine and fir trees, eventually to arrive, head spinning and breathless, back at the village. Back to a warm chalet, friendly faces, a cosy bar. The knot of anxiety in my stomach tightened and a shiver ran down my spine.

Jamie, happily shouting out the names of all the peaks in view, seemed immune from such thoughts and I said nothing. Les Droites and our route across the glacier to it were still hidden behind L'Aiguille Verte and so Jamie suggested climbing up the ridge above us to a spot that looked like it might offer a sneaky view. We dumped our sacks on the terrace and grabbed our axes.

On the snowy platform we met two men from the ski-patrol who were setting off on a final sweep down the hill. Swarthy, fit-looking guys, with weather-beaten faces, they stopped to ask us of our plans. In broken French we replied that we intended to climb Le Face Nord des Droites.

'Ah oui, bon,' they replied. 'And you know there is forecast some snow on Tuesday?'

'Yes, we know.'

'D'accord. Bon chance!' they wished us. They skied off and we started plodding up the broad snowy ridge.

Unaccustomed to the thin air, I found myself panting heavily as I toiled up the slope on Jamie's heels, and despite the low temperature and the weakness of the evening sun, I soon built up quite a sweat. Fortunately we only had to climb a couple of hundred metres before we arrived at a large platform on the ridge. From the edge of this platform we found we could peer out across the cheerless north face of the Verte and get a sidelong glimpse of Les Droites. Looking, as we were from this vantage, directly across the face we intended to climb, we were unable to pick out much detail. The lower ice field was entirely hidden by a projecting buttress of the Verte but we could see a series of icy grooves higher up which looked fairly continuous and reassured us that the route was probably in condition. The face looked cold and uninviting.

Below us we could see most of tomorrow's approach route, down to the Argentière Glacier, then continuing up the glacier, below the north face of the Verte, to the foot of Les Droites. We took note of the position of some possible false trails in the descent to the glacier, then sat on some rocks and watched the sun sink behind the Aiguilles Rouges.

Warm, flame-red light bathed the surrounding peaks, and they looked like they might thaw with the last rays of the day, but the alpenglow soon faded and we were left alone on the mountainside as the blue chill of night descended.

Quickly we got to our feet and stomped back down the hill to get some dinner and make preparations for the morning.

Jamie got the stove going on a picnic table on the terrace and while he prepared us a large meal of pasta, vegetables, tinned fish and tomato sauce, I got on with sharpening up the ice gear. I suspected we would be encountering some pretty hard ice and wanted all the equipment to be in top order – sharp enough to remove an appendix, as Jamie put it. Besides, I always found there was something therapeutic at such times in engrossing myself in a task of close focus, occupying my troubled mind with simple concentration.

By now the darkness was total, save for the beams of our head torches, and the soft twinkle of lights far away in the valley below. The temperature was dropping sharply and when Jamie had done his stuff, we wolfed down the meal, probably our last hot food for a while, then had a final brew before packing up shop.

I discovered that the main door into the station was still unlocked so we moved inside to avoid a night out in the open. While laying our mats out on the wooden floor and repacking the sacks for the morning we heard the faint sound of a television floating up from somewhere in the building.

On investigation we realised we were sharing our home for the night with two *téléférique* engineers. Every night during the winter season, two engineers have to sleep up there in case the winding machinery is frozen up in the morning. The guys were friendly and didn't mind us sleeping in their building. We chatted to them in their cosy little bothy for a bit and they kindly gave us some water to fill our bottles, saving us from having to melt snow with the stove. Then they wished us well with our climb and Jamie and I returned to our floor to turn in for the night.

CHAPTER TWO

Les Droites

I SLEPT THAT NIGHT, but not deeply, the gnawing contemplation of tomorrow's trials preying heavily on my mind. Attempting to banish all such thoughts from my head, I kept telling myself that this was no unusual sense of foreboding but the normal build-up of anxiety that I suffered before a big climb, an anxiety I had learnt to suffer and ignore, knowing that the rewards of perseverance would make it all worthwhile in the end. Still I slept fitfully.

I thought also about Anna and about our parting earlier in the day. These partings were becoming more difficult it seemed. We'd been seeing each other for nearly three years now and our commitment to one another was growing.

We had first met through several mutual friends at various rounds of social events in Edinburgh where Anna was working at her friend Flo's restaurant, cooking and waiting on tables. The restaurant was just up the street from where I lived and I often found myself glancing casually through the windows as I walked past, hoping to catch a glimpse of the pretty blonde girl with the lovely smile and attractive eyes. Anna, I found out later, would similarly keep an eye on the window in the hope of spotting her friend Chris's skinny climbing mate as he strode down the street.

Eventually, with a bit of a prod from the aforementioned mutual friends who were growing impatient with the lack of proper action, we got together and things took off from there. As the months slipped by and Anna and I began to spend more and more time together, our desire turned to affection and affection grew into passion, and before we knew it we had fallen head over heels in love with one another.

We loved each other's company, shared the same tastes in food, drink and culture, and always got along really well together. A little over a year after we started going out, the tenants who had been staying in my flat moved out and Anna and I moved in together.

Anna wasn't a mountaineer although she had done a bit of rock climbing and some scrambly hill walking. In fact, a few years before I met her, she'd taken a nasty tumble after losing her footing in the snow on the exposed mountain ridge of the Aonach Eagach in the Scottish Highlands. She was lucky to escape that fall with only bad bruising but her confidence had suffered and she had done little on the hills since. Perhaps that partly explained why Anna felt so nervous about me going up into the mountains. I knew that she wanted nothing but the best for me, that she wanted me always to follow my heart, but I knew also that she suffered every minute that I was away, and that in turn made me feel bad about going.

I never managed to reconcile the mixed emotions I felt about leaving Anna to worry while I went away climbing. Pig-headed, I left them unresolved and went anyway, knowing that everything would be fine again when I returned home safely, although each time I went away I felt worse about going. This was the issue that I turned over in my head as I lay on the floor of the *'frique* station that night, trying to sleep.

Jamie too slept little, possibly barely at all. When I opened an eye in the small hours, I saw his dark form pacing about over by the window, silhouetted by the stars. Perhaps he too was feeling the tension, or thinking about his girlfriend, Alice, or perhaps he was just anxious to get going. I didn't ask him but turned over and went back to sleep.

I woke at 5.00 a.m. to the soft roar of the petrol stove.

'Time to go,' said Jamie.

I groaned. 'Do we have to?'

'Yes. Come on.'

'What's the weather?'

'It's the same. Perfect.'

I groaned again. This was always absolutely the worst bit for me. Getting out of a warm sleeping bag into the freezing morning to face the realisation of the previous night's dread. It was enough to make me half hope for bad weather. Then I could roll over and go back to sleep and we could get the first *'frique* down in the morning and go to a café for breakfast and relax. Perhaps sometimes I more than half hoped.

However, the weather was indeed fine and so with one final groan I heaved myself upright and began to get ready.

With a grin and a couple of biscuits, Jamie handed me a steaming brew.

'Come on, you'll feel better once we get moving.'

'Yeah, right. Once I'm wading through knee-deep snow in the dark with a massive great sack on my back. Then I'll feel better.'

'Stop whingeing and get ready.' Jamie was always a good morning person. Always shamelessly bright and cheerful. Me, I hate the mornings. I'll sleep till midday given the chance, and if forced to rise at an unnatural hour, remain stiff and grumpy for a good couple of hours.

We quickly ate our frugal breakfast and got all our gear packed up. Sacks were swung onto our backs, then it was out into the crisp night air, ready for action.

We stopped on the snowy platform to put crampons on and tie into one of the ropes in preparation for the glacier, then set off down the slope we'd spied out the previous evening.

The walk-in started well, the first few hundred metres being downhill through pleasantly soft snow. We soon came down onto the Argentière Glacier and bore to the right to follow it up under the foot of the mighty north face of the Aiguille Verte. Darkness yawned around us, cold and vast. Our route was now gently uphill and we sank in the snow to our knees with each step. We took it in turn to break trail, puffing heavily with frosty breath. I was soon sweating like a pig and cursing my own folly for torturing myself like this.

God, I hate this. I hate it so much.

I felt physically sick with pent-up tension and my body screamed in complaint at such a high level of activity at this unaccustomed hour.

I hate this. I can't even remember why I'm doing this. I feel grim.

Jamie, stomping a trail through the snow in front of me, sang to himself as he laboured, some Dylan number with all the words wrong. 'I was standing by the side of the roooad . . . Paint falling off my shoes . . .'

As we marched, the strong beams of our head torches occasionally picked out a *sérac* looming up ahead of us or a faint shadow in the snow warning of a possible crevasse hidden beneath the surface. We picked our way round these obstacles carefully but on the whole our way was hazard free and we made good progress considering the difficult underfoot conditions.

'We'll meet again someday in the avenooo . . . China loving blues . . .'

We had aimed to reach the foot of the climb just before dawn but daylight, filtering over the horizon, was beginning to creep up on us. As the stars began to wink out one by one, the dark wall of mountain above us slowly began to reveal itself. Huge black buttresses, indiscernible in detail, emerged from the gloom, too monstrous in proportion to comprehend. Between them, silver ribbons of ice and snow hung like sheets, ghostly in the half-light. Far above, the jagged crest of the mountain ridge showed its outline against the lightening sky. The whole sight was completely awesome and quite threatening. A chill of apprehension ran down my spine and Dylan stopped his singing.

We could see the shape of our objective, Les Droites, rising before us now and it wasn't long before we could make out the details of our planned route. The great ice field was unmistakable – a vast white curtain, draped over the bottom half of the mountain. Above it reared the headwall, greatly foreshortened from our perspective, defending the summit ridge. Through the headwall we could make out a number of discontinuous icy rivulets, hinting at breaks in its fortifications through which we might make our escape.

We stopped for a short while to eat some chocolate and discuss our line of attack. Jamie, having climbed Les Droites a year and a half previously by its great north-east spur, was more familiar with the mountain than me, and was able to point out and name many of the different lines that tackle the face: the Ginat Route, the Courneau-Davaille, the Colton-Brooks. We intended to begin up the original Courneau-Davaille route but higher up it would be likely that we would link sections of various routes together, depending on conditions.

We set off again, now up the steepening slope leading to the foot of the face. Half an hour of hard toil brought us to the *bergshrund*, a wide crevasse separating the approach slope from the main face and the first obstacle of our climb. We stamped out a small ledge in the snow just below the *bergshrund* and began to gear up. It was broad daylight by now and I gazed up at the face, rearing impossibly overhead.

There is something fantastic about Alpine peaks – a quality of incomprehensibility and intangibility. Compared to our lowly and lush Scottish hills, which always feel so close and real, the mountains of the Alps seem somehow beyond the constraints of scale, as if they are too big for the eye to take in. The harsh quality of the light lends a feeling of unreality and you have the sensation that the whole scene is merely a painting on a stage backdrop, or a mirage, that might at any moment shimmer out of sight.

The sense of unreality, and the ever-present knot of anxiety in my stomach, made me feel detached and numb, as if I wasn't really there. I geared up like a robot, pre-programmed with the routine, and spoke little to Jamie who was concentrating on what he was doing, intent on getting started quickly. Jamie volunteered to lead off first and I deferred, happy to let him get the ball rolling.

Moving together we traversed upwards and leftwards, following the lip of the *bergshrund*, its dark chasm gaping like a hungry mouth. Soon we came to a point where the gap narrowed and the ice wall opposite appeared climbable. I settled down in the snow beneath the *bergshrund* to belay Jamie's ropes and, without further ado, he set off. Striding confidently across the crevasse, he established himself on some rather rotten-looking ice on the far side. The wall was almost vertical and Jamie had to hold himself in a strenuous position as he swung each axe in turn, usually several times before feeling the satisfying thunk of solid ice beneath the crumbly surface. Pieces of the rotten ice broke off with each blow and clattered away out of sight into the void below. I held my breath as I watched him struggle on, whacking in his axes and kicking in his crampons, slowly progressing up the steep wall. Soon he reached an easing in the angle where he stopped to place an ice screw, holding on precariously to one axe while fumbling with the screw in his other mittened hand. Ice screw in and clipped to the rope, Jamie continued and disappeared over the top of the initial wall, leaving me alone, paying out the ropes and listening for the call to follow.

The ropes snaked their way upwards at a steady pace and a few pieces of ice occasionally tumbled down from above. When there was about five metres of rope left I shouted up a warning to Jamie. A muffled reply floated down. A couple more metres of rope disappeared upwards then there was a pause. After a short while I heard Jamie's voice.

'OK, climb when you're ready.'

'Climbing,' I yelled back, took a deep breath and began climbing.

My heart in my mouth, I strode across the gap and found myself suddenly ensconced on steep ice. Cold and unfamiliar with the new terrain, I moved slowly and clumsily at first, kicking my feet and swinging my axes harder than necessary, knocking off large blocks as I went. My heavy sack tugged at my shoulders, trying to lever me off, and I had to work hard to keep my balance. Fortunately, despite the rotten crust, the ice underneath was good and I was able to get good solid placements for my tools. Unable to linger long on the steep ground, I hurried upwards and it wasn't long before I reached Jamie's ice screw. Gingerly, holding tightly to my left axe, I let go of the right axe, unclipped the karabiner from the rope and unscrewed the small tube of titanium from the ice. With the screw safely clipped to my harness, I drew breath and carried on. The angle relaxed a bit now and with it the quality of the ice improved. Jamie came into view once again, waving to me from his stance cut into the ice slope above. I smiled at him and continued climbing.

When I reached his stance we grinned at each other. I realised then that the weight on my mind had lifted, the knot in my stomach had dissolved, and I suddenly felt a whole lot better. Now I remembered why it was I came here. Now I knew why I forced myself out into the mountains, and suffered the anxiety, the stress, and the discomfort. The extraordinary sense of freedom, of independence from the everyday world, of sheer purity, made it all worthwhile. Exhilarated, I breathed the crisp morning air deep into my lungs and felt the strong throb of blood pulsing in my veins.

I chopped myself a foothold in the ice alongside Jamie while he tied off the belay and passed me the leading gear.

There was no time for dawdling so I set off immediately. We were now in a wide, open couloir, or gully, which led upwards and slightly leftwards to a steeper wall guarding the entrance to the great ice field.

The ice was good now, quite hard and occasionally brittle in places, but mostly firm and yielding to axe picks and crampon points. I began to find my rhythm. Right axe up, left axe up, swinging each one hard enough to bite the ice, but not too hard to risk shattering it. Right foot up, left foot up, trusting each kick of the crampon to give a good foothold. Repeat. Keep the movement smooth, regular and relaxed, conserving energy as much as possible. There was going to be a hell of a lot more of this to come.

After 20 metres or so, I felt the need of some security. I picked out a likely spot for an ice screw placement and cut out a small foothold below it. I then stood up on the foothold and whacked my left axe in nice and firmly. With the pick of my right axe I cut a small notch in the ice, then sank the right axe in securely out of the way and left it, freeing my right hand to place the screw. Fumbling with the karabiner in my large mitten, I managed to remove a screw from my harness. The air temperature was around −10°C and when I held the karabiner in my teeth for a moment I instantly felt it freezing to my lips so removed it quickly. I pushed the threaded end of the screw into my pre-prepared notch and turned. After a couple of false starts it began to bite, squealing satisfyingly as it turned through the ice. Soon it was in to the hilt, nice and tight. Bomb proof. I clipped one of the ropes in to the karabiner, retrieved the right axe, and carried on climbing.

'Runner on!' I shouted to Jamie.

Even with practice, the whole procedure of placing an ice screw takes some time, as does the second man's job of removing it. If we were to make quick progress on this climb we would have to use the screws sparingly. I climbed on until I heard Jamie shout that the rope was running out. I cut myself a small foot ledge, stood on it, and placed two ice screws, tying carefully into them. In the event of one of us falling these were the only pieces of equipment that secured us to the mountain, so for good measure I sank an axe up to the hilt and tied into that too.

'Safe, Jamie!'

I put Jamie on belay and he was soon climbing up to join me.

As he climbed I was able, for the first time that day, to gaze out at our surroundings. The view was incredible. The glacier already looked a long way below us, serene and virginal, a motionless river of whiteness, its smooth surface untouched save for our tiny trail of footprints, just visible to the eye, marching up to the foot of the climb. Ahead stood the majestic peaks of L'Aiguille du Chardonnet and L'Aiguille d'Argentière, bathed in golden morning sunlight. To both sides, sombre north faces sulked in cold shadow, dark and inhospitable. The sun would not see its way to shine on our cheerless face that day. We wouldn't enjoy the warmth of its rays. Still, we could draw comfort from the blueness of the sky and from the radiant landscape around us.

Jamie arrived at the belay enthusing about the quality of the ice, took the leading gear from me, and carried on up. In this way, leap-frogging each other and taking it in turn to lead a pitch, we would continue all day. This meant minimum fuss at each belay stance, maximum speed, and an equal share of the workload.

It was good to be climbing with Jamie again. I had the utmost confidence in him as a partner in the mountains and I felt secure and relaxed climbing with him.

When we'd first met eight years before he was really still a beginner. His father had introduced him to climbing and other outdoor pursuits when he was a child living on the family farm in Zambia and on summer holidays to the European Alps; he and his two brothers were always encouraged in the spirit of adventure.

21

I had often heard Jamie tell the story of how he had first decided that he wanted to be a climber. One day, on a holiday to North Wales, sometime after the family had returned from Zambia to live in Oxford, Jamie and his older brother Mat were sent out on a cycling trip to get them out of their parents' hair for a while. At the time Jamie was about twelve and Mat a more knowledgeable fourteen. They were cycling down Llanberis Pass when Mat called a halt to go and look at a famous rock climb he knew about. It's quite a big hike up to Dinas Cromlech and the final scramble up to the foot of the great open-book of Cenotaph Corner is not straightforward, but the intrepid brothers somehow got themselves all the way to the start of the climb. There they sat and ate their sandwiches, while Mat explained with authority that Cenotaph Corner was the hardest rock climb in the world and that it had only been climbed by one man – Joe Brown. Jamie was very impressed.

Back in the early 1950s when the corner was first climbed, Mat's exaggerated story would have been partly true. Nowadays, however, the climb is a fairly standard trade route, a milestone on any aspiring climber's wish list, but gazing in awe up at that remarkable vertical slash, rising between perfectly smooth rock walls, Jamie believed his big brother, and he resolved to come back one day and follow in the footsteps of the legendary Joe Brown.

So it was that on going to university Jamie embarked on his career as a climber, which he pursued with the passion of religion. It began with rock climbing in Scotland, Wales and northern England, and snow and ice climbing in the north of Scotland. He wasn't unusually talented as a climber, but what he lacked in technique he made up for with a remarkable amount of tenacity and determination. He could be really quite punishing on himself, as witnessed by his large hands which were invariably bloodied and scabbed from extended battles with vicious jamming cracks – his favourite style of rock climb. At some time during this period, Jamie revisited and climbed Cenotaph Corner, but by then its ascent was little more than a formality, and Jamie had other targets in mind.

He soon progressed from UK climbing to Alpine mountaineering where he excelled himself in the ascents of many hard climbs over a number of seasons. In the past few years he had been on a couple of lightweight, low-budget expeditions to the Himalaya, both of which were notable for their audaciousness in choice of objective. The first trip was to the spectacular, unclimbed Shark's Fin on Meru Peak in the Gahrwal Himalaya. The second was to Savoia Kangri in the Karakoram, at the time one of the highest unclimbed peaks in the world. It was unfortunate that both trips were plagued by bad weather and were ultimately unsuccessful in their primary aims, but in failure Jamie gained a lot of valuable experience and there was no doubt that he was destined to be a very successful mountaineer. His career had just begun.

I on the other hand was less ambitious than Jamie. I felt well aware of the fact that in a few months I would be thirty and that I was no longer a youth. As the years passed I was gradually becoming more and more settled and no longer felt such a need to push life to the extremes. Sometimes I found it difficult to square this relaxing of attitude with the burning desire that had fuelled my climbing when I was younger, and felt that I wasn't pushing myself hard enough.

Like Jamie I had begun my climbing as a teenager, inspired by my father's tales of climbing during his university days. As a comfortably off, reasonably intelligent, middle-class adolescent, presented with a world of opportunity and choice, but unable to choose anything in particular, I felt that in climbing I had finally found an activity that was truly worth pursuing. Climbing was so different from anything else I did. It was so much more real, so alive. There was real risk in climbing, real challenge and real beauty. Not like the sports we did at school for which I had no enthusiasm or talent, running knock-kneed around muddy fields chasing a slippery wet ball and being jumped on. In football and rugby I was always the last standing in line to be picked for the team, but I was actually good at climbing.

I wasn't a strong climber, not to begin with anyway, and on steep rock my puny arms would quickly fade and my fingers uncurl, but I knew instinctively how to use my body to its best advantage – to wedge a knee behind a flake or brace shoulders and feet across a groove – and conserve the power in my arms as much as possible. I learnt to read the patterns in the rock and quickly figure out and execute sequences of moves without pausing to deliberate and tire.

Of course I often found the climbing frightening – I wouldn't have enjoyed it so much if I didn't – but I also learnt to measure my ability and accurately judge the difficulties ahead of me. By assessing and managing the risks, and with the occasional injection of youthful recklessness, I was able to push myself regularly to the limit of my capabilities. This exploration of my own boundaries was one of the chief attractions of climbing for me.

Before long, my strength improved as did my confidence and I found I was managing harder and harder climbs. Growing up in the leafy suburbs of Glasgow, I learnt my craft on the local outcrops and surrounding hills with a couple of willing schoolfriends, eventually venturing further afield into the Highlands, the Lake District and North Wales. When I left home for university I met many more like-minded people and it was then that I bought into the climbing dream wholesale, to the sorry detriment of my studies.

Since then I had been climbing at a high standard for over a decade, and had climbed in many countries all over the world. As well as rock climbing, I had learnt the skills of snow and ice climbing and mountaineering, and I had made many wonderful ascents of rock faces and high peaks in far-flung places. My climbing took me to incredible parts of the world, introduced me to all sorts of different people, and brought me experiences that I had never dreamed of as an unseasoned teenager, clambering on the scruffy, graffiti-scrawled little outcrops in and around Glasgow.

Climbing had also led me to my current career. After leaving university I had drifted aimlessly through temporary jobs for a few years, not finding anything that really inspired me. Then I heard from some friends that there was good money to be made by climbers in abseiling, using ropes to access difficult worksites on tall buildings, bridges, oilrigs and the like. So I began work as a rope access technician. I wasn't experienced in the various construction and maintenance tasks that I became involved in, but I learnt fast and was quick and confident on the ropes and soon progressed to supervisor level. The work was often hard and demanding and involved many antisocial hours, but it was also very varied, often spectacular and exciting, and always physical and rewarding. I now worked for an Edinburgh-based firm and divided my time between supervising jobs on the ropes, and teaching new technicians in the company's training facility. Climbing was now part of every aspect of my life.

We climbed for a couple more pitches up the wide couloir until it brought us to the steeper section and an apparent impasse. For a while we thought the way ahead might be blocked, but, hidden from below, a smaller gully, narrow with rocky walls, snuck its way leftwards out of the cul-de-sac. This provided the key to gaining the ice field.

The gully reminded me a little of Point Five Gully on Ben Nevis, back home in Scotland. It was steeper than the previous pitches had been and the strain on arms and shoulders was great, but it soon yielded to Jamie's strenuous assault and before long we were both standing in awe at the foot of the great ice field.

It was a vast expanse of blue-white ice, about 500 metres high and 400 metres wide, sloping upwards at about 60 degrees. Its surface was rippled by dozens of vertical flutes and runnels, caused by the scouring action of snow and ice falling from above. Too great to suffer significant melting during the summer, the field survives, cloaking the foot of Les Droites for season after season.

Looking up at this huge ocean of ice and the menacing headwall above made us feel quite small. We paused to drink some water from our bottles and eat a few biscuits – our second breakfast – then Jamie, in his practical manner, broke the inertia.

'Right then. Let's deal with it.'

We set off. Pitch after pitch of fairly repetitive climbing followed, never extremely difficult but never easy. It was a case of getting our heads down and working at it, really hard graft, trying to cover as much ground as possible before nightfall. In places the ice was iron hard and so we weaved in and out of the shallow flutes and runnels, trying to pick out the lines of softer ice. Generally the softer stuff was white and bubbly in appearance, as opposed to the blues and greens of the harder water ice or, tougher still, the almost impenetrable grey ice.

In this way we progressed, slowly but surely, in a fairly direct line up the ice field. The climbing was enjoyable, but it was also very wearing, especially on the calf muscles, which bear the brunt of the strain when standing on the front points of crampons. There was never any let-up in the slope, the ice field being unrelenting in angle and unbroken by ledges or rocks. We couldn't cut ledges large enough to be of any relief to aching calves due to the very hard nature of the sub-surface ice. The best we could do was to cut out small footholds at each belay stance, and lean back in our harnesses, hopping from foot to foot, in an attempt to rest each leg in turn.

We didn't chat much, mainly because we spent very little time together, one or other of us always climbing while the other belayed. We both kept shouting to a minimum. When we passed each other on the belay stances we would exchange a few cheery words and maybe discuss particulars of the route or some other technical detail, but mostly we remained quiet, each secure in the knowledge that the other was equally invigorated by the fantastic surroundings. Exaltation was unnecessary, superlatives inadequate.

Belaying Jamie up one pitch, I leaned back in my harness and listened to the sound of the mountain. Apart from the light tinkle of ice falling from Jamie's axes 30 metres below, the silence was complete. Absolute silence. There wasn't a breath of wind, nor was there a living creature to be seen.

Then, drifting out of the still air, came a faint sound, a high-pitched buzz. I scanned the valley and at first didn't see anything. Then, there it was! Far below us, floating over the glacier, a tiny single-engine plane, looking for all the world like a child's toy. Jamie turned to watch it as it cruised away down the valley and out of sight, before returning to his work. Tourists probably, enjoying a spectacular sight-seeing flight.

It reminded me of another time, another climb, a couple of summers previously when Jamie and I, and two other friends, were on the second day of the Walker Spur on the Grandes Jorasses, not far from where we were now. We were high up on the spur, approaching the summit, when a helicopter thundered into view and bore right down on us. It hovered only yards away from us so that we could clearly see its passengers, a rich-looking couple, he in a smart suit and she in a fur coat. The helicopter lingered long enough for the couple to get a good view of us climbers, and then buzzed off, leaving us once again to the peace of the mountains. I remember at the time feeling strangely violated by this intrusion, that our hard-earned privacy had been disturbed. With hindsight though, I suppose that it is us climbers, who use the facilities in the towns, who take advantage of *téléfériques*, cable cars and mountain huts, and who are always keen to keep our money in our pockets, who owe a greater debt to the community of people who live and work in the Alps, than do the well-off tourists who come to see the mountains and are happy to spend their money.

It's a busy place, the Alps, in summer. Now, in the winter, Jamie and I were alone.

Later on, we spotted a pair of ski-mountaineers, gliding gracefully down the glacier, which by now was far, far below us. Those were the only people we saw.

We were making good progress now, but time was marching on and we would soon have to find a spot to spend the night. We had been heading for a shallow rocky spur which protruded from the ice field just below its top. This we hoped would offer some sort of level ground on which we could dig a bivvy, and would place us in a good position to approach the headwall first thing in the morning.

Jamie arrived at the foot of the rocky spur and I led off up it, looking for a suitable place. The spur rose as a series of rocky bulges, separated by sloping icy terraces. I was hoping to find either a sheltered spot beneath one of the bulges, or a flat ledge on top of one, but they were all disappointing. Bulge after bulge proved to be sloping on top and the ice had done a good job of filling all the gaps below. The bulges were quite steep and I found my way over them with difficulty, although it was a relief to have a break from the monotony of the ice field. Before long I had run out of rope and still hadn't found anywhere suitable to stop. Dusk was gathering now and, rather than mess about, I decided to bring Jamie up and let him search on his way.

Jamie began to climb, and he too had no luck in finding somewhere, until ten metres below me, he stopped. After a short while I heard his shout, so I climbed down to join him, reversing with difficulty the last few moves. He was at the foot of one of the bulges, at a place where two large lumps of granite met at an angle. In the space between the two rocks was a small alcove, big enough for half a body. It wasn't exactly a five-star bivvy spot, but it was a start on which we could improve so we began to prepare our accommodation for the night.

First I made sure we had a really bomb-proof belay with plenty of gear in the crack between the two rocks. Then I set about attempting to extend the level section of ice out from the alcove, chipping away at the sloping ice. Jamie, meanwhile, began excavating a separate ledge below and parallel to mine, cursing as the debris from my own digging streamed down onto his worksite.

After about half an hour's chiselling we had created what approximated to a rather short and narrow pair of bunkbeds. Home sweet home.

It was dark now, the temperature was dropping, and we began the tricky procedure of getting ready for bed. Sleeping mats, bivvy bags and sleeping bags had to be made ready, equipment stowed and secured, and ropes and anchors organised – all without letting go of any loose item for a second. Hardest of all was removing our boots, crampons and all. I'm absolutely petrified when taking off my boots on the mountain, for fear of dropping one. If one of us were to lose a boot, we would both be in very dire straits, but both of us preferred to sleep with our boots off so that our feet could be kept warm during the night. It's very easy for your feet to go numb, immobile in their boots, and to not even realise it.

Sitting on my bed, freshly hewn from the ice, I gingerly took off each boot in turn and stuffed them both securely into my sack, which hung safely in the alcove. Keeping the rest of my clothes on, I wriggled carefully into my pit. I then adjusted my anchor rope to stop me from sliding off the ledge.

Jamie, who took charge of the stove as usual, got on with preparing the meal, or Burns Supper, as he called it, it being Burns Night: cheese, biscuits and a mug of hot chocolate. The stove tended to melt its way into the ice and so had to be held at all times. Jamie was therefore unable to extend to any further culinary complexity, but continued to melt snow to refill our bottles. These we kept in our sleeping bags to prevent them freezing overnight.

We enjoyed our frugal meal, happy to be safely tucked up and relaxing on our relatively secure little ledges. I always loved this part of a multi-day climb the most. When the day's toil is over, it's great to be able to lie in comfort (or partial comfort) and soak up the incredible atmosphere of the situation, watching the stars emerge one by one, reflecting on the day's progress, speculating on the climbing to come, and generally feeling at one with the mountain. The experience is incomparable.

We chatted for a short while, sharing our elation.

'Well, this certainly beats going to work,' said Jamie after a pause.

'That's because it's probably less effort and less stressful than your work,' I replied with a smile.

Jamie's job was a characteristically demanding one. After university he had forsaken his chosen subject of Geography and gone to Leeds to do teacher training. Then, as if mainstream teaching wasn't challenging enough, he had moved into caring for children with special needs. He had since moved back to Edinburgh where he lived in my flat with Anna and me, and had taken a job in a Dr Barnardo's home as a care assistant.

Every single day Jamie would come home with some crazy story or other of what his kids had been up to: running away, getting in trouble with the police, throwing tantrums. Most of them came from broken homes and had fallen through the net of foster care. Many of them had been abused or had learning difficulties. Every day Jamie suffered verbal abuse, sometimes physical abuse, but he resolutely accepted this as part of the job, responding to it by giving the children the care and patience that they really needed. By comparison with what Jamie did, my own job – abseiling off huge oilrigs in gale-force winds over stormy seas – seemed easy.

However, that all felt a long way off now. The sky was full of stars and the surrounding mountains had vanished into the darkness of night. We were both tired and it was quickly growing cold so we said goodnight, sank deep into our sleeping bags and turned in.

CHAPTER THREE

Mal Temps

It WASN'T EXACTLY a good night's sleep. My legs kept sliding off the narrow shelf, and I constantly had to heave myself back into position. A slight breeze had picked up, shifting fine particles of ice about the face of the mountain. These particles were funnelled between the two rocks, and every so often, a rivulet of spindrift would come pouring into the alcove, directly onto my head. I zipped myself into my bag. Jamie was up in the middle of the night, chipping away with his axe, attempting to improve his position, but on the whole, the night passed in relative comfort, and certainly I got a good amount of dozing in before it was time to move.

I woke with a start, unaware that I'd been asleep, confused by strange dreams. It was still dark but Jamie was already moving about, getting the stove fired up for the morning brew. I gave my usual morning groan of complaint.

'Stop moaning and find the biscuits,' suggested Jamie.

Another continental-style breakfast of bourbon crèmes and hot chocolate and it was time to get ready for another big day out on the mountain. Getting out of our bags, booted up and equipment ready to go was worse than the reverse operation the evening before, our limbs being stiff and clumsy and our fuddled brains only half warmed up, but by the time it was getting light, we were set to go.

It was Jamie's turn to lead and he set off, traversing leftwards to regain the top section of the ice field. When it was time for me to go, I said farewell to our little hotel and started to climb, feeling rigid, slow and awkward after our cold night. As I climbed, though, I soon warmed up, and my climbing began to feel natural again as I relaxed into the by now very familiar sequence of movement.

We were approximately halfway up the face now, and would have to move quickly today if we were to reach the summit and complete the most difficult part of the descent by nightfall. The headwall was only about three rope lengths away, and we had to decide at which point to find a way through the initial steep section. The wall rose up above us as a series of steep granite slabs, then the angle fell back a little into a confused mix of snow, rocks and icy grooves, which led eventually to the shattered summit ridge. The initial steep slabs were breached in several places by great smears of white ice, drooling down the rocks from out of sight above. We settled upon the largest and most central one of these ice smears, and took a diagonal line in the direction of its foot.

It was another clear and windless day, the sky unbroken blue. As with yesterday, the temperature was round about $-10°C$, but the stillness of the air ensured it was easy to keep warm.

An hour and a half later, we were established at the foot of the ice smear. I led off, eager to leave the interminable field of ice behind. The smear gave steeper climbing, although similar in nature to what had gone before. I had to be more careful with the ice here, however, as it tended to shatter off in great big dinner plates which would then tumble down towards Jamie who cowered uncomplainingly below. I reached the end of the ropes before the top of the smear and so had to take an uncomfortable stance, hanging from ice screws. I called to Jamie to get a move on and he soon arrived at the belay, took the gear, and shot off. Now it was my turn to suffer the barrage of cascading ice, and several large lumps landed square on my helmet, sending an unpleasant shock through my spine. Fortunately, Jamie was soon out of sight over the top off the smear, and shortly came the call to continue climbing.

Above the ice smear were several grooves offering upward progress. We chose the one that led slightly leftward, which was the general direction we wanted to trend. The ice in the groove was good and when we reached the top of it we were presented with further choices of route. We continued in this way for many pitches, wending our way leftwards and rightwards, through icy grooves and runnels and across areas of more mixed, rocky ground. The route-finding was quite intricate and the climbing very enjoyable and absorbing.

At about 2.00 p.m. I suddenly became aware of a few flakes of falling snow. I looked up in surprise to see banks of clouds appearing from behind our summit ridge.

Shit.

'Jamie!' I shouted. 'Here's the snow arrived! Better get a move on!'

Snow. No big deal really – we could easily cope with a little falling snow. It was just slightly worrying to know that the weather was no longer perfect. The spell of settled weather was over and who knew what was in store next? Snow had been forecast and was forecast to pass over quickly. Hopefully this would turn out to be the case but in the mountains you just never know. We could only hope that this wasn't the precursor of some even worse weather. I didn't want to get caught out in a storm.

The snow wasn't a problem at first. It was quite light and whisked around our heads in energetic flurries, like autumn leaves in a doorway, then disappeared off down the face, too busy to settle anywhere.

We redoubled our efforts but were really already moving as fast as we could manage. At a belay stance, we met for a conference.

'What do you think?' asked Jamie.

'I think this is OK.'

A devil of whirling flakes danced between us, beautiful in the soft afternoon light, yet cold and threatening.

'Yeah it is, we're all right with this, but don't you think it would be a good idea to head rightwards – straight to the *brèche*?'

I thought about this for a moment. The Brèche des Droites was a small notch in the high summit ridge of the mountain from where the descent route down the other side began. It was the gateway to our quickest escape from the face. By heading diagonally rightwards, straight for the *brèche*, we would save valuable time. We would also miss out on the summit of the mountain. The *brèche* is only a few metres lower than the summit but for a mountaineer there's nothing quite like standing on the very highest point of a mountain, to be able to turn through 360 degrees and be overshadowed by nothing, to feel for just that one moment that you are on top of the world. It would be a disappointment not to savour that moment on this occasion. Nevertheless our objective was primarily to climb the mountain's north face, not to reach its summit, and it was now more important to get down off the hill quickly.

'OK,' I conceded, 'I suppose you're right. We'll save the summit for another time.'

We climbed on, taking a general rightwards line now, still weaving in and out of the icy grooves and runnels that streaked the face.

Then, quite suddenly, the snow got a lot worse. Heavy clouds were now rolling over the ridge, boiling down into the valley, and the beautiful view was soon gone. Snow started to fall harder and harder, dumping itself onto our shoulders and rucksacks, heavier than I could remember ever seeing snow fall.

Shit. Shit. Shit.

A chill spasm of fear spread up my spine, through my shoulders and down into my arms. The hairs on the back of my neck prickled. This was bad news. The scales had tipped and the weather was now definitely against us.

However, conditions were only to get worse as the snow, piling onto the face of the mountain higher up, funnelled down the grooves and runnels that we were climbing, sweeping over us in great waves of spindrift. Each wave hit us like a dark blast, powerful, blinding and penetratingly cold. The waves shot past with an ominous rushing, hissing sound, a sound that only emphasised the utter silence of our mountain surroundings. It began to dawn on me how very alone we really were.

There was no choice but to battle on. Retreat would be too slow. The quickest and safest route off the mountain from here was up to the *brèche* and down the other side.

We were at the foot of a steep icefall now, probably the steepest we had yet encountered, and as we could find no alternative way round, I launched up it. Avalanches of snow came rushing down the icefall in unbearable, suffocating waves. As each wave hit, it was the most I could do to hold on tight, waiting for the torrent to pass. The snow did its utmost to force me off, thundering down on my back and shoulders, trying to wrench my sack from me, and piling up between my legs and the ice, attempting to lever me off. It penetrated the crevices in my clothing, forcing its way up my sleeves, down my neck. I literally couldn't see my hands and axes in front of my face.

Then, after about ten seconds, the wave would pass and I would climb as quickly as I could before the next one hit a few seconds later. The placement of ice screws was quite out of the question, and I climbed on upwards without protection, driven by pure fear, until I reached the top of the pitch.

I shouted, but there was no way Jamie could hear me, so I gave a couple of sharp tugs on the ropes to let him know that he could climb.

I stood hunched on the stance, belaying Jamie, as wave after wave of snow swept over me and down onto Jamie below. The snow piled up on the uphill side of me faster than I could brush it away, and the weight of material kept threatening to push me off my small stance.

Jamie arrived, his grey face set in an expression of determination.

'This is grim,' he admitted.

'Let's just keep going, shall we?' I replied.

Our progress was considerably slowed now, but we reckoned that we couldn't be more than five or six pitches from the top, so we struggled on. Visibility was down to about 15 metres between snowstorms, zero during them, so route finding became difficult. We kept on in the rough direction of the *brèche*, picking the line of least resistance.

I fought my way to the top of one groove and found myself in a dead end. Above me was an overhanging wall, and to the left, blank slabs. What, from below, had looked like a continuation gully to the right, turned out to be a different gully line altogether, separated from mine by a steep drop. I realised I was looking at the Ginat route, which climbs the fault line on the right side of the face in its entirety. The Ginat route finishes at the Brèche des Droites and it would be a good route for us to follow, but there was no way into it from here.

34

I brought Jamie up until he was in shouting distance, and explained that I had reached a cul-de-sac. Instead of coming up to join me, he made a traverse leftwards, at the foot of the blank slabs. Crossing some difficult mixed ground, despite the unrelenting bombardment of snow, he was able to gain further groove lines on the left. He was soon level with my stance, then he disappeared up and out of sight.

When the ropes came tight, I dug myself out of the building snow, and attempted to climb back down the groove. I couldn't get very far, however, as the ropes were still tight, pulling me upwards and leftwards, and Jamie wasn't giving me any slack.

'Slack!' I shouted, but no response. I shouted and shouted but to no avail. After a while I began to get panicky about the amount of time I was wasting. I dithered, not knowing what to do. I wanted to climb down and left, but the ropes were forcing me up and left, across the blank slabs. Jamie obviously had no idea what was going on, and unless I took some action, I was stuck there.

Eventually I decided that there was nothing for it but to let myself pendulum across the slabs. I didn't like the look of the swing at all but standing there wavering I was wasting valuable time. Without further delay, lest I should have a change of heart, I leaned my weight onto the ropes and, praying that Jamie had a good hold of them, I stepped out of the groove.

My crampons clattered and scraped on the rocks as I swung, accelerating out of control, across the icy slabs. Snow and rocks rushed past me in a blur until I eventually ground to a halt on the far side of the slabs. I swung my axes into some ice, got my feet established on some holds, and breathed a sigh of relief.

I was now in a position where I could regain Jamie's route and climb up to join him. When I reached him I cursed him for not paying me out any slack. Apart from the continuing snowstorm, there was a growing sense of gloominess in the air, and we realised that the light was failing.

'We could stop here for the night,' suggested Jamie. 'Those rocks over there. We could dig out some sort of ledge and get some shelter in the lee of that wall.'

Looking at the hopeless spot Jamie was suggesting I admired his optimism, but I just couldn't see us getting any shelter whatsoever on this face, nor did there seem any possibility of creating a ledge big enough for the two of us to lie or even sit on.

'I think we should press on for the *brèche*,' I argued. 'We must be nearly there and we've much more chance of getting a decent bivvy spot there.'

Jamie agreed, so we carried on.

Fortunately the climbing was easier now, although it didn't help that the snow was now building up on the surface of the ice, necessitating large amounts of snow clearance before each placement of the axe, which was hard work and very time-consuming.

We found a ramp line that led up and right and followed this for a couple of miserable pitches. Before long we were climbing by torchlight.

The snow swirled and danced eerily in the beams of our head torches. All that I could see as I stood on my belay stance was the hypnotic display in front of me, and Jamie's bobbing light fading in and out of view. I felt very vulnerable.

Leading up the next pitch, I suddenly felt a rattle in one of my axe picks. I took a closer look and discovered that the bolt that held the pick had come loose.

Christ. That's all I need.

To lose an axe now would be a disaster. However, there was nothing I could do in the middle of the pitch, so I carried on, trying to rely on the other axe as much as possible, and avoiding hard blows with the faulty axe, lest the vibration should shake out the loose bolt.

Thankfully, I got to the top of the pitch without further incident, and when Jamie joined me, we got an Allen key from one of the sacks and retightened the bolt.

I felt very tired now.

'I've had enough of this,' I moaned. 'Surely we must be nearly there?'

'Don't worry,' said Jamie. 'We'll get there soon.'

Jamie's next pitch brought him to the end of the ramp. He paused at the top, then his head torch vanished from sight. When I followed on up, I found that the ramp finished at a short drop which was easy to descend and I joined Jamie in a wide, open couloir, disappearing upwards into the darkness.

'I think this is it!' said Jamie, excitedly. 'The *brèche* must be at the top of this *couloir*!'

I led on upwards, the incessant spindrift beating down on me. Too cold to stop and attempt to get any protection, and too tired to care any more, I climbed blindly on until, disappointed once again, I reached the end of my ropes before coming to any *brèche*. Working now on autopilot, I constructed a perfunctory belay and brought Jamie up. Without a word, he joined me, took the gear, and set off into the darkness. This time, however, before running out the full fifty metres of rope, Jamie gave a shout, muffled in the snowy darkness, and halted.

Soon came the call for me to follow, accompanied by a tug on the ropes, and I began climbing again. As I climbed, the *couloir* became narrower and steeper until suddenly, as I peered upwards through the falling snow, I saw that the beam of my torch no longer picked out the snow slope above, but disappeared into inky blackness. My heart leapt. A few minutes later I was sat beside Jamie on the Brèche des Droites, and we whooped and cheered with joy to anyone who would listen to us. We embraced, grinning with relief at having survived our ordeal, both agreeing that that had been one of the most unpleasant epics we had survived yet.

This was no time for congratulation or reflection though, and we immediately curtailed our celebration to take stock of the situation.

Unfortunately, although the *brèche* was the gateway to our descent from the mountain, it was a bitter disappointment in terms of space and comfort. The place was a notch in the high, razor-back ridge which forms the crest of Les Droites. On both sides, to the east and west, the mountain ridge rose up above us, flanking the *brèche* with steep rocks.

Dropping away to the north was the steep gully we had just fought our way up. To the south fell a similar gully, disappearing into the darkness, down which we would descend in the morning. The two gullies met each other at the point where we were sitting, in a knife-edge crest of snow and ice. The knife-edge, which we sat

37

astride like a saddle, was about three metres in length, between the walls of rock on either side. It didn't appear that there was anywhere where we would be able to rest.

We discussed the possibility of climbing the west wall of the *brèche* to where we could see a snow slope that offered a glimmer of hope. We might be able to dig out a ledge or better still a snow-hole where we could spend the night. However, we decided against this as the climb out of the *brèche* looked quite difficult. We were already very fatigued and in all probability the snow slope would turn out to be as iron hard as every other slope we had encountered.

We decided to make the most of the spot where we were. If we could at least get a little rest, the snow should stop by the morning, and we would be able to make a quick descent.

We decided to work on the east side of the *brèche*, it being slightly wider than the west side, and because Jamie had already uncovered an excellent rock spike on the east wall which would make a suitable belay.

Digging away at the snow and ice with the adzes of our axes, we attempted to cut down the knife-edge to form a level platform. It took about half an hour of hard work, but eventually we had made ourselves a surprisingly acceptable ledge on which the two of us could just lie, side by side. There was no shelter whatsoever from the elements, and nothing to keep us from rolling off the edge on either side, but at least we would be able to lie down and get some sort of rest.

We began the laborious business of getting the bivvy ready: sleeping mats down, bags out, trying to avoid letting the fast-falling snow get in. Equipment was stowed, boots safely tucked into rucksacks, unavoidably jostling each other on the tight, icy ledge.

As soon as we were both organised, we drank the last mouthful of our water with a toast to the morning, then zipped ourselves into our solitary cocoons, to dine privately on a few squares of chocolate and wait for the night to pass.

CHAPTER FOUR

Trapped

During the night the wind got up. I decided that this must mean a change in the weather and therefore the end of the snow, and I lay awake, too uncomfortable to sleep, listening to the wind battering the nylon of my bivvy bag. To my side I could feel the weight of Jamie's body, pressing against me. I knew he would also be awake and listening. As I lay there, willing on the dawn, I reflected on the previous day.

That really had been a close call. Too close for comfort. We had had to pull out all the stops and I don't think either of us could have carried on much longer in those conditions. Perhaps we had been foolish to go out in the winter with a less than perfect forecast. Perhaps we had been foolish to venture out at all on this kind of climb in the winter time. Then again we were both mountaineers and as a mountaineer you have to take risks in order to achieve your goals. If you don't take any risks, you'd never go out of your house. You'd stay at home, wrapped in cotton wool, whiling your life away in the safety of your armchair. Nevertheless, I supposed, maybe it's a question of balance. Everyone, every mountaineer, has to decide what risks are acceptable to them in the quest for their own personal goals. We all have to draw the line somewhere. Perhaps I would draw the line just a little earlier in future. Assuming we got ourselves down from this awful place.

39

Once again I felt thankful that I was climbing with Jamie. If nothing else Jamie was a survivor and he could always be relied upon to pull through whatever the circumstance. The previous two winters he had made attempts on the formidable North Face of the Eiger and survived some very severe storms during epic retreats on both occasions. His two Himalayan expeditions both involved enduring some particularly atrocious weather and two summers ago he had climbed through the most appalling storm on the Central Pillar of Frêney on Mont Blanc, during which several other climbers perished. Jamie was as tough as old boots all right, and in conditions like these it was good to be with him.

The storm didn't let up during the night and several times I had to unzip myself to clear away the heavy build-up of snow that threatened to bury and suffocate me in my bag. I dozed on and off, but my consciousness never drifted far from the cramped ledge where my body lay shivering.

I woke to see daylight filtering through the fabric of my bivvy bag, and hurriedly unzipped to survey the day. My heart sank when I emerged to discover snow falling every bit as thick and fast as it had been the previous night, only now it was driven by a strong north wind.

I gave the body next to me a nudge and presently a tousled mop of ginger hair appeared, followed by Jamie's familiar but tired-looking face. He gave me a smile, then grimaced towards the heavens.

'This isn't looking good,' I said. 'There's no way we're going to manage the descent in this.'

'Well, what are our options, then?'

'Either we attempt to go down, or we sit it out here, I suppose. What exactly is the descent like?' Jamie had gone down that way before, after doing the north-east spur of Les Droites eighteen months previously, although on that occasion, in the summer, there would have been little snow and ice present in the gully.

'As far as I remember, it was quite straightforward: about ten or twelve abseils, mostly equipped, down to the Talèfre Glacier. From there it's a straightforward descent to the Couvercle Hut.'

'Well, the abseil points will all be buried at the moment so that will slow things up, and I really don't fancy going down there in this wind and snow. The spindrift will be worse than it was last night.'

'OK, well at least we're safe here, so let's stay put. The storm can't go on for ever.'

The cold wind was biting at our faces so we both retreated into our respective shells.

It was a hard decision to make, whether to go or whether to stay. More than anything, I just wanted to be off the mountain now, back in the safe, familiar world of the valley. Back in the comfort of the chalet, with Anna and our friends, eating large amounts of hot food and drinking, laughing, relaxing, and then the glorious luxury of a soft, warm bed.

Instead I was stuck here, perched on this ridiculously inhospitable spot, freezing cold, zipped into a body bag, unable to move, being buried alive by the incessant snow.

To attempt a descent now, though, would certainly be foolhardy. Conditions in the gully would at best be extremely dangerous, at worst downright suicidal. The most sensible course of action was to wait for the storm, which was more severe and had lasted longer than forecast, to pass. Then we would be able to make the descent in relative safety. Perhaps this afternoon we would be able to make it to the Couvercle Hut.

So I whiled away the morning hours, lost in thought and dozing occasionally.

Jamie and I were unable to chat much. We had to shout to make ourselves heard through the bivvy bags and the snow, and over the constant noise of the wind. So we kept communication to a minimum, only occasionally shouting out to ask after each other. I didn't have a watch and would sometimes shout for an update on the time.

Mostly, however, we were alone, wrapped in icy shrouds, with only our wandering thoughts for company, only our own body heat for warmth.

By about 2.00 p.m. it became apparent that we would be going nowhere that day. Our morale was low and sinking further. Time for something to eat. I suggested to Jamie that we do a stock check of our provisions. We'd already eaten any sweets which we had in our pockets, so we emerged from our bags to look in the sacks. Both rucksacks were completely buried and it took Jamie some time to excavate them, working as quickly as he could in the unpleasantly chilling gale. Meanwhile, I attempted to clear snow from our ledge. The snow, as it fell on us, would tend to work its way down either side of us, and as we moved about, it was eventually building up underneath us, gradually filling up the space which we had cut for ourselves, forcing us off our ledge. I swept away as much snow as I could, trying to restore the ledge to prime condition.

When Jamie announced that he had located all the food, we both retreated thankfully to the safety of our quarters. Jamie then listed off the inventory.

Food: one bag of pasta and dried soup (useless till we got to the hut and could cook it); one large bar of chocolate; one packet of biscuits.

Liquid: none.

The lack of anything to drink was more serious than the lack of food. We were both already parched after yesterday's exertions and my mouth was as dry as a packet of cream crackers. If we didn't take in liquid we would soon become dehydrated and weak, and as getting the stove going was impossible in our current position, the best we could do was to nibble small pieces of snow. This eased the pain in our mouths and lips, but had little effect in rehydrating our exhausted bodies.

Jamie broke the chocolate bar in two and passed one half over to my berth. We ate separately, greedily enjoying the sticky, sweet squares that were our breakfast, lunch and dinner for the day.

Then there was nothing left to do but wait and hope – wait for night to fall, and for day to follow night, and hope for a let-up in the vicious weather that might let us escape to safety.

Eventually, darkness fell. The storm raged on without a hint of abating, and we resigned ourselves to another miserable night.

I was by now excruciatingly stiff and uncomfortable. The little ledge wasn't long enough for me to lie out full length and so I lay mostly on my side, with my knees brought up towards my chin. I couldn't turn around much for fear of pushing Jamie from his equally precarious perch, and so I spent most of my time in the one cramped position. The snow, which worked its way underneath us, would gradually thaw with our body heat, and refreeze to form ice. Our sleeping mats were becoming buried beneath this thick layer of solid ice which we were now lying on.

The ice beneath me was hard and unforgiving, and my bony hips were getting bruised and painful. The ice also became polished and slippery, and the ledge was turning into a skating rink, making staying in position a constant struggle.

Staying warm was also a constant struggle. I was well wrapped up, in all my clothes, and also in my sleeping bag, but each time I poked my head into the outside air, clouds of spindrift would come billowing into my bivvy bag. It was impossible to prevent this from happening, and a good reason to avoid too many external excursions. The uninvited snow would soon melt, and gradually my prison cell was becoming damp. My sleeping bag was particularly affected and was slowly becoming sodden.

In an attempt to stay warm, I would wriggle and shiver, working on one limb at a time. I would also massage my feet from time to time to keep the circulation going in my toes. By carrying on like this, I kept myself going through the night.

Jamie, I knew, was suffering as much as me, but it wasn't Jamie's habit to complain.

I wondered how Anna was feeling now. Jamie and I had said that we might be back as late as Thursday and it was still only Wednesday night, but she knew that we hadn't been expecting weather like this, and she was bound to be distraught with worry. I guessed that she wouldn't be sleeping either. How selfish it was of me to put her through this. I debated whether she might have alerted the rescue services by now. Possibly. I hoped she had.

CHAPTER FIVE

The Valley Scene

Anna watched the cable car as it clanked out of the station and began to sink away. She could just make out my hand, waving to her through the window as the car disappeared over the brow of the hill. She turned and walked towards the café to meet our friends, a sick feeling of apprehension rising inside her.

She was used to my going off like this. I'd done it many times before in my ceaseless quest for adventure, but it was never easy for her to deal with. So far, I'd always returned, safe and sound, glowing with the fresh thrill of my latest conquest, telling the tale with shining eyes and a grin as wide as my face. She knew that essentially I was a safe climber, cautious and level-headed, and she knew that with Jamie I couldn't be in better company, he being as competent and as assured a climber as you could ever hope to find. She knew that we made a good team and would most likely arrive back at the chalet on Wednesday afternoon, bursting with superlatives and tales of derring-do.

However, Anna also knew the risks involved. She was no great mountaineer, but she understood what was involved and she was aware of the dangers that we would face. She knew that however well we climbed, however careful we were, and however many precautions we took, what we were undertaking was essentially a hazardous activity and there was a chance that we might not come back.

Anna always found my climbing difficult to come to terms with. Despite my constant reassurances, she hated the thought of me deliberately seeking out and facing danger. On the other hand she realised that in many ways my love of climbing defined who I was, shaped my personality, and was woven deep into the very core of my being. She knew how much it meant to me, so with half her heart she blessed my love of climbing, and with the other half she cursed it.

Resigning herself to a few unsettled days of worry, she joined the others, and they continued their day's snowboarding in the sun.

When the lifts began to close at four o'clock, the five of them descended to Argentière to rejoin the rest of the group who had all enjoyed a great day on and off the pistes, boarding and skiing.

The mood was buoyant in the chalet that evening and everyone agreed to go out for a meal in a local café to celebrate the successful start to the holiday. The residents of our chalet met up with the others in the nearby apartments, and together the British contingent numbered over twenty. Also present was our friend Julian Cartwright, a talented young mountaineer, Jamie's regular climbing partner, and a work colleague of mine, fresh from the second winter ascent of the very difficult Leffeuer Route on the North Face of Les Drus. Jules was raving about the climbing conditions and reassured Anna that Jamie and I would have no problems. The humour of the party was high and Anna did her best to put her worries behind her and join in with the spirit of the evening.

On returning to the chalet that night, Anna found the note that I'd left for her on her pillow. She slipped the scrap of paper into her wallet, vowing to keep it until I'd kept my promise to return. Several times in the night she woke and reached out her hand, only to find a cold space in the bed beside her. In the small hours of the morning, she found herself awake with an uncontrollably racing heart. Tiptoeing downstairs to get a glass of water and to try to calm herself down, she came across Stu Fisher, also awake. The two sat together for a quiet chat. Stu, a doctor, reassured Anna that her thumping heart was just due to anxiety. He also told her of the dozens of times that his son had caused him sleepless nights. How time after time he had lain awake, waiting for Jamie's return from difficult Alpine peaks, extended Himalayan expeditions, or exploratory trips into the African bush.

Stu also knew that it was he who had first instilled in Jamie a sense of adventure, from childhood canoe journeys up remote Zambian rivers, to early family trips to the Alps where easier peaks were conquered. He understood that the passion which was Jamie's driving force and lifeblood was not something that could be quashed or tempered, but was part of the very heart and soul of what Jamie was all about. To love Jamie was to know his passion and to accept the risks which formed part of his way of life. It could never be easy though, and the threat of tragedy was a constant concern.

After talking for a while Anna padded back upstairs to try and get some sleep.

Monday was a very similar day to Sunday. The weather was beautiful, the snow was still great, and everyone had another day of excellent skiing and boarding. Anna, with a similar group to the previous day, took the bus down the valley to the resort of La Flégère, where they had a lot of fun bashing the pistes until they were thoroughly exhausted. The sun shone all day, sprayed snow sparkled in the wake of speeding boards, and the mountains hung like a backdrop framing the picture postcard scene.

Monday evening was Burns Night and the Scottish contingent had brought with them supplies of haggis for the traditional Burns Supper. Sat around the chalet's large dining-room table, tucking into their haggis, neeps and tatties, and drinking whisky, the assembled party made a round of toasts. When Anna's turn came, she proposed a toast 'to absent friends', almost choking on the lump in her throat as she did so. A murmur of agreement rippled round the table and everyone raised their glasses to absent friends.

When the party was over, Anna settled down to a second night shared with the cold empty space.

Tuesday dawned once again a fine day. The team chose an area known as Le Brévant, next to La Flégère on the north side of the valley, for the day's venue. The snowboarding was going well there, and it wasn't until just before noon that Anna noticed a vast bank of clouds marching in from the south-west. Immediately her heart rose into her mouth. It wasn't long before the building cloud had enveloped the whole of the Mont Blanc Massif before her, and shortly afterwards a few delicate flakes of snow began to fall on the pistes of Le Brévant. Quickly the snowfall got heavier, until soon a thick white veil of heavy flakes fell all around. To the snowboarders this was good news. The snow on the pistes had been getting more and more chossy and carved up as the days of sunshine went on. Some fresh snow was just what was needed to rejuvenate conditions, but Anna knew that for Jamie and me the snow would only mean added danger, and for her, therefore, it meant added worry.

Still, knowing that we would most likely be able to take care of ourselves, and taking consolation from the fact that at least it wasn't windy, Anna once more put her concerns to the back of her mind, and tried to enjoy the greatly improved snowboarding conditions.

Later in the afternoon she descended back to Chamonix with a couple of the others, where they bumped into Stu. He was obviously concerned about the deteriorating conditions too, and went with Anna and the others back to the chalet to discuss the situation with Jules.

Anna was unable to judge how Jamie and I might be affected by the weather, which, even down in the valley, was pretty horrible. Jules was concerned but upbeat. He argued that by now we should have completed the climb, and that as long as we could reach a hut or find somewhere to dig in, we would be absolutely fine. Stu said that it would be better to err on the side of caution, and the three agreed that if there was no news and no improvement in the weather by first thing in the morning, then they would alert the PGHM. It would certainly do no harm to let the rescue services know that we were out there.

Most of the group went out to the pub that night after dinner, but Anna stayed in and watched the snow falling, silent and dense, ethereal in the soft light of the window. She went to bed early, hoping to get a little sleep in the peaceful couple of hours before the noisy return of the masses.

On Wednesday morning the weather had not improved. In fact, it had deteriorated. The snow fell as thickly as before, but it was accompanied now by a strong wind from the north, making conditions in the valley quite unpleasant. Anna and Stu got up early to catch a bus into Chamonix, where they found Jules in his gîte and the three of them went to report their concerns to the PGHM.

The PGHM, the Peleton du Gendarmerie des Hautes Montagnes, is a division of the French police force dedicated to providing rescue cover in the high mountain areas of the Alps. It is a small but highly committed and motivated force, priding itself in its unparalleled expertise in the field of mountain rescue. Its officers are fully trained policemen, but they are also qualified mountain guides, talented climbers, and all-round lovers of the mountains. If anyone could help Jamie and me, it would be the PGHM.

Anna, Jules and Stu walked into the austere PGHM building. On the walls were maps of the area, speckled with coloured push pins, and glass-framed photographs – black and white images of young men, officers fallen in action during the forty-year history of the force. High-ceilinged with a tiled floor, the place had a cold, serious feel to it. From behind a Formica-topped counter, a grey-haired, severe-looking officer in uniform asked how he could help them.

The three explained their relationship to Jamie and me, how we had gone to climb the North Face of Les Droites, were still not down from the mountain, and that they were worried that we might be in trouble. The grey-haired man frowned as he carefully took down all the details of the situation. This matter would be taken very seriously, he said. Please wait.

They stood at the counter, looking through to the room at the back where the officer and his colleagues spoke into their radio. Anna looked at a large map of the area on the wall in front of them and picked out the locations of the various huts. Eventually they sat down to wait.

After they had been waiting for half an hour or so, the grey-haired man returned, this time accompanied by another serious-looking officer.

They had radioed all the huts in the area, they said, but there was no response from any of them. The weather was too bad to fly a helicopter. An attempt to find the climbers on foot was also out of the question, but a search and rescue mission was being prepared and they would be ready to scramble as soon as the weather improved. There was nothing else that could be done for the moment.

The officers were unable to provide any words of reassurance. They took a contact mobile number and said they would call as soon as there was any news.

After leaving the PGHM, Anna, Jules and Stu decided to pass the time as best they could, to make the most of the snow and head for the slopes at Le Tour. They stopped off at the chalet to get their equipment, Jules taking my snowboard and boots that were lying unused, and got the bus up to the lifts. However, when they got there, the lifts weren't working due to the strong winds, so they sat and drank tea in the café at the bottom. The atmosphere was tense as the three of them tried to be positive, but each knew what the others were thinking.

In the afternoon, the lifts reopened, and they set off upwards to the slopes. By the time they arrived at the top chairlift station, Anna was already freezing cold, could see nothing in the raging blizzard, and could barely move in the waist-deep powder snow that covered the piste. Setting off down the first run, she soon lost sight of her friends, and got about a hundred yards down the slope before tumbling and becoming buried in the cold, suffocating powder. It was too much. All alone, tears rolling down her cold cheeks, she slowly and arduously pulled herself and her board from the clawing snow. Cold and wretched, she ploughed her way slowly back up the hill, dragging her board behind her. Then she took the chairlift back down to the café, and sat there waiting for the others to return.

Back at the chalet that evening there was still no sign of Jamie and me, and the snow and wind continued unrelentingly. Anna turned in for an early night, but once again had slept little when the dawn light crept into her room.

CHAPTER SIX

A Shock in the Night

THE LONG NIGHT wore on. The constant noise of the wind outside indicated the lack of any break in the weather, but at least the wind kept the snow from building up on us so quickly, lessening the need for expeditions outside for re-excavation.

Drifting in and out of a shallow sleep, encapsulated and hidden from the outside world in my frigid nylon shroud, I began to imagine I was elsewhere – on another mountain, another time, or in a snow-hole somewhere in Scotland, somewhere else, anywhere else. Then I couldn't remember where I was, and thought that perhaps wherever I was I wasn't really there but somewhere else. And then I thought that perhaps this was what it was like to slip into the confused beginnings of hypothermia, and I shook myself awake in a panic.

No. I'm not hypothermic. I'm still fine. Body temperature still fine. Back to sleep.

When I opened my eyes again, it was light once more. As usual, a powerful north wind was tearing through the narrow gap where we lay, bringing with it thick snow like there was no tomorrow. My despair deepened. When would we be allowed to leave this hell hole?

Jamie was awake too and we met for a debate, docking together openings in our bags, so that we could see and speak to each other without letting the snow in.

'What are we going to do?' I demanded to know. 'We can't just lie here for ever.'

'I know,' said Jamie. 'I don't think I can take much more of this. I think we should try to descend. It would be better than just lying here, freezing to death.'

'Yeah, but at least we're safe here. If we wait here till the weather clears then we can get down no problem. Or perhaps a rescue helicopter will show up.'

'The weather might never clear.'

'Don't say that, it's got to.'

We carried on deliberating for a while and eventually decided to go, both of us wanting to do something proactive rather than suffer any longer where we were.

'Come on. Let's get out of here,' said Jamie, casting the deciding vote.

So we began to move, emerging fully dressed from our frosty cocoons like strange, giant insects, dazed after our long sleep. Ponderously we attempted to get our equipment together, struggling against the force of the gale, our bodies stiff from immobility. The attempt lasted about five minutes.

'This is hopeless,' screamed Jamie, the wind tearing the words from his lips. 'We can't do this.'

Glad that he had spoken first, I immediately agreed, and sixty seconds later we were both zipped up in our bags again, back in our own personal sub-worlds.

I lay huddled in my customary position as the latest infiltration of spindrift melted and further dampened the atmosphere, not to mention my spirits. Now I really was beginning to despair of ever getting off this terrible mountain. The longer we waited, the weaker we were becoming, and we were already pretty exhausted by our ordeal so far. It seemed to me that our only chance now would be a rescue. I hated the thought of suffering the ignominy of having to be rescued. I didn't fancy having my pride dented like that, but if push came to shove, I'd take that helicopter ride down the hill.

Jamie and I had another conference and discussed for the first time the possibility of being rescued.

'I still would rather get down under my own steam,' insisted Jamie. 'When the weather clears I think we should set off straight away.'

'But Jamie, we're probably already too weak to make it. We haven't drunk, eaten properly or even moved for almost two days. Anyway, I reckon the rescue team is ready and waiting already. As soon as there's a break in the weather, the helicopter will be here within minutes. We'll not even have had a chance to set off down. What do you want to do, say no thanks to them?'

'Well no, but I don't want to lose all my gear. We'd probably have to leave it behind.'

'Well, I don't give a shit about my gear,' I said, exasperated at Jamie's stubbornness. 'I just want to get down the quickest way possible. Anyway,' I teased him, 'it's mostly my gear.'

We lapsed into silence.

'What's for lunch?' I asked, some time later.

'Well, unless you fancy uncooked pasta, we've got dry biscuits or dry biscuits, but I don't think I could manage them.'

I tried to eat a biscuit but it was hopeless, like playing the game where you attempt to eat cream crackers as quickly as possible, only to end up with a mouth full of unswallowable pulp. My mouth was just too dry so I gave up.

After that, we whiled away the hours in our separate prisons once again, hoping for a change in our fortunes.

I discarded my sodden sleeping bag, which had become frozen and worse than useless, pushing it to the bottom of my bivvy bag. I still felt just as warm without it. My next problem was that I needed to go for a pee. I hadn't been for nearly two days and although I had drunk very little water in that time, my bladder had continued to fill. I was now getting desperate. Guessing that the nearest public conveniences were probably some distance away, and my movements being somewhat restricted anyway, I was going to have to go where I lay. I struggled and fumbled with the various layers of zips, Velcro, clothing and harness that were in the way and eventually, getting out of my bivvy bag as little as possible, I managed to pee into the snow beside me. I attempted to push the resulting yellow snow over the edge of the *brèche*, then retreated with relief into the bag, hoping that I wouldn't soon be presented with the other, more problematic call of nature.

Some time in the afternoon, I sensed a commotion going on next to me. Hurriedly, I stuck my head out of my bag to see what the problem was.

'What are you doing, Jamie?' I asked. He was frantically digging his rucksack out of the snow and appeared to be on a mission.

'Emergency!' he gasped as he dug.

'What?'

'Emergency! Is this an emergency?'

'I suppose so.'

'Well, in that case we should have our emergency Kendal mint cake!'

With a flourish, he produced a large bar of mint cake from a hidden pocket in his sack.

'Genius!' I cried, overjoyed at the thought of such an unexpected treat.

We'd both completely forgotten that Jamie always had an emergency supply of mint cake stashed away in his sack. Each Christmas, his granny, worried about her most errant grandson, would present him with a bar 'just in case' and Jamie would obediently carry the bar on his travels until it disintegrated, or was replaced by next year's bar.

I had been there that Christmas, sat politely in Mrs Winder's front room, as the ritual giving of mint cake took place. At the time I had been more interested in the rich aroma of steak and kidney pie drifting through from the kitchen, and had thought nothing more of the mint cake.

Now the mint cake was of prime concern and we immediately set to the business of consuming it. Jamie opened the plastic wrapping to reveal the battered and soggy contents – more of a mint mush than a cake. The mush was roughly divided into two halves (by the tried and tested 'I cut, you choose' method). We shouted out our thanks to Granny Winder, and then wolfed down the wonderfully sweet, minty pulp without further ceremony.

A minute later, our feast over, we each retired to our private bags to lie back and savour the sugar rush, and to lick our sticky lips. I couldn't remember a sweet bar ever tasting so good.

There was no hint of any mitigation in the weather that day, and we gradually resigned ourselves to the prospect of a third night at that bitter place, cast before the pitiless wind.

The nights were the worst. I hated the nights. It was colder at night-time, and the ceaseless wind seemed more savage. Time dragged its heels in the darkness of night, and the cold hours would stretch on forever. It was at night-time that my thoughts turned from the general practicalities of survival on the mountain top, to dreams of the friendly but unreachable world going on in the valley. Only a few short miles away as the crow flies, it might as well have been a thousand. How warm must everyone down there be, and how wonderful to be able to eat and drink as much as they want, and curl up in a cosy, soft bed, or in front of a blazing open fire. I promised myself I would never take the simple pleasures in life for granted again. And what about Anna? She would be absolutely beside herself with worry by now. She wouldn't know if we were alive or dead, or whether she would ever see us again. Would she ever forgive me when I eventually did return? I wouldn't blame her if she didn't. I wished there was some way I could let her know that we were still all right.

Some time in the small hours of the morning I was woken from my shivering reverie by a nudge in the small of my back.

'Jamie!' came the muffled call. 'Jamie! Are you awake?'

'What's wrong?' I responded.

'I'm very cold. What about you? Do you think it would be a good idea if we got into the same bag?'

I realised immediately that he must be very worried. Jamie would put up with the most extreme physical discomfort without a word of protest and there was absolutely no way he'd complain of being cold unless he was really suffering.

It would certainly make a great deal of sense to share a bag in order to stay warm. It would just mean we would be even more cramped and restricted in our movements. Warmth was our first priority though.

'OK, let's do it. What about if I get into yours?' I suggested. 'It's bigger than mine.'

We put our head torches on and emerged into the night. This was going to be difficult. Rather like trying to get into the same pair of trousers as another person while lying on a vaulting horse, if you can imagine such a thing. I wriggled out of my bivvy bag, leaving the defunct sleeping bag behind, and brought my legs over to Jamie's side of the ledge. Jamie opened his bag, which had a zip along half of its length, and I got my feet in. Then came a lot of wriggling and kicking and squirming about, with elbows in faces and knees in groins. Try as we might we couldn't get in a position where we could bring the sides of the bag, which were flogging madly in the wind, in together to close the zip. Somehow we ended up changing positions, and were still struggling away when the bottom suddenly fell out of my world.

First I felt myself sliding over the icy surface of the ledge. Before I could react to stop myself, there was no more ledge and I was falling, plummeting out of control, into the abyss, towards a horrible untold fate. I was aware of the ice accelerating past my face, and I opened my mouth to scream. Snow and space and darkness whirled around my head, swallowing up the scream before it could be uttered. I had a brief vision of a body, broken and lifeless, lying at the foot of a frozen mountain.

Then the falling stopped, as quickly as it had begun, and I was left hanging in my harness, brought to a halt by the rope.

Disoriented, rigid with fear, and gasping heavily, I looked around to see what had happened. Thankfully Jamie was still sitting safely on the ledge above me. I had fallen off the ledge, down Jamie's side – the gully that we had climbed up. The rock spike, our main anchor, had been above Jamie's side of the ledge. My anchor rope, which held me from falling down my side, had been too long to prevent me from falling down the other side. I was now hanging from it, my face pressed against the ice, a few metres below the ledge. I'd also taken along Jamie's bivvy bag, which was still wrapped around my legs, threatening to fall off at any moment. The wind howled around my spinning head.

I looked up at the light of Jamie's torch.

'Jamie!' I screamed. 'Jesus Christ! Help me!'

'It's OK!' yelled Jamie. 'Don't panic. You're OK. You've got to climb the rope.'

'I can't! Help me!'

'Yes you can. Come on. Try.'

I'd taken my gloves off to wrestle with the bivvy bag zips and was bare handed. I grabbed hold of the icy rope in front of me and heaved with all my might, dragging the deadweight of my body and legs in the bivvy bag behind me. I tried to lock off with one hand while making a grab for the rope higher up with the other, but my grip failed and I slumped back down.

'I can't fucking do it!' I shouted, a tide of panic welling inside me. My fingers were numb with cold and I was almost vomiting with fear.

'Yes you can!' screamed Jamie. 'Just try again.'

This time I felt a monstrous wave of adrenaline course through me. With a stream of curses, I hauled myself up hand over hand, clutching for all I was worth on to the frozen rope. I reached Jamie's outstretched hand and made a lunge for it. Clinging on to his arm for dear life, I clambered up and heaved myself back on to the ledge.

'Oh, Jesus!' I wheezed, sprawling myself across the ledge. 'I really thought I'd had it then. That scared the shit out of me.'

'Quick,' barked Jamie. 'Get into the bivvy bag!'

I allowed Jamie to reorganise my anchor so that I couldn't slide off the ledge again, and meanwhile I wriggled into Jamie's bivvy bag, the bigger of the two, which I'd fortunately managed to hang on to during my struggle. Jamie had already got into mine.

Once I was safely wrapped up in the bag and lying horizontally again I began to calm down. Gradually my breathing slowed and my pounding heart settled.

My worries weren't over yet, however. My fingers were still white with cold and there was no sensation in them which was a great cause for concern. I rubbed them and blew on them and held them in the warmth of my crotch but still the circulation wouldn't return. If I couldn't warm them up I would be in big trouble. Frostbite in the mountains is a killer and frozen fingers now would leave me very vulnerable.

Eventually, after several minutes, I felt a warm tingle growing in my fingertips. Very slowly the sensation increased, and before long I was suffering the full, excruciating, but reassuring pain of hot aches in both my hands. The hot aches always accompanied the return of blood to my hands after a spell of numb cold and the pain was often strong enough to make me feel physically sick.

I shook my stinging hands, willing them to come off the ends of my arms, and shouting, 'Ow! Ow! Ow!' until I thought I couldn't possibly stand it any longer. It was several more uncomfortable minutes, however, before the pain finally subsided. My mittens, soaked and frozen, had disappeared somehow in all the confusion so I dug out my spare mitts and put them on.

By now the tears were streaming down my face, and when I caught Jamie's eye, shining in the light of my torch, and saw the Cheshire grin on his face, I couldn't contain my emotion any longer and choked out a strangled cough that was half laugh, half sob.

Jamie followed suit and before we knew it we were both in fits, laughing out loud at the ridiculousness of the night's episode.

We came to a compromise arrangement with regard to bivvy bag sharing. Jamie lay in the smaller bag up to his waist and I had my legs in the big bag. We kept the top half of the big bag unzipped and managed to wrap it round both of us so that we were sheltered from the wind and snow but could huddle together to share body heat.

This system was quite awkward, making it difficult for either of us to move without letting in a blast of cold air, but on the whole we were able to stay significantly warmer. Another important benefit was that, being face to face, we could chat to one another. This would help a lot in passing the time and keeping our spirits up.

We settled down to rest for the remainder of the night. I was still cold and frightened after the shock of my unexpected departure from the ledge and the ensuing struggle but Jamie helped me warm up again and did his best to reassure me that we were going to be OK.

Later on, lying there sleepless, I reflected on our state of affairs. Things were getting serious now. What had brought us to this dire situation? I wondered. Why had we come here? I was supposed to be on a snowboarding holiday for God's sake. What point in the chain of events leading up to this horrible night had steered our respective fates in this particular direction? My mind wandered back to that crazy, wet hill climb, less than a month ago, when we had talked for the first time about doing an Alpine route on this trip. Perhaps that day was to blame.

It was 2 January 1999, the second day of the New Year and the second day, for both of us, of particularly tenacious hangovers. We were staying in Brackenclose, the Fell and Rock Club hut at the foot of Scafell Pike in Wasdale, and the weather was predictably atrocious. Bored of reading books and playing games with our companions, cooped up in the stuffy hut, Jamie and I decided to go out and get some exercise, despite the lashing rain that beat against the windows.

'OK then,' said Jamie, 'let's go and get changed. I'll meet you outside in ten minutes,' and he disappeared off to his dorm.

I went into the other dorm where I was sleeping and got into my warm clothes. I pulled on my big mountaineering boots, waterproof trousers, waterproof jacket, hat and gloves and generally prepared myself for a foul weather day on the hill. When I stepped out of the hut into the cold, rain-soaked landscape of the Lake District, I found Jamie jogging up and down on the spot, dressed in leggings, a single thermal top and running shoes.

'Oh,' I said, looking at Jamie's lightweight attire. 'When you said, "Let's go for a quick run up Scafell Pike," I didn't realise you meant literally running.'

'Of course I did. You don't want to hang around in weather like this.'

With that, Jamie set off up the stony path at a sprint. Eyeing his receding figure for a moment, I sighed, then I lumbered on after him. I knew exactly what he was playing at. He was being deliberately competitive. Not in an outward, point-scoring, first-past-the-post sort of a way, but in his more usual non-verbal, gauntlet-throwing sort of way. By launching off at this breakneck speed Jamie, I knew, was tacitly challenging me to keep up with him. I knew also that it was a challenge that I couldn't refuse. Overburdened with clothes as I was, I would certainly never beat him, but I was damned if I was going to let the bugger burn me off. Nor would I, for my part, admit to him that I knew that this was a race. I knew of course that he knew I knew it.

We toiled up the steep hillside, Jamie setting a screaming pace, me labouring hard on his heels, the two of us locked in unspoken pursuit. It was too steep to keep up a running pace but we fought on up the hill, hands pushing hard on our knees for greater power with each step.

I was soon soaked. Rain outside soaking in, sweat inside soaking out. Soaked through. Even my feet, perspiring in my heavy boots, were soon wet through, but I pushed on, keeping the rubber studs of Jamie's shoes in my sights. I stuffed my hat and gloves into my pockets and opened all the zips on my waterproofs in an attempt to cool off.

As we climbed up into the thick cloud, in which the top three-quarters of the hill was hidden, Jamie started to pull away and he was soon lost in the swirling mists ahead of me. Then I came round a bend in the track and found him waiting for me, sheltering in the lee of a large boulder.

'Are you all right?' he asked innocently. 'Want to stop for a rest?'

'No, no,' I replied as casual as possible while desperately trying to control my breathing. 'We don't want to hang around. Let's just push on.' So we continued.

The path led us up the pretty, wooded banks of Lingmell Gill onto a grassy spur called Brown Tongue. Brown Tongue eventually gives out onto the desolate boulder field of Hollow Stones. From the top of Hollow Stones we took care to find the correct path which leads up steep, rattling screes to the high mountain pass of Mickledore.

Funnily enough it was on this same path that Jamie and I had first met, more than eight years previously. It was on an Edinburgh University Mountaineering Club meet to Wasdale, in my final year. We arrived at the campsite, just below Brackenclose, late on the Friday night and it was dark and starlit; someone suggested climbing up to Mickledore and sleeping there so that we would be first to the rock climbs in the morning. A group of us made the 2,500-foot ascent, stumbling up the steep path in the dark. On the way I got talking to a keen young first-year. As club president I was a little overproud and didn't often make much effort to befriend freshers. This guy seemed different though, and I soon discovered that we shared many common interests and a similar outlook on life, not to mention the same first name. We got to discussing our respective plans for the morning, and had talked our way up most of the rock climbs on the mountain before we reached our lofty bivouac spot.

It was then that I realised with embarrassment that I'd completely managed to forget my sleeping bag. It was a chilly October night and I spent it shivering in a rocky niche, wrapped in all the clothes I could borrow, while the others snored around me. Ironically, in the morning I discovered I'd been lying next to an emergency stretcher box which had a sleeping bag in it.

Unfortunately on that occasion our high bivvy and early start didn't do us much good. We were up at seven and by eight it was raining. It rained for the rest of the day, so it was in the Wasdale Inn that evening that I next met Jamie Fisher. I didn't even recognise him, having never seen his face during the dark march of the previous night, and paid little attention in the dismal morning, but over a few pints we hit it off well and our friendship grew from that day on.

Jamie turned left at Mickledore and began the last 500 feet of ascent over rough ground to the summit of Scafell Pike, at 3,210 feet the highest point in England. He began to pull away from me again and had just disappeared into the mist when the giant summit cairn loomed ahead. There he was waiting when I arrived, every muscle in my legs screaming with lactic acid burn and my heart trying to beat its way out of my chest.

'Fifty-eight minutes,' said Jamie, looking at his watch. 'Under an hour. That's not bad going.'

A simple statement which simultaneously confirmed the end of the competition and declared us both to be winners, the role of loser being discreetly transferred to the clock. That's how competitions with Jamie usually ended. With the one exception of squash, in which he was a merciless slayer, he was too modest to ever claim victory for himself. If you joined in one of Jamie's games you'd probably end up bruised, battered and exhausted, but invariably you'd be richer in memories and shared experience. Of course the greatest prize of all was to earn a place in one of Jamie's legendary tall stories, countlessly told, exaggerated out of all proportion, and listened to by many.

Jamie's storytelling, his gregarious nature, amenability and generosity made him universally liked. During his time at Edinburgh University he was at the core of a large and diverse group of mountaineering friends and was a popular president of the mountaineering club in his final year.

Jamie was no angel though. In fact he could be stubborn, headstrong and unreliable, and the two of us were often bickering and arguing, mainly about Jamie's lack of contribution to the housework. He also had a reputation for episodes of wild, hedonistic behaviour, during which anything could happen, and often did. He had an extremely mischievous streak and it seemed that trouble often sought him out. Or it might be fairer to say that he often sought trouble out. Going out for a drink with Jamie was never a quiet affair. However, he had an equally strong sensible streak, and usually managed to maintain a healthy balance of fun and seriousness in his activities.

In the eight years that had passed since our first meeting, Jamie and I had become very close and we had shared many experiences – from sunshine climbing trips in Spain to serious mountaineering expeditions in the Alps, hillwalking and bothying in remote Scotland to adventurous sea-cliff climbing in North Wales, hill races and mountain marathons, we had done a lot together. As partners in our various activities we were well matched. When travelling light, I was usually faster than Jamie. With heavy loads, he was the stronger. I was the expert at technical rock climbing, we equalled each other on snow and ice, and Jamie was the better at tackling big mountains. Certainly there was no one that I'd feel more secure with as a partner for any expedition.

With the pressure of rivalry now lifted, we trotted together at a more relaxed pace down the hill, this time taking the path over the subsidiary summit of Lingmell.

'Have you decided about Chamonix yet?' I asked as we jogged down the hill.

'I'm not sure I can afford it,' said Jamie.

'It won't be that expensive. The flights are cheap and there'll be loads of people to cover the cost of the chalet.'

'If I go to Cham I'd rather go climbing than snowboarding, especially if the weather's good.'

'Well, we could take our gear, just in case,' I conceded. 'If it's nice weather we could do a short route and spend the rest of the week on the slopes.'

This got Jamie interested and we spent the rest of the descent talking about possible routes until the conversation broadened into a discussion of our other plans for the year ahead. So much to do, so little time. We arrived back at Brackenclose full of optimism for the future and wondering what adventures the last year of the millennium might have in store for us.

CHAPTER SEVEN

Helicopters, Tea and Biscuits

THE MORNING ARRIVED, but it brought with it no sign of a change in the weather. The north wind still blew, ripping through our notch in the ridge, and the snow still fell, racing with the wind in thick squalls.

By now we were becoming resigned to our continuing ordeal. There was no question of attempting a descent that morning – there was just no way we'd make it in that blizzard. Not in our fatigued state.

We passed the time chatting about climbs we'd done, climbs we'd like to do, our work, our friends, and anything else that cropped up.

I pointed out that as it was Friday today and Jamie's flight, which was non-changeable, was on Saturday, he was most likely going to miss his plane home. I laughed as Jamie, for the second time this trip, cursed easyJet.

'What's the first thing you're going to do when you get down?' I asked, changing the subject.

'Have a bath,' said Jamie promptly. 'And I'll have a huge pot of tea with about twenty spoons of sugar. And I'll also have several bottles of Yop.'

'You what?'

'You know, that yoghurt and milk drink. I'm going to drink lots of that.'

'Have you ever had Yop?'

'No, it looks disgusting, but it's what I really fancy right now. Plus loads of soft fruit.'

Personally I had never liked yoghurt drinks but at that moment a sweet milky yoghurty mixture seemed really appealing to me too and I imagined pouring the delicious thick liquid down my parched throat. The idea of soft fruit appealed too. In fact I couldn't imagine ever wanting to eat anything but nectarines and pears ever again.

We carried on talking about future meals and other luxuries for a while.

'How much of a lull in the weather do you suppose they'll need to get to us in the helicopter?' asked Jamie, changing the subject again and subtley admitting that a rescue was realistically our best chance of getting out of there now.

'Well, I guess there'll have to be a clearing in the clouds, or else they won't be able to find us, but I reckon these modern helicopters can fly in pretty strong winds.'

'Not as strong as this, though?'

'Uh ... No. I don't suppose so.'

We talked about our friends down in the valley, whose skiing and boarding holidays would be coming to an end soon.

'I reckon we owe them all an apology,' I said.

'Yeah,' agreed Jamie, 'and they haven't exactly had good skiing weather either. What about Anna?' he asked. 'Do you think she'll be very upset?'

'Oh yes,' I said. 'She's going to kill me.'

'No she won't, she'll just be relieved to have you back. It'll all be fine. My dad's going to kill me,' he added.

I had been rubbing my hands together when I suddenly noticed that blisters had formed all over the backs of my fingers and on my knuckles. They were bluish-yellow blisters, taut with liquid and numb to the touch. My instinct was to panic, thinking that the fingers must be dead and would drop off at any minute, but Jamie was immediately reassuring.

'Frost nip,' he diagnosed dismissively. 'It'll heal.'

It reminded me of Jamie's role as expedition doctor on his last trip to the Himalaya. He knew little about medicine but then

64

neither did anyone else on the team and as his father was a doctor he was reckoned to be best qualified for the job. In the remote areas of Pakistan through which they passed, the locals always asked for medicine, so on many occasions Jamie would hold surgery, dishing out aspirin, Elastoplasts, and sympathy in equal measure.

I would have to be extra vigilant and take greater care of my hands now. The skin on my fingers must have become frozen during their brief exposure last night. They had thawed out and there was no serious damage to the fingers but the damaged skin would be at more risk now, the circulation of blood reduced and the chances of freezing again would be higher.

I was lucky it hadn't been worse. If my fingers had become any more frozen, down to the flesh or even to the bone, the tissue might have been destroyed and the fingers would become useless. I would then be helpless, unable to take care of myself. I carefully replaced my mittens over my blistered hands.

We sank into silence again.

'I spy with my little eye,' announced Jamie all of a sudden, 'something beginning with . . . S.'

'Snow,' I said with a sigh.

'Yes. Your go.'

'Um . . . I spy with my little eye, something beginning with . . . BB.'

'Bivvy bag?'

'Yes.'

Thus we passed the time, intermittently dozing, chatting and playing games to keep ourselves sane.

Early in the afternoon I was attempting to have a nap when I was roused by Jamie, shaking me vigorously.

'Look!' he exclaimed. 'It's clearing!'

I shoved my head into the open air and sure enough, on the north side of the ridge, the clouds were beginning to part, and for the first time since Tuesday afternoon we could see glimpses of other mountains in the range.

'Yes!' I shouted, willing the clouds to disappear. 'Come on. Come on. You can do it. Come on, clear!'

We watched, tense with anticipation, as the awesome scene slowly revealed itself. At first there were just holes in the swirling clouds, opening for a moment to reveal a few jagged peaks, then closing, just as quickly, but as we watched the holes grew larger and more frequent and we could see long chains of snowy peaks, like teeth, stretching into the distance. Eventually the windows in the clouds merged together and we were able to look on the entire vista through trailing wisps, which boiled up into the sky. The view was incredible. Our old friends L'Aiguille du Chardonnet and L'Aiguille d'Argentière sat proudly in front of us. Behind them were stacked row upon row of fang-like mountains, as far as the eye could see. It's easy to forget what a vast range of mountains the Alps is. Below us, now a long, long way down, we could see part of the glacier, gleaming white.

The clouds were mainly gone now, but the wind remained powerful.

'I think they might come now!' I shouted excitedly. 'I bet we'll see the chopper within an hour.'

'I hope you're right,' said Jamie.

In fact we didn't have to wait that long. It was only a matter of fifteen minutes or so before we heard the unmistakable deep throb of a helicopter.

We waited with bated breath.

'There it is!' shouted Jamie.

Far below us, somewhere at the bottom of the face, we could see the small dark machine, rising effortlessly towards us. It was scanning its way up the face, searching for us, and we waited impatiently for it to reach us. Within a few minutes it was upon us, thundering spectacularly overhead.

Jamie leapt to his feet and hailed the chopper as it passed over, giving the international distress signal of outstretched arms waved up and down to the sides. The helicopter acknowledged us, circling round above us several times, before rolling sharply to the side and shooting off, back down towards the glacier, and out of sight round the shoulder of the Verte.

We looked in horror as the object of our salvation disappeared.

'Where have they gone?' asked Jamie.

I thought about it.

'I suppose they had to find us first, to check out where we were. Now they know where we are they'll have gone off to prepare the rescue. They'll be back soon.'

'Yeah, you're probably right. Shit, I'm freezing. Let's get back into the bags.'

We got settled down again and waited patiently for the return of the cavalry, chatting longingly about steaming baths and hot meals.

About fifteen minutes later we heard the beating of rotor blades once more. Eagerly we looked out and quickly spotted the chopper, racing towards us. Hanging below it we could see a tiny figure, dangling like a spider from the threadlike winch rope.

Jamie and I cheered and shouted.

'We're going to be rescued!' we screamed at each other, and embraced with relief.

Soon the helicopter drew closer, its human cargo swinging to and fro beneath. As it approached the gap in the rocks, between which we lay, we could see that the machine was being severely battered by the wind. It pitched and rolled, desperately trying to find its balance, but the buffeting gale tossed it about like a plaything. The man hanging perilously below was also tossed about, and several times swung dangerously close to the rocky walls on either side. Slowly, the helicopter eased its way into the frighteningly narrow gap, the blurred tips of its blades seemingly inches away from the rock. Then a monstrous gust of wind roared through and the pilot was forced to abort. The helicopter lurched outwards and upwards, and its helpless passenger was jerked along after it. The machine wheeled round in a great arc and regrouped for another attempt.

Several times, the helicopter crew tried to land their man in the *brèche*, but each time they were beaten back by the ferocious and unpredictable gale. For a while, the brave man on the end of the wire was hanging only five metres away from us. Once again, however, he was wrenched out of reach as the helicopter shot upwards. This time the helicopter dipped away towards the glacier, and disappeared from sight.

Jamie and I looked at each other with grey faces.

'They'll come back. They've got to come back.'

After a tense wait they did come back, this time with a different helicopter – a smaller yellow one. It too circled round us several times, bucking visibly in the gusting wind, before retreating to the open air above the glacier. As before, it returned with the rescuer hanging from the winch line. The new helicopter battled for some time to bring the man in to land, but it too was constantly forced back by the wind. Eventually the man was again hanging only a matter of metres away from us. I felt sure I could make out his expression of pity as, for the final time, the helicopter pulled back and the man was whipped away.

We watched in dismay as the second helicopter vanished behind the shoulder of the mountain.

'Maybe they'll go and get a longer winch line or something,' said Jamie hopefully.

But even as he spoke, the clouds were rolling back in, slowly obscuring the mountains and the glacier, closing the curtains on our hopes of being rescued that day. Soon the cloud was a thick cloak, screening us off from the rest of the world, and we were alone on the mountain once more.

Neither of us said a word. I felt a lump rise in my throat.

Jamie broke the silence. 'Fancy a cup of tea then?'

I looked at him, incredulous.

'Are you being serious?'

'Well, I guess we're here for another night, so we may as well give it a go while the snow's off.'

So we buried our bitter disappointment in the task of attempting to make a brew. We got everything we needed out of the rucksacks as quickly as possible: stove, fuel, pan, lighter, mug, tea bags. Then we retreated swiftly to the shelter of the bags. Once inside we devised an arrangement whereby I raised myself up on my left elbow, and Jamie raised himself on his right elbow, thus lifting the roof of our mini-tent and creating a small space for the stove between us. We each then had one arm spare to tend to the stove, although it was tricky keeping the top of Jamie's bag, which formed our roof, from breaking free and flapping madly in the wind. One of us would then hold the stove with our free hand (if set down on snow or ice, it tended to melt its way in), while the other held the pan, packed full of snow, over it.

It was awkward work, and we had a couple of eyebrow-singeing incidents which threatened for a moment to set fire to our bivvy bag, but once we had the stove under control, we started to make progress. It took several loads of snow to make just a mugful of water, and once we had the water, it took an absolute age for it to begin to boil. Eventually though, we managed to produce a steaming mug of wonderful hot tea. We shared the mug, accompanying our slurps with much praise and noise of appreciation. We also took the opportunity of dunking a few of our dry biscuits, turning them into a sweet mush, which slid gloriously down our throats, in great contrast to the undunked version.

I still felt like crying with the disappointment of having had our rescue so cruelly cancelled, but this unexpected supper went a long way towards providing consolation.

Once our nectar was all gone we relit the stove, and set about preparing another brew, which we drank with equal gusto, and then a third, until the biscuits were all gone, and the stove spluttered out, the fuel all burnt. The heat which the stove had provided, giving warmth to our enclosed space, soon faded away, and the air once again turned chilly.

It was growing dark now and we settled ourselves down for our fourth night at the *brèche*, fifth out in the open, drawing the bivvy bag round us tightly for protection from the penetrating wind. The highs and lows of the last twenty-four hours had taken their toll on us, mentally and physically, and we were both glad we'd finished the day with a boost to morale.

'They'll be back for us in the morning,' I said. 'Let's just hope that the wind drops in the night.'

Jamie grunted.

That night was much the same as the previous three, but with less snow. We lay side by side, shivering the hours away and praying for the dawn. The hours seemed to creep by impossibly slowly and I wondered if perhaps we were trapped in some unimagined purgatory, condemned to spend the rest of eternity interned in this icy prison.

Our situation was indisputably dire now. I thought back to the many scrapes and epics which had punctuated and enlivened my climbing career, but none of them compared to this. Only on two occasions had events conspired to take me beyond a level of danger with which I felt comfortable. Only on those two occasions had I truly felt that the situation was out of my control and I had been in a position of very serious risk.

Once, in the Cairngorms of Scotland, I was caught in an avalanche. Trying to find our way to the start of a climb in Coire an Lochain, my friend Andy Hume and I went slightly off route in thick mist. Aware of our error we changed course and began traversing the top of a wide snow slope to regain our original path. Suddenly I realised that the slope consisted of dangerous wind-slab snow – a foot-thick layer of windblown snow lying loose on an older, hard-packed base. I turned to Andy who was a short distance behind to warn him, when I felt a strange sense of disorientation. Quickly I looked down but the snow in front of me was stationary. However, the odd feeling of being in motion continued and too late I realised that the whole slope on which I stood was moving off down the hill. Andy, safe at the edge of the slope, could only watch as the snow carried me helplessly off into the mist, shouting out a single expletive as I disappeared.

As the snow accelerated, time seemed to slow down and the whole avalanche went into slow motion. At first I was standing on a huge raft of snow moving as one body. Then, as it gathered speed, the raft started to break into smaller slabs and I struggled to remain upright. For a moment I hoped I might be able to ride the avalanche out, but then it surged over a steeper section and the flow at once became turbulent. I was tossed hopelessly about like a rag doll in the midst of a torrent of rolling snow. Eventually (it seemed like a long time but was probably only a few seconds) the movement slowed, and remembering with unexpected clarity my winter skills training, I started to swim through the fluid snow, paddling for all my worth with my hands and axe, until I regained the surface of the moving mass just before it ground to a groaning halt.

I pulled myself gasping out of the snow as it immediately began to set as hard as concrete. I had fallen about 400 feet and every crevice in my clothing was filled with snow. I was badly shaken, chilled, and a little bruised by my own flailing ice axe, but otherwise unharmed. A lucky escape.

The other occasion occurred a few years earlier, on Ben Nevis, when three friends and I set out to attempt Point Five Gully despite poor ice conditions. We climbed the long initial snow slopes of Observatory Gully and took a belay on a snow ledge at the foot of the first steep ice pitch. Martin Reynard and John Irving were climbing first, followed by Stone Elworthy and me. Martin was about fifteen feet up the rotten ice of the first pitch when without warning both his axes ripped out and he fell, plummeting past the belay ledge where the other three of us stood. John held the rope but as it came tight the belay failed and John was pulled off after Martin. Together they tumbled out of control down Observatory Gully. Unfortunately they fell either side of Stone and he was also pulled off by their rope. Now there were three falling bodies and just me left standing on the snow ledge. I wasn't attached by a rope to Martin or John but I had just tied into the opposite end of the rope to which Stone was attached. I watched in horror as fifty metres of neatly coiled rope whipped off down the hillside. I had about three seconds to prepare myself and brace futilely before the inevitable jerk on the rope came and pulled me down after the others.

The next thing I knew I was somersaulting head over heels down the steep upper slopes of the gully – head, feet, head, feet, impacting with the snow. For a few moments I thought I was in for a really nasty fall. Fortunately, however, Observatory Gully is a concave slope with a broad, easy angled outflow into the lower reaches of the corrie and quickly, as the angle eased, I stopped cartwheeling but continued shooting down the gully in an uncontrolled slide. As the angle gradually eased still further the pace of my descent began to slow and I managed to right myself into a sitting position. Below me I could see the others, also upright, sliding down the slope on a great mass of surface snow that we had brought down with us. Finally the whole mass of snow came creaking to a halt with the four of us sitting on top of it, strung out like a row of corks over about fifty yards.

Miraculously we were all entirely unhurt. A little shaken obviously, but without a scratch or a bruise, thanks to the layer of soft surface snow that had cushioned our tumbling. If the gully had been icy, as it often is, it might have been a different story.

What was damaged was our pride, especially when we were faced with the scorn of some passing Glaswegian climbers who had watched the whole debacle from below. The worst of it was that my axes were still at the top, planted neatly in the snow where I'd left them before being so rudely torn away. Our unexpected toboggan run had taken us over 600 feet down the hillside and I had to plod all the way back up, and all the way back down, before the four of us scurried away, nursing bruised egos and vowing to return for revenge another day.

These incidents, frightening and dramatic as they were at the time, were really just momentary losses of control, over in a flash. They were good material for pub stories but had never really given me cause to consider seriously the whole nature of the climbing game. Perhaps in a way they only served to make me feel even more invincible.

Now, shivering on this uncomfortable little ledge, I felt anything but invincible. Jamie and I had never talked about the possibility of not making it. The possibility of never being rescued, of freezing to death, our stiff corpses only being discovered in the spring, still lying side by side in the snow. We'd never talked about this prospect – we probably never would. Not a very constructive topic of conversation when you're trying your best to survive. I was sure we'd both thought about it though. I knew I had and I couldn't imagine that Jamie, determined as he was, hadn't at least given it passing consideration.

I thought about the likelihood of death. I wondered what it might be like to die. Whether it would be a gentle drift into oblivion, a simple, endless, dreamless sleep, or whether perhaps it might involve something more spiritual, some kind of afterlife. Impossible questions which, like anyone else, I'd pondered many times before, but which now seemed so much more immediate, so much more directly concerning to me. I shivered, for once not because of the cold. And what about the others? The people left below to mourn our passing. Our friends. Our families. Our girlfriends. How would they feel? How great a hole would we leave in their lives if we never came down from this mountain?

I shook myself back to reality. The helicopter would come for us tomorrow. There was bound to be another break in the weather some time, and this time they'd be ready with a plan to get us out of this dreadful spot. We just had to hold on till tomorrow and not torment ourselves with morbid thoughts.

The night drifted on, and so did my thoughts. I just couldn't free my mind from the cruel twist of fate that had brought our escape so tangibly close, so near it had seemed like certainty, only to snatch it away from us with such unkind callousness. I felt angry. Cheated. Unfairly treated. We'd suffered enough now. We'd done our time and learnt a lesson that we wouldn't forget. Now it was time for the happy ending. The eleventh-hour rescue and a tearful welcome at the helicopter pad. Surely it was time for us to go home?

The morning arrived, and with it came a terrible wind, stronger than any we had so far experienced. A wind that tore the blanket of clouds from the mountains leaving them naked, raw and exposed to its shocking force. Huge plumes of spindrift streamed from the mountain summits in great white streaks across the sky, like jet engine vapour trails. With it, the Siberian wind brought a bone-chilling drop in temperature. We had no thermometer, but the air temperature was certainly well below $-25°C$, which, combined with a wind speed of at least 120 kph, created conditions of the utmost severity for us unfortunate, stranded climbers, at the full mercy of the elements with only our puny bivvy bags for shelter.

There was nothing to discuss that morning. There was nowhere we could go to get out of the wind. There was nothing we could do to improve our situation, and there would be no rescue that morning. Not until the wind dropped. The azure blue sky above seemed only to mock us hurtfully with its irony. The sun, whose watery rays might have given some solace, remained hidden behind banks of clouds in the south.

Jamie and I huddled together, desperately trying to conserve warmth. We didn't talk much, saving our breath, but tried to sleep, in the hope that on waking we would find it all over.

Then Jamie spoke. 'What hill are we on?'

'What?' I asked, mystified.

'What are we doing here?' he continued, his voice slow and drawling.

Oh shit!

It dawned on me what was happening. 'Jamie!' I shouted. 'Come on Jamie! You remember where we are! Where are we, Jamie?'

'I don't know. I can't remember,' he said dreamily.

'Yes you can, Jamie!' I insisted, shaking him and rubbing his body with my hands. 'Come on Jamie! Tell me where we are!'

I was petrified. If Jamie wouldn't respond to my questions and I couldn't help him to warm up, his hypothermia would quickly get worse. He would become unconscious and die within hours.

'What hill are we on Jamie? Where are we?'

'Oh. We're on the Droites. I remember.'

I carried on questioning Jamie while rubbing him vigorously and soon I was getting quite sensible answers out of him.

'Shit, you frightened me,' I chastised him.

'I was just asleep,' he protested, 'and woke up a bit confused.'

'Yeah right,' I said, but let it drop.

We huddled together as tightly as possible after that, wrapping our arms round each other, and chatted as best we could over the constant racket of the bivvy bags flapping in the howling wind, lest one or other of us should slip unnoticed into the insidious grips of hypothermia.

'Remember the time we climbed the Forth Road Bridge?' I said, attempting to cheer ourselves up. 'That was a pretty exciting night.'

'What I remember is the state of my own and Finlay's hands afterwards,' moaned Jamie, and we both laughed at the recollection.

It had been one winter's night, several years ago, when Jamie, Finlay Bennet and I had hatched this particular plan. Nocturnal building climbs and rooftop traverses have always been a pastime of mischievous young mountaineers the world over, and the students of Edinburgh University were no exception. Jamie and Finlay had been particularly enthusiastic participants in this sport, and had covered much of the skyline of Edinburgh by night. Once they'd spent a night in police cells after being caught climbing a 200-foot crane.

However, no one we knew had climbed the Forth Road Bridge, and I reckoned it was just begging for an ascent. Jamie and Finlay were only too keen, so one night at 3.00 a.m. we drove out to North Queensferry in my rattly old Ford Fiesta and parked in the shadows beneath the north end of the bridge. Casually, we sauntered up along the footpath to where one of the great suspension cables sweeps down to road level. A video camera played down on the carriageway nearby but we decided to chance it. We waited for a break in the traffic, then hopped over the fence and onto the giant cable. The cable was easily wide enough to walk on and had wire handrails on either side. We climbed quickly up the ever-steepening slope, invisible once we were above streetlight height, but conscious that we might already have been spotted. It was a climb of 300 feet to the top of the great tower and we were breathless by the time we arrived. The summit of the mighty bridge was a cold and windy place so we took a couple of triumphal photos and set off back down straight away. It was only when I reached the bottom again that I noticed that the gloves I was wearing had become shredded by hundreds of tiny frayed wire ends as I'd run my hands down the cable handrails. I thought nothing more of it as the three of us jumped back onto the footway and ran back to the car. As we drove up to the main road a police car passed in the opposite direction. We couldn't tell if they were coming for us but we didn't stop to find out and shot straight back to Edinburgh, racing on adrenaline. It was then, as we were celebrating our victory, that Jamie and Finlay noticed their hands. Neither had been wearing gloves and, numb with cold, neither had been aware as their hands were lacerated with hundreds of tiny cuts just like my gloves. They were a gruesome bloody mess. Thankfully the wounds weren't as serious as they appeared and healed quickly but I still have a grisly photo, taken in Jamie's flat later that night, of the four outstretched, blood-smeared hands.

We tried to cheer each other with memories of other happier times, but there was to be little happiness for us that day, and there was no respite whatsoever from the evil storm which raged on furiously. We longed for even the shortest break in the weather, as we knew that the rescue team would be ready and poised for when the chance came.

The chance never came though, and eventually the light of day abandoned us once more to the mountain, and the icy gale continued its assault, deep into the cold black night. Lost in the fury of the elements, we lay clinging to one another, our lives inconsequential to the colossal forces of nature.

CHAPTER EIGHT

News in the Valley

LYING THERE HELPLESS on the mountain, I could only imagine what Anna and our friends were going through down in the valley. It was only much later that I learnt the details of their agonising wait for news.

By Thursday morning, many of our friends were now finding the severe weather conditions too unpleasant to contemplate venturing onto the slopes, so Anna found herself with further companions with whom to pass the time while waiting for developments. One friend suggested a trip to the swimming baths.

The Chamonix swimming baths are an elegant modern facility, set in the bustling heart of the town, with picturesque views out to the mountains. The two girls spent the morning enjoying the luxury of the warm water, the steam room and the sauna, which seemed such a great contrast to the cold and inhospitable world outside, still visible through the pool's large picture windows. Anna had spent the past few days shivering constantly with anxiety, but the heat of the sauna, steam room and pool forced her body to relax properly for the first time in days.

She floated placidly in the gently rippling water, and watched the endless snow driving past the windows as she tried to imagine what it must be like for Jamie and me, fighting this monstrous weather, day after day, without food or shelter. She longed to find out what our fate had been and where we were now. Shivering in a snow-hole in the middle of some glacier, waiting for a chance to bolt for freedom? Battling at that moment towards a life-saving mountain refuge or down into the safety of the valley? Or were we already frozen to death, helpless on the bitter icy face of the mountain? Perhaps we had plummeted to our deaths, pitched down measureless precipices of ice and rock. Or had we been buried by a killer avalanche, suffocated under a thousand tons of snow, set as solid as concrete? Or worst of all, had we disappeared down some hidden crevasse, been swallowed by the immutable glacier, never to be seen again, until decades later when our ice-mangled corpses would come tumbling out of the glacier snout, preserved for history? Two years previously Jamie Fisher himself had discovered such a body – the body of some unfortunate climber from Leeds, whose fate had remained unknown since the 1970s, his relatives left to wonder and to wait for nearly thirty years.

Anna shook herself from her morbid reverie and swam a length of the pool. They would come back, she told herself. They would come back. They had to. She knew that it would do no good at all for her to worry herself into a state, imagining all the possible disastrous fates which might have befallen us. She knew that she should force herself to think positively, wait patiently, and Jamie and I would no doubt appear in our own good time, dismissively pooh-poohing everybody's concerns for our well-being. Still, she couldn't help herself feeling that she should be preparing herself for the worst.

That evening, the increasingly unsettled group of friends went to a busy Argentière bar to unwind, play some pool, and generally try to ease their growing sense of concern. Anna tried to join in, but with the thought of Jamie and me spending another night out of contact, she felt too overwhelmed to drink, wanting to remain sober to be able to deal with any news that might arrive. The others tried to get her to join in the pool tournament but she was unable to come out of her shell, the anxiety making her shaky and restless.

After a while she decided to go home and try to get some rest. One of the lads walked her back to the chalet and as they marched down the snowy road he tried to offer some words of comfort, but really there was nothing he could say. The night air was so cold that Anna had to take out her earrings as the metal was freezing her ears.

Later on, alone in the chalet, Anna looked out of the window at the deep footprints that she had left in the snow. When she went to bed, an hour later, they were completely covered over.

By Friday morning, over a metre and a half of snow had fallen in the valley since it had started on Tuesday afternoon. It was so deep around the walls of the chalet that people were able to jump from the first floor windows into the drifts unharmed. This game provided an amusing diversion, culminating when one of the girls threw herself in head first and had to be dug out.

That morning Anna, Stu and Jules went into Chamonix to see if there was any news from the PGHM. There was none, although they were hopeful of getting a break in the weather to fly their helicopter. They would let them know if there were any developments.

The three went back out into the streets of Chamonix, aimless and listless, eventually settling in a café to drink the day away with coffees, teas and beers. Later on they wandered into a cinema and whiled away an hour or two absorbed in some mindless English language movie, before installing themselves in another café to continue their vigil.

Towards the end of the afternoon, a tall, bespectacled, grey-haired gentleman rushed into the café in a state of excitement. He obviously knew Jules and without introduction he immediately started talking ten to the dozen. Jules rose to shake the man's hand, and when he was able to get a word in, introduced him to Anna and Stu.

John Wilkinson, an old family friend of Jules, was an Oxford don and a mountaineering old timer who had moved to France to spend his retirement writing, skiing and doing the odd bit of climbing. His wife was the well-known French author Anne Sauvy, and together they divided their time between their apartment in Paris, where Anne taught at the Sorbonne University, and their chalet in Chamonix. Anne, who had written a documentary of the work of the PGHM, was the only civilian in the valley permitted to possess a radio tuned to the mountain rescue frequency. John had news.

There had been a break in the weather. The PGHM had managed to fly over Les Droites. They had located Jamie and me, on the top of the mountain, and we were both alive. However, it had been too windy to rescue us. They had tried but the helicopter had been in severe danger of being dashed into the mountain. The weather had closed in again and the PGHM were waiting for another chance to attempt a rescue. They were hopeful for tomorrow, although the forecast was cold and windy.

Anna's heart leapt in a confusing mixture of emotions. We were alive! That was the best news she had had all week. We were alive and the PGHM knew where we were. Knowing that was infinitely better than knowing nothing and only being able to hope and wonder vainly. We were alive, but we were still stranded. The PGHM had tried and failed to rescue us, and unless the weather improved we would stay stranded. The forecast for tomorrow wasn't good. Who could say how much longer Jamie and I could last up there? Perhaps we were already at the limit of our endurance. Perhaps we wouldn't last the night. The idea of us being trapped up there in that horrendous weather didn't bear thinking about.

Stu, firing John with a barrage of considered questions, was obviously going through the same thought processes. Jules helpfully pointed out that, having survived so far in those atrocious conditions, we must have a reasonable bivvy spot, and there would be no reason why we couldn't continue to survive. The others were all glad to accept Jules's analysis.

After the change in the situation had been discussed and dissected as much as it could be, John suggested that, in the hope of cheering themselves up a little, the three of them should join him and his wife for dinner that evening in their chalet.

Anna, Stu and Jules accepted the invitation, happy for the chance to have a break from the crowded and often claustrophobic communal living of their own chalet. Later that evening, the three of them arrived at John and Anne's beautiful Chamonix residence.

Built onto the hillside on the north flank of the valley, their stone and timber chalet offered unrivalled views across to the stunning Aiguilles, high above the other side. Inside the cosy living room, a pair of elegant cats strolled along the sills of enormous picture windows, and the outside world of darkness and snow seemed distant and unreal, as if viewed on a television screen.

Anna was introduced to Anne Sauvy, who was an extremely kind and sympathetic lady. She was no stranger to the dangers of the mountains, having herself made many difficult climbs in her younger days, and having spent her life writing about the dreams, adventures, successes, failures and tragedies of mountaineers and mountain people. Anne explained how she was permitted, for her work, to listen in to the radio conversations of the PGHM. Day after day she would tune in to their broadcasts, collecting material for her book, and building up a picture of the life and work of the men of the mountain rescue service; she was often the first to hear of any news from mountain rescue operations. She promised to keep Anna posted if there were any developments in the attempts to reach Jamie and me.

Resigned now to a sixth night of waiting, Anna sat down with the four others to a fine meal of pheasant stew and wine. Conversation drifted on, but every now and then Anna would catch herself staring out of the window into the blackness where she knew the mountains to be, and willing us, with all her heart, the strength to hold on a while longer, to hang on in there. Occasionally she thought she noticed the others doing the same.

When Anna got up on Saturday morning, the sun was shining, and her hopes leapt. Then, when she noticed the enormous plumes of spindrift streaming across the sky from every mountain summit, she realised how windy it must be and her hopes sank again, leaving her feeling more dejected than ever.

Stu and Anna had arranged to meet Anne Sauvy at the PGHM in the morning so they took the now familiar bus journey into Chamonix and once more entered the sombre vestibule of the PGHM building. This time Anne was there to introduce them to the duty officers, and to translate as they explained what was going on.

The officers drew diagrams of the mountain, detailing the *brèche* where Jamie and I were stranded. They explained how it had been too windy yesterday for their helicopter to get near to us, so they had enlisted the help of a private helicopter company, whose machine was lighter. The lighter machine had got close to the *brèche* but had been unable to land or get directly overhead. Their plan now was to land a man on the ridge, who would then be able to descend to reach us.

However, the wind was still the problem. One of the men pointed to the spindrift plume trailing from the summit of the Verte. That streak of snow was over a kilometre long. The wind speed at that altitude was estimated to be 130 kph. A solid wall of wind was barring even entrance to the Argentière Glacier basin. As things stood at that moment, their helicopters were grounded.

Clutching on to Stu's arm, Anna emerged from the PGHM, nursing the battered remnants of the fragile hope that she knew was all she had left. This new weather was even more awful than the endless snow. By comparison, the snow had seemed almost soft and warm, in an insulating sort of way. In its place, this terrible, soulless, tearing wind was utterly without mercy. The air temperature had plummeted, and even in the valley Anna could feel her exposed flesh quickly beginning to freeze. She couldn't even begin to imagine how it might be possible for life to be sustained up at that tiny notch on the mountain the officer had tried to draw.

Anna decided to phone my parents and let them know what was happening. She had held off for as long as possible in the hope that all would turn out to be well, not wanting to call them without some sort of encouraging news. She didn't want them to have to worry as well as her, but the story was obviously becoming newsworthy and they would have to hear sooner or later. Better to hear from her than from the television.

Calling from a draughty phone box, she caught my mother and father, Catherine and Howard, just as they were leaving their house to go to a wedding. Contentedly engaged in preparing for their much-anticipated day out, the news that their son was stranded on a mountain top, feared dead, caught them from behind like a rugby tackle.

As Anna spoke to my father, he sounded quiet and scared. His replies were limited to 'Uh-huh', 'Yes', and 'OK', but then it probably isn't possible to make much conversation when someone is breaking the news to you that your son is in perilous danger.

There was of course nothing that they could do. Anna filled them in on what was happening, then left them to carry on to their wedding, coping as best they could with the sudden and unexpected burden of anxiety on their shoulders.

The rental of the chalet was coming to an end that day so Stu and Anna arranged to stay in one of the apartments up the road that had been rented for an extra day. In the afternoon they hugged and said goodbye to all those in the party who were leaving, and the rest of the day was spent shifting all their stuff, plus Jamie's stuff and mine, to the apartment, and returning the rented snowboards and skis. Before they knew it, another day had slipped by, and still their loved ones had not been returned to them.

Anna went to bed with a very heavy heart that night. Time, she knew, was running out.

CHAPTER NINE

The PGHM

As ANNA TOSSED AND TURNED, sleepless in her bed, Jamie and I were struggling for survival on our little ledge. It was so cold now – colder than I could have possibly imagined. I wasn't certain how long I could hold out and I clung to Jamie desperately for warmth, just as he clung desperately to me. But there was no escape from the biting wind and all we could do was huddle together and wait.

Not knowing what else to do I found myself praying for the rescue to come, begging to whoever would listen for the helicopter to come and save us. I began to despair. What if they'd given up? What if after the failed attempt on Friday afternoon, the PGHM had decided that it was too difficult, too dangerous to reach us, and that there was nothing else they could do? Would we be left here for ever?

If only I'd known just how hard the brave men of the PGHM were trying to rescue us, I might have held out hope for a little longer. It was weeks, even months before I learnt their story, piecing it together from the accounts of those involved, and it was only then that I fully realised just how important it was for them, just how much it meant to them, to get us safely down from the mountain.

* * *

The PGHM

Capitaine Blaise Agresti, commander of the PGHM, gathered his men together in the upstairs briefing room of their headquarters, a look of concern on his face. It was two days now, forty-eight hours, since the three worried Brits had come in to the office and registered their concerns for the overdue climbers. During those two days, he and his men had been able to do practically nothing to help. Agresti was proud of his rescue team and their extremely high rate of success in bringing stricken climbers down from the mountains, and the current enforced lack of action was frustrating.

However, there was nothing that could be done. Snow was falling at an incredible rate – up to 10 centimetres an hour. There was more snow than anyone in the town could remember, it seemed. And with visibility down to more or less zero, the helicopters couldn't fly and a rescue mission on foot was impossible.

This weather had arrived on Tuesday afternoon, and although some snow had been forecast, no one had predicted just how severe it would be. A huge area of low pressure, totally covering the North Atlantic, had brought Arctic winds in from the north-west. At the same time, an equally large area of high pressure over the South Atlantic was feeding winds from the south-east. These masses of cold and warm, moisture-laden air had collided over Europe, causing a heavy snowfall. Due to the sheer size of the pressure systems the snowfall had proved unusually heavy and extended.

Agresti was just glad that more climbers hadn't been caught out. There was one pair who had been stranded in a mountain hut, but they had been evacuated after a day or two. Another pair of Russian climbers had also been missing, but they had turned up safe and well, after tunnelling their way across the Vallée Blanche to the Midi Station. The two British climbers, however, were of great concern.

Later on today, he told his men, the *météo* predicted a chance of an improvement in the weather. The team was to be ready to scramble at a moment's notice. Gilles Trousselier and Alain Place were the 'secouristes premiers à marcher', or first rescuers on duty, that day, and Daniel Poujol and Christian Bare-Guillet were the helicopter pilot and winchman respectively. The two climbers were thought to be stranded somewhere on the North Face of Les Droites or on the descent from the mountain, and it was there that the team should start looking.

When the briefing was over, Agresti wished the team good luck before they headed out to the helicopter station, known as the dropping zone, to make preparations for the anticipated search and rescue.

At about 2.00 p.m. their chance came. A partial clearing of the clouds offered the possibility of being able to reach Les Droites in the helicopter. The helicopter, an Alouette 3, was soon airborne and struggling in the strong winds. In order to cut down on weight, the team dropped Alain Place off at the Lognan ski station and continued up to the foot of Les Droites. Fortunately, the North Face of Les Droites was mostly cloud free by that stage, and it took only a few minutes to scan the height of the face.

Nothing was visible until they crested the ridge of the mountain and there, right on the *brèche*, were two small figures, waving frantically. Poujol circled his machine round a few times, as close as he dared go, while Trousselier and Bare-Guillet surveyed the layout of the land. It looked like it was going to be difficult. The notch in the ridge was quite deep and Poujol would have to hold the helicopter very steady while Trousselier was lowered down.

They pulled out and circled over the glacier while Trousselier got himself ready on the end of the winch line. Poujol then flew back over the *brèche* and attempted to bring the machine down steadily, but at that altitude the helicopter had little power and was unable to fight the gusting wind without careering about dangerously. The main difficulty was the strong updraft blowing up the North Face, which at any moment could toss the helicopter unexpectedly skyward.

After two vain attempts, the team pulled away from the face to prepare a different method of attack. This time Trousselier was lowered down on the full 40 metres of the winch line as the helicopter approached the *brèche* in the hope of landing him. He would detach himself from the line, and simultaneously attach one of the two climbers, to be carried to safety. The helicopter could then return to lift the second climber and Trousselier together.

Struggling with the updraft, Poujol managed to get Trousselier to within five metres of the climbers, but no closer. Each time he eased in towards the *brèche*, the vicious updraft would suck the helicopter upwards, swinging Trousselier about dangerously. After several determined tries, the helicopter once more pulled back.

Meanwhile, the PGHM had enlisted the help of a private helicopter company, Chamonix Mont-Blanc Hélicoptères. Their Lama helicopter had the same engine and rotor blades as the Alouette, but had a lighter body and a pylon-construction tail, rather than solid walled. The Lama was therefore capable of flying in stronger winds and remaining steadier in heavy gusts.

The Alouette was landed at the Lognan Station and Trousselier transferred to the Lama, piloted by the civilian pilot Pascal Brun. Brun took his Lama up to the *brèche* and attempted the same manoeuvre as the Alouette. Once again Trousselier got to within five metres of the climbers, but once again the helicopter was forced back.

It wasn't going to work. A different approach was required. Trousselier formulated another plan. While it was impossible to drop a man at the *brèche*, it did appear feasible that he might be landed near the west peak of Les Droites. From there he would be able to traverse the ridge a short distance before making an abseil into the *brèche*. The next difficulty would be getting himself and the climbers out of the *brèche*. If they were able, he could help them to climb up to the West Peak from where the helicopter should be able to pick them up. However, the two climbers were likely to be dehydrated and extremely fatigued from their ordeal, possibly incapable of making the steep climb out of the *brèche*. If necessary, Trousselier would be forced to share their little ledge for the night, and attempt an escape in the morning. His rucksack contained the equipment he needed along with hot drinks and provisions.

Before the team could implement this plan, however, the weather intervened and thick clouds swept in, shrouding the mountains in a dense cloak once more. The helicopters were forced to retreat to the valley, and as the afternoon drew to an end, the rescue team retired for the night, disappointed.

Capitaine Agresti reported the day's news to John Wilkinson and Anne Sauvy, who he knew well, and who promised to pass the information on to the British. They would be relieved to know that the two climbers were still alive, despite the failure of the rescue attempts. Then there was nothing that could be done but wait.

* * *

At 7.30 a.m. on Saturday morning, Daniel Poujol and the rest of the team were at the dropping zone, ready to go. The sky was free of cloud but the wind was blowing even more fiercely. In the control room, Poujol looked at the data that was coming in. The wind speed was 140 kph; the *météo* confidently predicted strong winds all day. With top speeds of 130 kph, the Lama and the Alouette would be unable to fly anywhere near the mountain summits.

Despite these horrendous conditions Poujol made two attempts to approach Les Droites that morning, in the hope of at least reassuring the climbers that they were still trying to get them down. The first flight was with *securiste* Philippe Debernardi, and the second was with Agresti himself. For Agresti it was the most terrifying flight of his career. It was hopeless.

The outlook for the stranded climbers was grim. The temperature in the valley was −25°C – 3,000 metres higher up, on the summit of Les Droites, the temperature would be more like −30°C. Combined with a wind speed of at least 140 kph, this would create conditions equivalent to −60°C.

Later on in the morning Blaise Agresti and Gilles Trousselier met with Anne Sauvy and her British friends to describe their efforts so far and to explain why no rescue could take place that day. They assured the worried party that the men of the PGHM were doing their utmost to get the climbers down and that another mission would be launched as soon as the wind allowed.

During the day, the team met to plan a strategy for the next attempt. The greatest difficulty had been the depth of the *brèche*, preventing the helicopter with its 40-metre winch line from getting close enough to the climbers. A longer winch line would be too unmanageable and heavy. Extending the line with a lighter climbing rope wouldn't work either, as the climbing rope would be blown about too easily and could get tangled, snagged, or even sucked into the rotor blades. However, it was proposed that the winch line could be fastened to the end of the climbing rope. The winch line was heavy enough to keep the climbing rope taut, and was stiff enough not to get blown about or tangled itself. The *securiste* could be dropped off at the west summit, and from there could make his way to the climbers. When he had prepared them to be lifted, the heli-copter would hopefully be able to bring the winch line close enough to attach to them and lift them off.

The forecast for the next day wasn't much better, but the hours immediately after dawn offered the hope of a little respite in the wind. The mission was planned for first light. Until then all they could do was pray that the two climbers were still alive and could hold out through the night.

At 7.30 a.m. on Sunday morning, Daniel Poujol was back at the dropping zone, monitoring the flying conditions. Finally the wind had dropped sufficiently for the helicopters to fly. The team held another briefing during which Poujol and Brun persuaded Agresti that the best man to pilot the helicopter was Brun's colleague, Cor-rado Truchet. Truchet was an extremely experienced and skilful pilot as well as being a qualified alpine guide. The only trouble was that Truchet was currently in the Val d'Aoste in Italy, enjoying the weekend off. The Mont Blanc Tunnel was closed and the roads were all blocked with snow so, while the rest of the team prepared the rescue, Poujol and Agresti made an illegal flight into Italy to pick Truchet up.

Poujol and Agresti then took the Alouette up to the Lognan Sta-tion with the two 'premiers à marcher', Philippe Pouts and Alain Iglesis, where they rendezvoused with the Lama, piloted by Truchet.

Also on duty at the Lognan Station was Jérôme Moracchioli, one of Chamonix Hospital's unique team of mountain doctors. Experi-enced mountaineers or even mountain guides, these doctors are experts in the field of high-altitude and emergency medicine. Along with the PGHM, one of these doctors is permanently on standby to assist in the rescue of injured or sick climbers. By giving immediate medical attention at the scene of the accident and before patient evacuation, the mountain doctors are able to save valuable time and often save lives that would otherwise have been lost. Due to the extreme difficulty of the mission today, however, Moracchioli would be going no further than the Lognan.

The men hurriedly made their final preparations, aware that the clock was still ticking. It seemed almost too much to hope that the stranded climbers had survived the night, but if they had then with every passing minute their chances were diminishing.

When all was ready, Truchet, his winchman and Iglesis set off in the Lama to carry out a recce. Conditions were still very turbulent when they reached the summit of Les Droites. As they approached the *brèche*, their hearts pounding, they hoped against hope that they weren't already too late.

CHAPTER TEN

A Rescue

ON SUNDAY MORNING the rest of our party were due to return to Britain and Stu and Anna were forced to move once again. This time, to be closer to the centre of things, they took rooms in a hotel in the middle of Chamonix, whose name, Hotel Le Chamonix, belied its modest nature.

The pair had moved their belongings to their new quarters and were sitting in the tiny hotel bar, drinking coffee, waiting and hoping, when Anna heard the buzz of a helicopter flying outside. She rushed to the door and just caught sight of the machine, flying low over the town and disappearing out of sight behind the buildings.

When she came back inside to tell Stu, the television, flickering silently in the corner, attracted her attention. The television was showing pictures of a helicopter, and a team of men, strapping on crampons. It then cut to a map of France, and a graphic pinpointed the town of Chamonix.

It was on the news! There was a rescue going on!

Anna and Stu raced up the hill to the PGHM building, a couple of hundred metres away. Arriving breathless, they demanded to know what was happening.

The duty officer confirmed that two climbers had been evacuated from the mountain.

Were they alive though? implored Stu. The officer was vague about this. Both had been taken to hospital. One was definitely alive. Stu and Anna were having difficulty understanding the officer's French. The other might be alive but may have been unconscious or have sustained a serious injury.

Then Miles Bright, the man who had arranged the chalet for us, rushed into the building. He told Stu and Anna that he had just come down from the Lognan Station where the rescued climbers had been brought for immediate treatment before being ferried to the hospital. There was no doubt, he said, as to the condition of the two climbers, and they might as well know the simple truth now.

One was alive. The other was dead. He didn't know which was which.

Silence fell over the room. Anna and Stu were both completely derailed. This was an outcome which neither of them had prepared for. They had been through this whole nightmare together, bolstering each other up, united by their common concern. They had prepared themselves for the worst – never to see their loved ones again. They had urged each other to keep hoping for the best – the safe return of the two itinerants. Neither of them had thought for one moment that one climber might be rescued alive and the other not. How could it be that one of them would get their Jamie back and the other one wouldn't? How could the one look the other in the eye ever again?

Anna immediately found herself hoping that it was her Jamie who had survived. The guilt that swelled inside her at thinking the thought tore her apart. Was Stu currently going through the same awful mental dilemma? she wondered. Were they both, at that moment, wishing with all their hearts for it to be their Jamie who was alive, loathing themselves for, by default, wanting the other to be dead? Neither of them seemed able to speak.

Anna thought about the crumpled note in her pocket, which she had carried with her always since Monday, and which read, 'See you soon xxxx'. Was it true? Would she see her Jamie again now? Or was Stu to be reunited with his son? Was she to be reunited with just a lifeless corpse? Had the note been a lie? It was all too awful to think about. They would have to go to the hospital now to find out.

The PGHM gave Anna and Stu a lift across town to the hospital in one of their transit vans. Jules and another friend, Jacqui Austin, who had been waiting outside, came along for moral support. Feeling like she was going to be sick, Anna followed the others into the spotless modern building. They were asked to wait. Anna sat next to Stu, holding his hand. Still she didn't dare entertain hope that one or other of us was the survivor for fear of finding herself wishing the other dead. Her head swam in a sea of confusion.

The two sat silently side by side as the moment when their wait would finally be over bore down on them with the inevitability of a freight train.

CHAPTER ELEVEN

The End

WE'RE NOT GOING to make it. I know now that we're going to die. Ever since our hands froze I've known that we're not going to make it through the night.

I don't remember exactly what happened. It all became too confusing. I remember we were fighting the wind for the top of the bag. We kept trying to pull the edges under us and keep the zip done up tight, but the wind kept tearing the bag away and it would flap about uncontrollably. The wind had also scoured the ledge clean of snow and it was just like a rink of solid ice; we kept sliding about and the bag wouldn't stay where we put it, and then there was some problem with the zip. After I'd finished fixing the zip I found my fingers were white and frozen at the ends and I couldn't put my hands back into my gloves. Jamie's fingers where the same and we knocked our hands together and they went clunk, like frozen chops. And we laughed. I think we both realised then that all hope was lost.

I don't know how long ago that was. Five minutes. Five hours. I don't care anyway. I can't get any sense out of Jamie any more. He just keeps shouting at me, 'It's time to go! We've got to go now!'

I don't understand what he's talking about, but he just keeps on shouting, 'We've got to go now!'

I don't seem to be able to think straight. Everything is in such turmoil. The wind is making too much noise in my ears and it stops my brain from working. All I know is the wind, screaming in my ears. And the bivvy bag – Jamie's one, which is brand new – it's gone. I don't know what happened to it. It's just gone. And now we are sitting in the open, fully exposed to the terrible wind, and Jamie is looking at me and shouting at me once more, 'We've got to go now!'

Still I don't understand, and as I look in his eyes I see nothing. No recognition. Just darkness. Then he looks down at the snow and he doesn't shout any more.

But now I understand. Now I realise that it's all over. The game is up. The mountain has won and there isn't going to be a happy ending this time. The hope which kept us going for so long is gone now, blown away in the wind, leaving behind it only certainty. The certainty of death.

I'm sitting down on the ice now, face into the wind. I've lost my mittens. Both my hands are frozen, claw shaped, like meat. I've got no boots on either, and my feet are frozen too. But I feel no pain. Just numbness.

Jamie lies beside me, face down across the *brèche*, like a culled deer on a horse's saddle. At first he fights and struggles, tries to escape. But soon he slows down and just lies there. I shout to him but he doesn't respond. I can't reach him. I can do nothing.

Occasionally he moves, an arm or his head, but less often now. I sit in the snow and watch, feeling detached. I have the strange feeling that I'm no longer on the ledge, but floating high above it, circling like a bird, or a spirit, or perhaps a helicopter, arriving too late. I'm soaring above the ledge and looking down on two frozen corpses, one lying, one sitting, both motionless. Two more mountaineers who have fallen victim to the mountains, their story of tragedy to remain forever untold. Two young men, in the prime of their lives, whose luck has run out, like so many before, and so many to follow, and whose friends and families will bear the burden of their loss.

I didn't expect this. I didn't see it coming. I'm still less than thirty and I'm about to die and I'm not prepared for it. Somehow I thought that this would never happen to me. Not like this. I think about Anna, who gave me her unquestioning love. I can't believe I won't see her again, not even to say goodbye. I promised her I'd come back. I've let her down. And my parents, who went through all the emotion and effort of bringing me up, and everyone else, I've let them all down.

I look across at Jamie. He doesn't move any more. I think he's dead, now. I've never seen a dead person before.

I wonder how long before I join him. I just want to drift off and join him now. It occurs to me that if I unzip my jacket, the end will come quicker. I try to grasp the zip of my jacket, but my hands are useless blocks of ice. If I could, I would stand up, to face the full force of the wind, and meet my certain fate head on, but the rope which tethers me has become frozen into the ice of the ledge and it stops me from standing. I am chained to the mountain, like Prometheus, at the mercy of the gods. I am so beaten by the forces of nature that I am unable to rise to meet my fate. I can only sit and wait.

I curl up where I am, and close my eyes. I think I feel drowsy now. I want to let sleep take me – to let it carry my soul silently and pain-lessly away, leaving my useless body deep in a slumber from which it will never wake.

I sit there, curled up, for what seems like a long time, and then gradually I slip into the waiting arms of sleep. But I am not released into the freedom of unconscious oblivion. Instead I begin to dream. I dream that I am still sitting there, hunched on the icy ledge, when a mysterious hole opens up in the snow, on the opposite side of the ledge. Figures emerge from the hole – shadowy figures which I can't identify or recognise. I can't seem to look directly at them – can only see them out of the corners of my eyes. I know that they've come for us – to take us away. They take Jamie first. They lift up his inert body, and carry him into the opening in the mountain. I wait for them to return. I want them to take me too. But they don't come back for me, and the opening in the mountain closes up, and then I'm awake again.

I look about. Jamie's body still lies there, his lifeless face pressed into the snow. There is no hole in the mountain. I'm still alive.

Then I notice the mountains in front of me. They are becoming lit by the diffuse light of dawn. As I watch, the light grows stronger and the peaks grow out of the darkness, monstrous and luminous like ghosts. One by one, the mountain summits catch fire, struck by the first, flaming rays of the sun. I gaze on, mesmerised, as the burning red light spreads across the whole of the savage and prehistoric landscape before me. I am convulsed by the violent beauty of it all, and I feel that my heart is being torn from my chest by the raw emotion that's welling up inside me. I am utterly defeated by nature's awesome and terrible power, and, able to do nothing else, I attempt to scream my fury at it. But my voice is torn from my lips by the force of the wind, so I give up, and continue to watch the spectacle in silent submission.

Gradually I become aware that the primal din of the gale is accompanied by another noise. A heartbeat. Faintly – a fast and constant pulse – getting louder. A helicopter.

I am long past reactions such as surprise, relief or joy. I watch with indifferent interest as the machine thunders into view. I look on, dazed and dispassionate as it soars up the face and swoops overhead like an eagle.

The helicopter wheels round in the sky and makes a further two passes above me. I wave a frozen hand, rigid as a garden fork, but make no other move. The helicopter retreats to open space above the glacier. I continue to look out at the beautiful mountains.

When the helicopter returns, it carries a man, hanging by a thread. This time the machine heads for the narrow ridge above the *brèche*. With difficulty it hovers, rocking in the unsteady wind, kicking up clouds of billowing spindrift, and sets the man down on the ridge. It then flies off, leaving the man behind.

I might watch the man more closely, but I am facing to the north, and it is difficult for me to twist my stiffened shoulders and neck round to face him. So I gaze at the mountains and wait his arrival.

The man moves fast. He has soon set up an abseil which brings him in one rope length to our bivouac. He reaches Jamie first and, bending over him, checks for signs of life.

Something revives inside me, as if I've found a glowing ember in my icy core, and I find the will to speak, miraculously in French.

'Il est mort,' I say.

The man ignores my words, but leaves Jamie's body and strides across to where I sit. He is a small, lean and wiry man, with brown leathery skin and steely blue eyes. His movements are quick and efficient and he breathes with fast, urgent pants. Around his mouth, ice is forming, as his warm breath condenses. He wears the blue mountain uniform of the PGHM, the French mountain rescue service.

He squats down beside me, unshoulders his pack, and fetches from it a steel flask. From the flask he pours a cup of steaming liquid.

'Buvez du thé!' he orders.

I sip the hot sweet tea as he brings the cup to my lips. It tastes wonderful but is too hot and scalds my mouth.

'C'est chaud,' I complain at the heat.

'Oui. Buvez!' he insists.

I finish the contents of the cup and he pours out another cupful.

'Du plus!' he says, so I drink some more.

He then puts away the flask and gets out a rescue harness. I help him get the harness on to me by shifting my weight as best I can while he pulls it underneath me. He does up the harness buckles with care, double-checking everything. Then he pulls out a knife, locates the frozen rope that binds me to the mountain, and slices through it with one swift stroke.

He takes a radio handset from his jacket and shouts into it some words of French that I don't follow. A brief reply crackles from the radio.

We wait for a minute or two. Suddenly the helicopter appears again, this time approaching from the south. Below it, it trails the winch line. The helicopter makes no attempt now to hover over the *brèche*, but flies straight over. The pilot must be supremely skilful for, as he makes the pass, the end of the winch line swings precisely towards us.

My rescuer, holding my harness attachment in one hand, deftly catches the karabiner as it swings past with the other hand, and in one movement clips it to my harness.

Immediately I realise what's going to happen, but have only about two seconds to brace before I feel the monstrous, stomach-lurching jerk and am whisked, spinning into space. The rock walls of the *brèche* rush past me, in a terrifying blur, then I'm flying through open air, high above the glacier, high above everything, suddenly free from the prison of ice that has incarcerated me for so long.

I still feel bewildered. My stumbling thoughts are disordered and incoherent. But one thing is clear: this isn't a happy ending. It hasn't all turned out fine in the end. I know that I am going home now, but I know that I am returning to a very different world from the place I left behind six days ago.

As I am flown away, I look back at the *brèche*, receding fast into the distance. The last thing I see is the man in the blue, crouching over the inanimate body of Jamie – my friend.

The helicopter soon sets me down. Everything becomes a confusion of noises and blurred faces. I feel a lot of hands, lifting me and moving me. A hard metal platform. Loud voices. Another helicopter. A gentle voice speaks to me, says something about oxygen. A gas mask on my face. A kaleidoscope of coloured stars. Then black.

CHAPTER TWELVE

A Hot Bath

First I hear voices. A clamour of urgent French voices, issuing instructions, shouting out orders. Then I am aware of scissors. They are big scissors and I am aware of them because they are cutting through my clothes. I am distressed about this because I need my clothes to keep me warm, and they are expensive clothes, but they are quickly pulled from me and I am naked, on a hard bed. Then I am wrapped in wonderful warm blankets and I feel the heat soak into me like water into a sponge and I forget about the clothes.

I feel hands, holding me under my arms and legs.

I hear, 'Un. Deux. Trois!' and I am lifted bodily and quickly set down again, this time in a sitting position.

My eyes swim into focus, and the fuzzy white shapes that surround me resolve themselves into people: doctors and nurses, hurrying about in white coats and uniforms. I am in a small bright hospital room, and am sitting in a brown plastic reclining chair, my body still swaddled in the blankets.

A nurse, a young woman, is sitting at my side. She holds a plastic cup, with a lid like a baby's mug, to my lips.

'Here. You must drink some tea,' she says softly. She tips the cup and, gladly, I drink the warm, sweet liquid.

Two other nurses are standing by a sink and filling buckets with hot water and disinfectant, and I wonder if they're going to wash the floor. However, I realise the water is for me when the buckets are placed on stools around my chair, and my hands and feet are immersed. I am being defrosted like a turkey, forgotten until Christmas morning.

A doctor approaches me. I presume he is a doctor because he is wearing a shirt and a coat rather than the uniform of the nurses. He is a tall man, with impossibly long thin limbs and the hunched shoulders of a man who has spent a lifetime stooping to pass through doors. His hands are long and bony and his gaunt face wears a kind and caring expression.

'I am Docteur Marsigny,' he says, 'I am the chief of the department of resuscitation and traumatology here. Can you please tell me your name?'

'Jamie Andrew,' I reply, meekly.

'Good. Now, Monsieur Andrew, I need to insert a tube into your chest in order to give you medicines.'

I put up no protest as he first injects an anaesthetic, then inserts a very large needle into my chest, pushing hard to get it under my collarbone. He frowns and tuts before removing the needle and trying again. Several times he fails to find the vein, explaining that I am very dehydrated and my blood vessels have partly collapsed. Finally the central line goes in and I am hooked up to a drip.

People continue to busy around me. I am fed more tea. My hot water buckets are changed. My blood pressure is taken and I have thermometers inserted into every orifice. I am carefully catheterised.

I don't know whether it's the rehydration, the warmth, the relief, the drugs or a combination of all of these, but I feel a rush of vitality charging into me. My head is spinning deliriously and I am soon buzzing like a man on speed. I chat to the nurses, babbling in the best, most fluent French I have ever spoken. I talk away, and I think the nurses are surprised to find their frozen patient suddenly so lively, although they don't always seem to understand my French. They are a cheerful bunch, and I feel that I'm in good hands.

Dr Marsigny strides into the room, a telephone in his hand.

'Yes ... Yes ... He is here. Would you like to speak to him?' He looks at me. 'Monsieur Andrew, it is your father. Would you like to speak with him?'

Surprised, I nod, and he holds the phone to my ear.

'Jamie?' I recognise my father's voice, but it sounds distant and brittle. 'It's Dad. How are you?'

'I'm fine,' I reply. 'My hands and feet are in buckets of water.' This is the best description of my situation I can come up with. 'Jamie's dead,' I add.

'We know. We're so sorry. Your mother and I have been so worried about you. We're so glad you're alive. I'm flying out to Geneva in the morning. I'll see you tomorrow.'

We say goodbye and Dr Marsigny takes away the phone.

After being thawed out, I am pronounced fully defrosted, and the next item on the agenda is a hot bath. I am wheeled out of the room, into a wide corridor, and into another room where a large steel bath is filling with hot disinfected water.

When the bath is full, I am lifted once more by the arms and legs, and lowered into the tub. Bliss.

I wallow in the hot pungent water while a nurse sits beside me, feeding me tea from my mug. We exchange conversation in a broken mixture of French and English and the inconsequential talk makes me feel relaxed and secure.

How strange it seems to be so suddenly snatched from the living hell of life on the mountain, to find myself warm and comforted, surrounded by friendly, caring faces, people who will look after me. I feel soothed and unburdened. I am aware that there are matters of great gravity that I will have to confront in the near future, but right now I am too shattered to care. I feel that I am in a dream, a soft protective dream, from which I have no desire to emerge.

Some time later, Dr Marsigny announces that it is time for me to go to bed.

'It is very important that you get some rest,' he says. 'I think you are very tired and you are going to have a hard struggle ahead.'

'What's going to happen to my hands and feet?' I ask, feebly hoping for some reassurance.

'It is too soon to say. You have very serious frostbite.' In his strong accent he pronounces this last sentence, 'You 'ave very serioz frozbite,' – for me, in the coming weeks, it is to become his catch-phrase.

A trolley is brought into the bathroom and I am lifted onto it. I am then wheeled through blue-walled corridors, and into a room, also blue walled, which contains a bed, a reclining chair, a sink, and various pieces of electronic equipment. This is to be my home for a while.

I am lifted onto the bed, and slid between smooth fresh sheets. Two of the nurses gently wrap my lifeless hands and feet in loose, dry dressings. My drip is rearranged, I am hooked up to an automatic temperature and blood pressure machine, then the nurses depart, wishing me a restful sleep.

I look around me and notice the window. Outside, heavy snow falls, and all is white. The storm continues.

CHAPTER THIRTEEN

The Worst Hour

A tall, thin doctor strode down the corridor, his thin battered leather shoes slapping with each step on the concrete floor. He wore an expression of utmost seriousness. Scanning the four pale people waiting there for news, he singled out and addressed Stu.

'I am Docteur Marsigny. Are you the father of Jamie Fisher?"

Stu nodded.

Marsigny crouched down in front of the seated Stu. He looked him in the eye and said, 'I am sorry. Your son is dead.'

Stu remained absolutely motionless. He said nothing.

Anna felt like she might wretch on the cocktail of emotions that ran through her. Her Jamie was alive. That was all she could think. After all the awful waiting, he had come back and he was alive. She hated herself for thinking it.

Tenderly, Marsigny asked Stu if he would like to see Jamie.

'Yes,' said Stu, his big voice suddenly sounding very thin.

Anna asked Stu if he would like her to come with him. She asked without considering how it would be to see the body, without measuring her dread. She just wanted Stu to have someone with him right now, the same way that they had been there for each other throughout the whole ordeal.

'Yes,' said Stu.

The pair followed Marsigny down the corridor and into a small silent room containing a single bed. Blinds were drawn across the windows. There, in the dim light, Stu and Anna said goodbye to Jamie.

Later, when Stu had regained his composure, he straightened up and asked Marsigny how I was. Marsigny explained that I was recovering from hypothermia and that I had very severe frostbite in all my extremities. For a minute or two Stu and the doctor discussed various technical issues, which Anna didn't fully understand, regarding the possibilities of complications and kidney infections.

Marsigny then asked Anna if she would like to see me.

Suddenly, Anna felt all her strength and resolve crumble, and all she could see was the frozen body on the bed, and a vision of me, motionless and blue also. She realised she couldn't face it. She wasn't ready.

When she said no, Dr Marsigny looked surprised. Anna felt she should explain, but she couldn't find the words. She just felt so terribly frightened. She muttered something about coming back in an hour and rushed off, Stu following on behind.

Back in the bar of the Hotel Le Chamonix, the pair were joined by the last stragglers of our party who hadn't yet departed for Geneva. Toying with their glasses of whisky, the sombre group drank to the memory of Jamie Fisher and to my swift recovery.

After a while, Anna felt ready to return to the hospital. One of our friends, Inge, a doctor, offered to accompany her and as they walked through the snow she tried to explain to Anna what it would be like in the hospital.

Anna wasn't to be afraid, she explained, if she was asked to put on a gown. Nor should she be upset if I was connected up to drips and electronic equipment or was wearing an oxygen mask. These were all normal medical procedures and nothing to be concerned about. Inge walked Anna as far as the door of the hospital, then, hugging her and wishing her luck, had to run back into town to catch the last bus to Geneva.

With butterflies in her stomach, Anna walked up to the reception desk and asked to see Jamie Andrew. After a short wait she was gently ushered to a room just down the corridor from the one where

Jamie Fisher had lain. Her escort left her by the doorway. Standing
on the threshold, Anna peered nervously in through the open door.
There, sat up in bed, tucked into a white sheet up to the waist, and
connected to an assortment of cables and tubes, was her Jamie, his
eyes turned towards the window. His face was drawn and hollow
eyed, but as he turned to look at her she saw with relief that he was
pink and warm and very much alive.

I am looking pensively out the window at the snow when I hear a
noise at the door. I look round and there, in the doorway, stands
Anna. Her face looks pale and tired, she wears an uneasy smile, and
I can see red rings around her eyes, but she is the most wonderful
sight I have ever seen. I don't suppose I'm looking particularly great
myself at the moment.

She comes over and sits down on my bed.

'Hello,' she says, uncertainly.

'Hello,' I reply. 'We've lost Jamie.'

'I know.' Then the tears begin to flow from both of us. I can't
move to embrace her but she leans down and hugs and kisses me.

'I'm so glad you made it. I thought I'd never see you again. I
thought you'd never come back.'

'I know, baby,' I say as I weep, 'but I did come back.'

We remain there for a few moments, wrapped in each other. Her
smell is so sweet, and her hair and skin are so soft. I can't believe I'd
given up hope of ever seeing her again. I no longer care about all the
pain and suffering I've been through, the pain and suffering ahead.
All that matters is that we are together, reunited again.

Then Anna draws back.

'The doctor says that I've to leave you to sleep. You're going to
need all your strength. I'll see you tomorrow.'

She kisses me on the forehead then backs out of the room, closing
the door behind her.

My head has no room left for any thoughts now. My mind is
blank. I settle back on the soft pillow and, before I can reflect on the
day's events, I fall swiftly into a deep and dreamless sleep.

Two Hospitals

CHAPTER FOURTEEN

Reality Bites

I WOKE GRADUALLY on Monday morning and for a few moments felt warm, secure and content. Then reality returned, flooding in like a grim tide into which my heart sank, as I opened my eyes to face for the first time my new world. Jamie was dead. Gone for ever. The recollection hit me like a brick wall. I couldn't believe it. Dead. As for me, I was alive, but God knows what was going to become of me. I'd never had cause in the past to learn much about the effects of frostbite. It seemed pretty obvious that I wasn't going to recover from this adventure intact, but what would I lose? Fingers? Toes? Hands? Feet? The only thing that seemed certain was that my life would never be the same again.

I felt like I had the most ferocious hangover of my life. My head throbbed, my mouth and lips were dry and sore, and my whole body was achingly stiff and uncomfortable. My hands and feet were still numb, as if they weren't even there at all, and because of all the drip lines and monitoring equipment I couldn't shift position or roll over. I could barely even move my head because of the central line in my neck. I lay still, imprisoned in the bed.

It began to dawn on me that although snow and ice had been exchanged for sheets and blankets, my sentence of enforced immobility was far from over. I had some relief only when a couple of nurses came in to raise the electric back to the bed and hoist me into a sitting position.

One of the nurses, a bubbly and effusive girl called Dominique, brought in a tray of breakfast materials and sat down beside me to feed me my first proper meal in a long time. I then had my first experience of what was to become the most hated of all the trials that lay ahead of me. Although seemingly trivial, I found being spoon-fed intolerable. The nurses who were forced to inflict this torture on me were of course wonderfully patient, and it wasn't the ignominy or loss of pride at having to be fed like a baby that made it so hard. It was simply the fact that eating is such a personal thing.

When being spoon-fed, the natural rhythm of eating is lost. A mouthful always tends to arrive too early or too late, or is too big or too small. I couldn't help but rush my chewing, try to swallow too soon, knowing that the person at the other end of the spoon, no matter how tolerant, would almost certainly prefer to be doing something else. The joy of food was lost. Eating became a chore rather than a pleasure. I would lose my appetite and all too often call a halt to the meal before being properly satisfied.

I had to be spoon-fed throughout my stay in France and it was to become more than a minor difficulty in the weeks of sickness to come when I needed every ounce of nutrition I could hold down. Even when Anna, whose infinite patience I could always rely on, took up the mantle of spoon-bearer, I still couldn't find it in myself to enjoy a meal. I had some insight into what it was like to be a small child, repulsing a proffered spoon and dribbling pureed vegetables down its bib.

Dominique chatted brightly about how she was going to take her little daughter snowboarding for the first time, as she made hunks of bread, butter and jam more palatable by dunking them into a bowl of hot chocolate, then popped them into my mouth which I presented gaping like a baby bird. I listened to her vacantly.

Dominique was young, attractive and energetic, like most of the nurses in Chamonix Hospital, an attraction of the hospital which didn't go unnoticed by the male contingent of my visitors in the following weeks. Chamonix, a lively and burgeoning town, unique as a centre for outdoor activities and tourism, is fortunate in that young people are drawn to the area, unlike so many other declining Alpine regions. The staff of the small but world-class hospital in Chamonix were representative of this trend.

After breakfast came what was to be the regular routine of a bed bath, followed by a change of bedclothes. The bed bath was a very thorough and fairly demeaning affair but one that left me feeling refreshed and purified. The change of bedclothes was a daily miracle whereby, while I was rolled from side to side, my sheets were removed from beneath me, replaced with fresh ones, and pulled smooth and flat, without any part of me touching the bare mattress underneath. As someone who could barely make a bed given all the time and space in the world, this regular act of magic was a constant source of wonder to me.

After they had changed my various drips and collecting bags, and taken notes from the temperature and pressure equipment, the nurses left me in peace.

I hadn't been absorbed in my thoughts long when Dr Marsigny came in, accompanied by a squad of white-coated physicians. Brushing pleasantries aside, they got down to the business of undressing and examining each of my limbs, pointing, gesticulating and arguing in a very Gallic fashion as they did so.

My hands and feet, which had been white and lifeless when the dressings went on, were still without life but had turned black and blue overnight. They were horribly swollen and looked as though they should be very painful, but I couldn't feel a thing. Also blackened, although I hadn't even realised at the time that they'd been frozen, were my right knee and my right ear. I begged Dr Marsigny to tell me what the outlook was.

Marsigny fired a sharp look into my eyes and took a deep breath.

'You 'ave very serioz frozbite,' he said. 'We don't yet know what is to happen to you. I think . . .' he paused for a moment '. . . that we will have to cut off something, but I don't know yet what we will have to cut. We first have to wait for the necrotic tissue to separate from the living tissue. We will have to wait and see.'

'But how long will that take?' I demanded, reeling at the thought of it all.

'I think it may take several weeks. Right now, the most important thing is to prevent infections from here,' he said, pointing at a blackened hand, 'from travelling up here.' He ran his finger up my arm. 'We are worried that you may then have poisoning of the blood and of the . . . How do you say? *Rein?*'

'Kidney,' interjected one of the other doctors.

'Yes, the kidneys. So right now we will wait, and we will give you some strong antibiotics to control the infections.'

He peered down to inspect my right hand. 'I want you to try to make a fist with your hand,' he said.

I strained the muscles of my right arm and watched as the swollen and bruised digits made the merest flickering of movement towards curling into the intended fist. I knew enough about the workings of the hand to realise that even this slight response was most likely caused by the pull of tendons from further up the arm. The hand itself appeared devoid of life.

We repeated the experiment on the other hand with similar results. Marsigny explained that it was the circulation of blood he was interested in, especially to the bones. If the circulation continued, there was hope of saving at least part of the hands.

My feet, almost out of sight at the other end of the bed, felt very remote and unrelated to me. My toes, which even when healthy had been unresponsive and powerless little monkey-nuts of pink flesh, were now utterly lifeless.

Marsigny and the others took photographs of my useless appendages, then the doctors departed, leaving one of the nurses to redress my limbs and tuck them back into the bed. She then left me alone.

So it was true. Barring miracles it seemed I was definitely going to lose parts of my body. But nobody would tell me what. More than anything I just wanted to know what it was that I would lose. An end to uncertainty. However, the doctors couldn't, or wouldn't, say and so I settled down to the unattractive prospect of waiting. Waiting for the necrotic tissue to separate, whatever that meant. Waiting for the executioner to proclaim life or death to my poor abused limbs. Waiting for a time when my life, so suddenly thrown into tumult, might begin to feel normal again. Over the coming days, and worse, nights, I was to have a lot of time to myself in which to sort through the confusion of dark thoughts which ran amok like demons through my troubled mind.

At first it all just seemed too much to take in. I suppose I was in a prolonged state of shock. To begin with, the grotesque monstrosities at the end of each arm and leg held no horror for me. The prospect of spending my life as a cripple in a wheelchair elicited no fear. The yawning chasm which until so recently had been filled by Jamie Fisher, larger than life, seemed unreal and meaningless in its emptiness. All the strangeness that surrounded me, in a turmoil of changed perspectives, felt distant and detached. I was a motionless rock in a world that had suddenly and inexplicably turned itself on its head. My mind was as numb as my inert hands and feet.

Soon though, as the hours and the days dragged on, the full weight of my concerns began to sink heavily and inevitably upon me.

At night my troubled thoughts seemed to ring round my head like silent screams.

What's happening to me? Where did all this madness come from? I didn't ask for any of this. I didn't see any of this coming.

I thought back again and again over the nightmarish events of Jamie's death and my salvation and just couldn't make sense of it all. Why had I been spared and he hadn't? Why? We had been in it together. Throughout the whole terrible time we had shared everything equally, our food, our drink, our shelter, our hopes. We'd both known that death was a possibility. We'd hoped and prayed together for a swift rescue. Neither I, nor I'm sure Jamie, had for one moment suspected that one of us might make it down without the other. We had lain side by side for four days and five nights, in mutual torment, until destiny, like a giant invisible axe, had suddenly and inexplicably split us apart.

Why had he been taken and not me? Jamie was so much tougher than me. He was the real hard man and I was just a part-time hard man imitator. What had been the crucial difference? Had Jamie perhaps worn one less layer of clothing? Was his blood circulation or metabolism less efficient than mine? Or had I lain in a more sheltered position than him, or had more than my share of chocolate, mint cake or tea? Was the difference down to the toss of the imaginary coin of fate, the random effect of the beat of a butterfly's wing in some far-off place? Or had the will of some greater being played a part?

I couldn't figure it out. All I knew was that the pair of us had been dragged to the edge of the void. Jamie had fallen, disappeared from sight, while I had been held on the very lip of that great precipice, face into the wind that blew from the darkness beyond, then been tossed back, without explanation, to face a new dawn and a whole new world by myself. What on earth could it mean?

I found it difficult to believe that he'd gone. I felt sure that I'd just missed him, that right at that moment he was holed up in some bar in the town, at a smoky table littered with glasses, haranguing an eager audience with the fantastic tale of our latest escapade. If I closed my eyes I could see him, with eyes like saucers and a grin wider than his face, expounding at length about the terribleness of the storm, the epic of endurance on the tiny *brèche* and the spectacular rescue. With each telling, the storm becomes fiercer, the ledge smaller and the rescue more heart-stopping. As the night wears on the storytelling is punctuated by raucous laughter and eventually degenerates into a melee of spilt beer and dancing on tables.

Or perhaps he was here in the hospital, in the room next to me. Perhaps he too was tucked up in bed being tended to by lovely nurses, with his hands and feet in bandages, wondering what the hell was going on. Perhaps we would continue our adventure together, learning to cope with our strange new disabilities, laughing with each other on the way.

But no. He was gone. I'd been with him as he died, watched helplessly through the clouded lenses of my own hypothermia. I'd sat with his unmoving corpse, waiting for my turn to die. He was gone and I knew that nothing would ever fill the space he'd left behind. I felt like a traitor, that I'd broken a pact of solidarity between fellow mountaineers, that I'd waited for him to die before callously hitching a ride out in a helicopter. I hated myself for having survived when Jamie had not. I felt like I oughtn't to smile or laugh ever again.

At home, rock climbing on my local outcrops near Edinburgh.

Jamie Fisher in his element climbing in the Himalayas.

above Jamie Fisher climbing steep ice at the head of the initial coulouir. This pitch provided the key to gaining the foot of the ice field.

left The ice field. An enormous expanse of ice, inclined at 60°, which gave many hours of consistently difficult climbing.

A view of the North Face of Les Droites showing the line taken. Marked are A: The Bergshrund, B: The Ice Field, C: The First Bivouac, D: The point reached when the storm struck, E: The Brèche des Droites, F: The descent down the South Face, G: The Summit of Les Droites.

above Bivouac on the first night. Not exactly a comfortable spot, but secure enough to get some decent rest before the second day of climbing.

right Day two. Jamie Fisher approaches the foot of the headwall.

below The weather breaks. Before long the snowfall was too heavy to contemplate taking any further photos.

Alain Iglesis at the Brèche des Droites while the rescue is taking place.

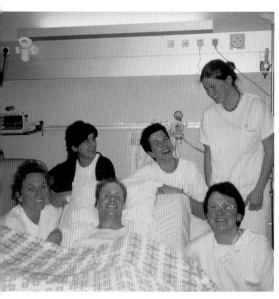

above Surrounded by nurses in Chamonix Hospital. Clockwise from the left: Dominique, Emmanuelle, Pascale, Raphaëlle, Patricia.

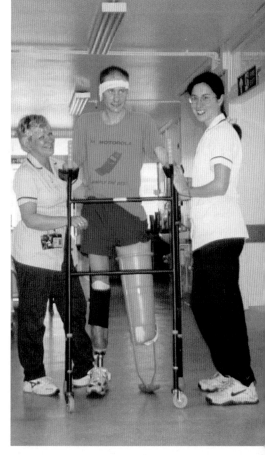

right Learning to walk with Doreen (left) and Joy; I'm wearing one prosthetic leg and one PPAM aid.

Somehow though, I knew in my heart that I had to smile and laugh again, and my smiles and laughs I saved for the many visitors who arrived at my bedside, some of whom appeared more traumatised and worried than me.

My first visitor on that first afternoon was Stu Fisher. He marched into my room with wide arms and a broad smile and gave me a big bear hug, exclaiming how relieved he was that I'd pulled through. I don't know how he found the strength to do that, knowing that his own son hadn't made it, but somehow Stu found room in his big heart to mourn for Jamie and to celebrate for me at the same time. He also confided that he'd had a chat with my doctors and that they were all good people. I was in safe hands.

I didn't know what to say to Stu. I couldn't express the shock and the numbness and the confusion that I felt, and I certainly couldn't bring myself to relate the events of the previous days, but I told Stu feebly how very sorry I was and that Jamie hadn't suffered when he died. Stu smiled at me and I saw the red rings around his eyes.

Stu was accompanied by Rob 'Sid' Tresidder, one of his oldest friends and climbing partners. Stu and Sid had once before suffered a great loss in the Alps when three of their mutual friends disappeared while climbing the Brenva Face of Mont Blanc. When Sid had heard what had happened to Jamie and me he'd flown straight out to be with Stu in his hour of need. Together, Sid and Stu – a more indefatigable pair of mountain goats you couldn't hope to meet – went a long way to cheering me up with their simple resolve to let life go on. They had both felt grief before, but had found a way to absorb the grief into their lives, refusing to let it defeat them. I promised myself that if Stu, with the help of his friends, could make it through, then so could I.

Jules Cartwright arrived. Jules was another young, ambitious and hugely talented climber, unusually professional in his attitude, who knew the risks of his game and had accepted that he might encounter death along the way. Jamie's death had upset him greatly, but he was determined that in no way would it shake his resolve to continue exploring and pushing his limits in the great arena of mountaineering. He knew that if it had been him that had been taken, in place of Jamie, Jamie would continue to climb.

Jules was full of praise for Chamonix Hospital. 'It's one of the two best hospitals in the world for treating frostbite,' he said enthusiastically, as if he'd already done a survey in case he ever needed to know in a hurry. 'The other's in Alaska.' He went on to list off the names of various famous mountaineers who had come to Chamonix from all over the world to have their frostbitten fingers and toes treated. It was reassuring to hear but I couldn't help wondering if they'd ever treated anyone with such bad frostbite as me before.

Anna came to see me too that afternoon. She didn't stay long, but sat with me as I drifted in and out of sleep, exhausted from the effort of talking to people. She came again in the evening and sat with me some more. Also that evening my father arrived, looking tense and concerned. He brightened visibly on seeing me, and was soon chattering away about how worried he and my mother had been when they'd heard what was happening, and how there'd been a barrage of journalists camped outside their front door all yesterday. I lay and listened, rueful of the amount of trouble I'd caused. Outside, darkness fell, the storm continued and snow fell on snow.

CHAPTER FIFTEEN

Uncertain Emotions

DURING THE NIGHT my back started to hurt. I was unable to move to alleviate my discomfort and slept little. I was feeling sick and slightly feverish, and to ensure finally that I didn't sleep, every twenty minutes the automatic blood pressure machine would inflate noisily and uncomfortably round my arm.

I lay awake, turning the events of the previous days over and over in my mind, desperately trying by force of will to rewrite the course of history.

What had gone wrong? What had been our fatal error?

If only we hadn't set out on that fated expedition with a less than perfect weather forecast. We should have just settled for a week of fun, playing in the snow. We should never have gone in the first place. If only we had gone lighter and climbed faster, we might have made it off the mountain before the storm struck. We might at least have made it to the Couvercle Refuge.

Or if we had stuck to the original plan and climbed to the summit of Les Droites and bivvied there, the helicopter might have reached us earlier.

If we had continued on the Tuesday night, up out of the *brèche* to the snow slope below the west summit, as Jamie had suggested, we might have been rescued sooner. Had I vetoed that idea?

Perhaps we should have attempted to make the descent. It would only have been ten or twelve abseils to the glacier. Perhaps we'd have made it, even in those conditions. Why had we just waited until it was too late? Were we guilty of gross and fatal procrastination?

Maybe we had given up hope too soon on that dreadful final night. Maybe we hadn't fought to stay alive as hard as we could have.

If only I'd been wearing inner gloves underneath my mittens, my fingers might not have frozen and we might have survived the night together intact.

As my head began to spiral out of control constructing endless combinations of events that might have produced happier results, I realised I was getting myself nowhere. There could be no 'what-ifs'. 'If-onlys' don't alter the facts. We can't change time. It runs like a river through our lives and we are powerless to swim against its current or alter its course.

I resolved that night to cast out my doubts, to convince myself that what was done was done, that I had no choice but to accept what had happened and get on with my life as best I could. But for many days, weeks, even months, I was unable to prevent those powerful thoughts of regret and contrition from creeping into my head, sinking me into a pit of depression.

I would say that the depression felt like having my heart torn from me, but that's not quite how it was. In fact it was more like my heart was the only organ that was left, beating impotently in my hollow body from which my stomach and guts and lungs had been ripped. Blood was still being pumped mechanically through my veins but my very reason for being alive was gone, my whole situation futile and unnecessary.

At other times, philosophising in the night, I would search for a way to somehow save Jamie, create a separate reality in which he could continue to live. It gave me comfort to think that perhaps each random event, like the tossing of a coin, caused the divergence of reality down two separate pathways, parallel, different, but equally real. I imagined every atom of time splitting as it passes by, creating an infinite number of universes containing all possible combinations of events. In many of those universes I would be the sole survivor. In others, it would be Jamie. In other versions still, neither of us or both of us might have lived. It cheered me up to think of Jamie, in his parallel universe, furious at being detained in hospital with anything so trivial as frostbite.

It was so strange to think that I would never see him again, that he was gone for ever. It wasn't just me who would miss him though. There must be so many other people who were thinking the same thoughts as me right now. His father, his mother, his brothers, his girlfriend Alice, his countless friends. How would they all fill the space that Jamie had left behind? How much pain and suffering would his passing cause? What about the kids he worked with? How would they be affected when their care assistant never returned from his holiday? What would be the cost of Jamie's death?

I woke in a cold sweat, the bedclothes twisted round my legs. Alone in the dark, I was unable to untangle myself and suddenly felt helpless and afraid. I shouted until Yvanne, the night nurse, came running. Whispering soft words of comfort, she straightened out my bed and mopped my brow.

Shift change was at seven o'clock. The arrival of the morning staff was always good news for me, signalling the end of another long night, with only my thoughts for company. In the daytime things felt brighter. There was more interest, more in the way of distractions and more chance of some news from the doctors, progress towards an end to my wait.

That morning, Tuesday, it was a nurse called Nathalie who came in with my breakfast tray of hot chocolate, bread and jam. Breakfast was the one meal of the day that I enjoyed, partly because it was simple and easy to eat, partly because it was such a relief that the night was over, and I wolfed down the soggy sweet hunks of bread.

After my bed bath, I asked Nathalie if she could shave my beard, as I now had well over a week's growth on my face. Nathalie went off to fetch a razor and presently returned with the bluntest, roughest piece of rusty steel I've ever had the misfortune to have scraped across my chin. Nevertheless, despite the scores of painful lacerations, it was a relief to be rid of my itchy facial hair. For some reason, I don't know whether it was a joke or just bad judgement, Nathalie also left one of my sideburns substantially longer than the other. Throughout my stay in France everyone who shaved my face continued this lop-sided trend so that by the end I looked decidedly odd, but as I could neither see nor feel my face, I remained happily oblivious.

At 10.00 a.m. the team of doctors and surgeons marched in and had another look at my hands and feet. I say 'my' hands and feet, but they didn't really feel like mine any more. They were now completely black, dry and withered in parts, especially the digits; swollen and oozing pus elsewhere. They looked for all the world like the ancient and leathery limbs of an Egyptian mummy, preserved for ever in some museum case. Certainly, in no way did they resemble the pink and lively appendages which I had been so used to owning throughout my life and which would wriggle and move at my command. Looking at the wizened, crooked little pegs that were once my fingers, I realised with dread that it was unlikely that many of them could possibly be saved. I tried to imagine a life without fingers, but couldn't.

Dr Marsigny seemed more concerned about my left leg. Of all my limbs, it had been the worst affected. The sharp delineation between pink and black flesh was well up my ankle, and the foot was looking quite swollen and putrid.

'You have an infection,' explained Marsigny, 'and we think it is coming from this foot.' He pointed at the offending article as if it was a disobedient schoolboy. 'Right now we are trying to fight the infection with antibiotics, but if you get more sick we will have to cut this foot. I think we may have to cut this foot anyway, but we want to wait as long as possible. You 'ave very serioz frozbite,' he added, in case I might have forgotten.

The good news was that my frozen knee had made a miraculous recovery, and I now had good mobility and sensation in it. The top layer of skin was dead, however, and over the following weeks it became grey, wrinkled and leathery. 'Peau d'elephant,' the nurses called it – elephant skin – and it eventually peeled off in large, satisfying strips.

The dead tissue in my right ear was also drying and separating off nicely. This I gathered was what they were hoping would happen in my limbs. The body's natural healing mechanism creates a barrier between living flesh and dead flesh, allowing the living flesh to repair itself and the dead flesh to dry and shrivel harmlessly, but until that could happen, the living material was at risk of infection from the dead. Hence all the antibiotics I was being given.

The doctors took their usual round of pictures for their album, then departed, leaving the nurses to tidy up after them.

I spent the morning, as I would spend most of my mornings, trying to kill time. To this day I have a pretty vivid mental map of the ceiling in that room, its plastic panels, fluorescent strip lights and the single air extraction unit. The walls were bare and all I had to look at in front of me was a stainless steel sink. Through the window I could sometimes see the heads of members of staff, arriving and leaving, clearing snow off their vehicles in the car park outside. Beyond was a steep wooded hillside, the trees rising thickly cloaked into the cloud. Occasionally a cable car would float silently into view – the Aiguille du Midi Téléférique. As the car climbed and vanished into the enveloping mist, I would count the seconds till its counterpart appeared, making the downward trip, and imagined the people inside, coming and going; skiers, on their way to make the fantastic descent of the Vallée Blanche; sightseers, hoping for a glimpse of the jagged mountain peaks; mountaineers hoping to climb them. I wondered if I'd ever ride in that cable car again. It seemed part of another world now.

My boredom was often relieved by the comings and goings of hospital staff. The nurses would come in regularly to see that I was all right, feed me drinks, and adjust my bed. Doctors would pop in from time to time. Blood samples were taken, drip bags were changed, I was X-rayed, and hospital orderlies would come and clean the room. Everyone would have a few words for me and most folk would stop and chat. I liked to practise my French and everyone liked to take a few minutes out of their routine to chat to the crazy Scottish climber with his garbled but enthusiastic attempts to speak their language.

I began to feel quite at home in that hospital. It had an atmosphere unique among all the hospitals I have visited before or since. Everyone was relaxed and friendly, and the quarrelling was always light-hearted. Often peals of laughter would be heard ringing down the corridors. The greatest blessing for me was that nobody was at all disapproving of the circumstances of my accident. Many of the staff, and all of the doctors, were mountaineers themselves and understood what Jamie and I had been doing up there. They realised that we weren't foolhardy, suicidal idiots who had recklessly brought about our own downfall, and it was generally accepted that we had been competent but unlucky. This was a great help to me in rebuilding my self-esteem.

At noon Nathalie arrived with my lunch. Lunch usually consisted of cheese, biscuits, fruit and yoghurts and I would certainly have enjoyed it in other circumstances, but I just didn't seem to have an appetite. What with the stress, the infection, all the drugs I was on, and of course the spoon-feeding, I just didn't seem able to force much food down. The best thing about lunch, however, was that it meant that it would soon be visiting time. Visitors were allowed all afternoon, from two to six, although they made an exception for Anna, and she was usually allowed to stay till lights out at ten. She would generally arrive at two, then leave me to my other visitors during the afternoon, and return to be with me in the evening.

After lunch that afternoon, I impatiently waited the hour and a half before my visitors would arrive. The moment Anna finally came through the door, my spirits rose. She, my dad and Jules had been to see the PGHM that morning in order to thank them for fighting so hard to save Jamie and me and so that they could be filled in on the details of the rescue.

Anna had brought a large bundle of mail with her, and we spent an enjoyable hour or so opening the cards from friends and relatives and reading through the sheaf of faxes that had come through to Anna's hotel. Happily this was to prove a regular feature of my stay in Chamonix. Every day, dozens of cards, letters, photographs and faxes would arrive, either at the hotel, or the hospital. I received messages of condolence and encouragement from scores, if not hundreds, of friends – more friends than I ever realised I had. Everyone had been terribly upset to hear what had happened, but they were all a 100 per cent behind me and wished me a speedy recovery. As well as condolences and well-wishes they would send me long, rambling letters, jokes, funny pictures and stories which kept me entertained through the long days ahead. It began to dawn on me that whatever happened to me over the coming weeks, I would have the support of an awful lot of people who cared about me.

I also received cards and letters from dozens of complete strangers who had heard about my story and wanted to wish me well. The most interesting of these were from other people who had suffered in similar circumstances in the mountains, or who were themselves amputees for one reason or another and wanted to share with me the benefit of their experiences.

In particular I remember one short note in a spidery hand:

> *Dear Jamie,*
> *When I was sixteen I lost both hands. Since then I've enjoyed an interesting, varied, full life, achieved independence, and a qualification which enabled me to earn a living, to marry and bring up two daughters. I wish you as much good fortune as I have enjoyed, because I'm sure you will meet as many good-hearted people as has been my happy lot.*
> *Yours sincerely,*
> *Cyril Wire*
> *P.S. I'm now 82 years old.*

It gave me a lot of strength to know that there were others out there who had been in predicaments comparable to my own and had somehow made it through.

Anna bought a folder to keep my letters in and it was soon bursting at the seams. My only regret was that I couldn't read the letters when I was on my own and bored. However, the nurses would stick the cards and photos to the walls with surgical tape and soon the drab blue room was plastered with colourful images.

Later on in the afternoon, my dad arrived with some of the newspapers, from home and from France. My story had created quite a sensation in the press and all of Monday's front pages in the UK had been plastered with headlines like 'ALIVE!' and 'Five Days in Ice Tomb with Dying Mate'. I didn't bother to read the hopelessly inaccurate stories they'd published. My parents' house, our neighbours and Jamie's mother had all been inundated with journalists clamouring for photographs and interviews. Here in France, the hospital and the Hotel Le Chamonix were under siege from an army of journalists, photographers and news crews from all over Europe, many of whom were prepared to resort to decidedly dodgy tactics in their aim to get what they wanted. Anna found the additional pressure of this unwanted attention quite upsetting, and sorely resented being followed from the hotel, and being snooped on from behind pot plants in the hospital foyer.

Dr Marsigny was doing a fine job of fielding all the questions about how I was getting on with typically terse and factual answers, but we decided that the best way to dissipate the demand for information would be to give a press conference. My dad and Jules arranged to do this the next day, and so on Wednesday morning they duly presented themselves in front of the world's press to answer as many questions as they could about what had happened and what kind of condition I was in. All the while, hidden away in the quiet backwater of intensive care, I remained almost oblivious to the circus that was carrying on outside.

Later on Tuesday afternoon, Anna took her leave and left my dad and I chatting and doing the *Scotsman* crossword, although Dad could rarely help himself from blurting out the answers as fast as he read out the clues. I couldn't really focus on the puzzle anyway. Towards the end of the afternoon, a call was put through to the phone by my bed and I spoke to my mother for the first time. She was understandably emotional and sounded very pleased to hear my voice. Like any mother might be, she had always been concerned about her only son being involved in the dangerous activity of mountaineering. In fact, when she realised that I wouldn't be dissuaded in my interest, she had paid for me to go on a rock-climbing course in North Wales, so that I would at least learn to do it properly. Nowadays she preferred not to know what I got up to, so that she wouldn't have to worry. Finally her worst fears had come true – or almost come true.

After talking to my mum for a while, I said goodbye and promised to come home soon. My dad then left me so that Nathalie could come and try to coax a few mouthfuls of beef stew down my unwilling throat. In the evening Anna returned to sit with me.

Anna was my constant companion throughout those troubled times. She was my shoulder to cry on when it all got too much. She was my psychologist and counsellor when my head couldn't take it any more. She was the light in my life when everything else looked black. In return, I tried to be all these things for her. As we sat and talked through those long quiet evenings, after the general hubbub of the busy hospital day had died down, I would realise that she faced the same difficulties as me, that she had lost a close friend too, that she was having to cope with strange and difficult circumstances, and she faced the prospect of forever living with disabilities as well. Then my problems didn't seem so great any more and I didn't feel quite so sorry for myself.

Sometimes we would chat about what lay ahead, speculating on how we might manage if I lost fingers, toes, hands or feet. Sometimes we talked about what had happened, how we both had suffered and what had gone wrong up there on the mountain, hoping to lay the past to rest. Or we would talk about Jamie, his life, his personality and his actions, knowing that by talking about him we could keep his memory alive. If things felt too heavy, we would chat about happier times, in the past and in the future, or play games or do crosswords. Often we wouldn't talk at all, but would enjoy each other's company in silence, lost in thought. Always we were there for one another.

CHAPTER SIXTEEN

My Left Foot

WEDNESDAY, MY FOURTH DAY in hospital, passed with little change in the situation. I'd had another bad night and the constant ache in my back and kidneys had been almost too much to bear. My general well-being was gradually deteriorating and I was having to be fed by drip as I could hold little food down.

One of the doctors to come and look at my limbs that day was Dr Jacques Foray, a retired world expert on frostbite. He was a friendly old man, but when he examined my hands and feet, he frowned and tutted along with the rest of the doctors. I don't know if he offered any advice to the youngsters after they'd left my room, but somehow I could picture him giving a Gallic shrug to the other doctors, before leaving the hospital shaking his head.

Dr Marsigny announced he wanted to send me to another hospital nearby in Bonneville to run some tests that would help establish which parts of my hands and feet might be saved. I was to go tomorrow. At least I would get a change of scenery for a while, I thought. He went on to explain how there were many new techniques being developed whereby plastic surgeons could rebuild the flesh around living bone in order to reconstruct damaged parts of the body. For example, in many burns cases, a patient's damaged hand had been inserted into an opening created in the abdomen. The body was then able to regrow the flesh around the bones. Finally, skin grafts would complete the reconstructed hand. Of course, this process took many months. I baulked at the idea of going round with my hands stitched into my stomach for months on end. I could see I was going to be in hospital for a long, long time.

In the afternoon Anna came to see me as usual, clutching the daily mailbag, then later on my dad arrived to tell me about the press conference while Anna left us to go and meet her friend Flo Kennedy. When she'd heard what had happened, Flo had immediately insisted that she should fly out straight away in order to look after Anna while Anna looked after me. Flo stayed out in Chamonix for two weeks, taking care of Anna, sharing the benefits of her skills as a professional chef, and being generally disapproving of men who insist on doing such activities as idiotic as mountaineering. Unfortunately she was unable to come and see me until later on in her stay as she had a stinking cold and didn't want to risk passing it on.

Anna returned in the evening to pass on Flo's best wishes. She also told me the sad but amusing story of how, earlier in the day, she had drunk her own private toast to Jamie. I had told Anna how Jamie's greatest desire when we'd been stuck on the mountain had been to quench his thirst with a bottle of Yop, the flavoured milk and yoghurt drink. Like me, Anna doesn't like yoghurt drinks but nevertheless she had bought herself a bottle of Yop and drunk it in Jamie's memory. I smiled at the thought of Anna forcing herself to drink the stuff just for Jamie.

Thursday came, and after I had been fed and bathed, it was time for my big trip out. I was gently rolled off my bed and onto a hard trolley. Two nurses wheeled me down the corridors to the waiting ambulance. As we pushed through the big doors into the ambulance bay I felt the sharp bite of the cold air and caught a whiff of diesel. I realised I was beginning to forget what it was like to be outside, spending so much time in my warm, sterile hospital environment. With a few jolts I was loaded into the back of a tiny little ambulance and my trolley was carefully strapped down. A young doctor, who was to accompany me for the day, climbed in beside me, and the nurses waved us off.

The bumpy journey down the valley to Bonneville wasn't as much of a distraction as it could have been. Lying flat on my back, all I could see from the windows was the sky and the snow falling out of it. Fortunately Bonneville was only forty minutes away, and I was soon being wheeled out of the ambulance and into the hospital. From what I saw of it, Bonneville hospital seemed a much more austere and unfriendly place than Chamonix, and I was glad I wasn't staying long.

The first stage of my test, called a bone scintigraphy, was to have a quantity of radioactive tracer fed into my central line. We then had to wait for a few hours to give the tracer time to travel throughout my circulatory system. My hands and feet could then be scanned with a scintillation counter to see which areas the tracer had reached and might, therefore, still be alive.

While we were waiting for the tracer to travel, the doctor and I were taken to a vacant room and left to have some lunch. The doctor had to spoon-feed me himself and, having obviously never attempted the duties of a nursing assistant before, was quite self-conscious and awkward about it. He was very sweet though, and tried to cheer me up by telling me about a woman he'd seen on television who had an artificial arm with which she could do all sorts of things. Even pick up an egg, he said.

I smiled, but privately I was thinking, 'Pick up an egg? I want a whole lot more out of my life than to be able to pick up a measly egg!' Was that really it? Was that the best I could hope to achieve in future – to pick up an egg? I was getting tense, aware of how much rode on the results of this test and feeling frustrated by having to wait.

When the time came to have the scan, I was taken through to a darkened room, and had to lie very still on a cold hard bench for a long time while a huge machine was manoeuvred into position over each limb in turn. For what seemed like an age, the one great eye of the scintillation counter peered minutely at each of my hands and feet, while I willed the blood to trickle back into my bones.

Then the scan was complete and the doctor and I were packed back into our waiting ambulance with a folder containing the unprocessed results; an hour later I was back in the comfort of my own little room where Anna and my dad were waiting for me.

They had had another day being harassed by the press, and in order to lance the boil of media attention once and for all, my dad suggested giving them a little of what they wanted. I agreed to let one paper come in and do a five-minute interview and photo-shoot on the condition that a sizeable donation was made to the PGHM.

A short while later, I found myself attempting to answer banal questions of the 'How sorry are you to have lost your friend?' nature. I was unable to speak about the climb and the rescue at all, but I managed to talk in general clichéd terms about how devastated I was about what had happened but how I was determined to rebuild my life and live it to the full once again. The three of us then grinned inanely for the cameras and the newspapermen left us in peace, delighted with their results. The story ran in all the national papers over the next couple of days, and after that the attentions of the press diminished significantly.

I said goodbye to my dad, who was returning to the UK, sure that I was in good hands, and optimistic that I was well on the road to recovery, and I spent the rest of the afternoon with Anna.

The uncertainty of the fate of my hands and feet was preying heavily on my mind now. I realised that at some point in the future the work of healing, amputating and reconstructing my body would be complete and I would be able to begin the processes of readjustment and rehabilitation; but not knowing when that point would be and what bodily condition it would find me in, I felt left in a continuing state of limbo, both mental and physical. I found it impossible to hold any sort of image of myself and so found it very difficult to imagine a future in which I might once again be contented, active, free, happy, or any adjective that might apply to everyday life.

I was therefore eager for news, good or bad, when Dr Marsigny and the two surgeons, Rik Verhellen and Guy Allamel came to see me that evening. They all had a very serious demeanour, so I knew immediately that it wasn't all good news. Marsigny showed me the printouts from the bone scintigram. The grey, blotchy images meant little to my untrained eye – I could make out the faint outline of my hands and feet but little else. Dr Marsigny explained that the tests had been inconclusive. There was a slight indication of some circulation in the bones but little to strengthen the doctors' hopes of saving them. To make matters worse, my infection wasn't responding to any of the drugs I was being given. The doctors now had grave concern for my health. The bottom line was that they wanted permission to remove my left foot.

I can't say I exactly reeled with the shock. Over the last couple of days Marsigny had consistently expressed his concern that my left foot was the main cause of the septicaemia that was polluting my blood. It was certainly obvious enough to me that it was the worst affected of my limbs, having the largest area of damaged flesh and having turned noticeably more pus-filled than the other three. But despite the fact that I knew in my heart that that foot was already dead and that it would have to come off, it still felt strange to be faced with the reality that it was actually going to happen. I was actually going to be an amputee. I suppose I had clung to the forlorn hope that a miracle cure might suddenly have swept in out of nowhere and made everything better. Now I knew that wasn't to be the case, and parts of my body were to be removed for ever, one by one, starting with my left foot. In a strange way I didn't feel entirely bad about this. Practically, it would be a relief to have the useless dead piece of rotting meat removed from my otherwise healthy leg, and mentally it felt encouraging to have the fate of at least one of my limbs sealed. At least that was something I could be certain about. I immediately gave my consent to the amputation of my left foot.

The surgeons were anxious to carry out the amputation without delay and the operation was set for first thing the next morning. The doctors departed, and as the nurse redressed my limbs, I snuck one last look at the condemned foot. It bore little resemblance to the pink, often sweaty and smelly object that I was accustomed to finding at the end of my leg. I thought about all the miles that foot had walked in the twenty-nine and a half years I had been its owner, all the hills it had climbed, all the balls it had kicked, the bicycle pedals it had pushed, the mountains it had ascended. Trying to look on the positive side, I thought wryly about the ingrown toenails and athletes' foot, the stubbed toes and the sores and blisters that would no longer bother me. I found it strange to think that the foot soon wouldn't be there any more. It was impossible to consider all the implications of that concept.

* * *

The next morning I was denied the daily pleasure of my hot chocolate, bread and jam, and given a thorough pre-operative scrub down. A pre-operative anaesthetic made me feel comfortably woozy. I was then shifted onto a trolley and began the strange upside-down journey down unfamiliar corridors, with unfamiliar ceilings, to where gowned figures, their inverted faces in masks, rolled me onto a hard, hard bed, where soon I was lost, deep in a senseless sleep.

When I came round, mysteriously returned to my bed, I gradually became aware of a dull pain in my left leg. I was also aware of the sweet, medicinal taste of oxygen in my nostrils. I tried to shift position to alleviate the pain but found I couldn't. Something was preventing my leg from moving. I turned my head and saw Anna, sitting by the bed. Seeing that I was awake she smiled and stroked my forehead. I smiled back and tried to say something to her but the words stumbled and failed on my lips. She gently shushed me and told me to lie still and relax. So I lay back while Anna told me that the operation had all gone fine. The oxygen tube taped to my nose was a normal procedure and I wasn't able to move because my leg was in traction.

Gradually I began to sober up from the anaesthetic and was able to chat a little with Anna. The downside of waking up fully was the gradually increasing pain in my leg that soon became quite intense. I was in traction, it seemed, because they hadn't closed the wound over my freshly cut bones, and were attempting to stretch the skin to cover them. The alternative to this would have been to cut the bones shorter in order to allow the remaining skin to close over them, but the surgeons had been anxious to leave the residual limb as long as possible to aid the fitting of a prosthetic leg in the future.

That night, lying flat on my aching back, grimacing with the pain in my leg, and unable to move with tubes, wires and the awful traction device, was my most uncomfortable to date, and I'm ashamed to say I spent most of it moaning and badgering the night nurse for attention and painkillers.

By the morning, however, I felt a good deal better, and was able to eat some solid food for the first time in thirty-six hours. I was released from the torture of the traction machine, and with the assistance of good old morphine, almost began to feel cheerful.

My mood was improved even more by the arrival in the afternoon of one of my closest friends, Chris Pasteur, his girlfriend Jane Herries, another friend Duncan Tunstall, and one of Anna's oldest friends, Judith Lane, who had all come out to Chamonix to be with us.

It was great to see some familiar faces in the midst of these strange days, and we were soon chatting and having a laugh just like old times.

Chris isn't known for beating about the bush, and his first enquiry after my health, in his usual brash manner was, 'How's your meat and two veg, man?' I assured him that everything in that department was fine and so, as she admitted weeks later, unknowingly alleviated a silent worry of Anna's.

Chris had also very thoughtfully brought from Edinburgh a couple of items of great medicinal value. Cheese and onion flavour crisps have always been my favourite panacea, never failing to provide satisfaction and comfort, and a can of Irn Bru, the tonic wine which cures a nation's maladies and self-inflicted ailments of the head, made me feel like I was back in Scotland again. Chris helped me to consume these remedies after which I felt ever so slightly better.

Later on, however, after everyone but Anna had left, I began to feel very ill again and spent another miserable night trying the patience of the night nurses.

On Sunday I fared little better and spent most of the day languishing in self-pity. When Dr Marsigny came to examine me on his rounds I begged him to tell me what he thought were the chances for my hands.

'Look at them,' he said. 'You tell me what you think.'

I stared down at the pathetic remnants of what used to be my hands, looking now more like holy relics than part of a living human being. The stench of rotting flesh filled the room.

'I think this one's dead,' I admitted, nodding towards my particularly desiccated left hand, 'but perhaps there is some hope for this one?' I indicated my right hand which still had areas of swollen reddish flesh.

'Perhaps,' conceded Marsigny with a gentle smile, but I knew that he was probably allowing me to cling to the final remains of hope

132

because he realised I had little else left. I knew also that the infections were getting worse and that Marsigny was deeply concerned about it.

My friends came to visit that afternoon, but I wasn't much company. Later on, a surprise visitor was Alain Iglesis, my rescuer. I felt flattered that he had come to see me and tried to express my gratitude at having been so courageously saved, but couldn't really find the words, especially with the halting mix of simple French and English we were using to communicate. Anyway, Alain brushed all compliments aside, not having come to be flattered. He laughed, however, when I told him that his tea had been the best tea in the world. As he left, Alain explained that he would return next week, this time in his capacity as a policeman to take down details for his report.

On that occasion I didn't glean from Alain many facts of the mission to save Jamie and me, but eventually I was able to piece together the whole story of what had been going on down in the valley during the five long days we were trapped on the mountain, and from Iglesis, Pouts, Truchet and Agresti I learnt of the final desperate attempt to get us down.

As the helicopter, piloted by Truchet and bearing Iglesis, approached the *brèche*, it immediately became apparent to the occupants that they were too late for at least one of the climbers. Lying face down in an exposed position, there seemed little hope that he was still alive. However, the other climber was in a sitting position and when they flew over, he moved. He was still alive, perhaps only just, and at the full mercy of the icy wind. They would have to move quickly to save him.

The helicopter pulled back while Iglesis was lowered out on the winch line. Truchet then brought the Lama in carefully and landed Iglesis near the west summit. As soon as he touched the ice, Iglesis sprang into action. While he set to work, the Lama retreated again to prepare the extended winch line.

The Lama was now accompanied by the Alouette, carrying Poujol, Pouts and Agresti. However, as they watched Iglesis traversing the narrow arête towards the *brèche*, Agresti became aware of a third helicopter hovering in the air over the mountain. It was a news crew from French television attempting to film the rescue. Agresti got on the radio and screamed at them to get out of the way, after which the uninvited helicopter reluctantly pulled back. The Alouette then returned to the Lognan to be ready to receive the climbers as they were evacuated.

Up on Les Droites, Alain Iglesis traversed along the knife-edge arête in only a few minutes. He was an extremely experienced rescuer and an accomplished mountaineer in his own right so he knew how to move fast over difficult ground. The final descent of 30 metres required an abseil and Iglesis spent some time excavating a suitable anchor point from the ice and rocks. He was in the full blast of the updraft now, and had to feed the rope out of his sack as he abseiled in order to prevent it from blowing about out of control.

Soon he reached the *brèche*. A quick check was enough to confirm that the first climber was dead. He was frozen solid. I was still moving though, and even mumbled a few words. Quickly Iglesis set about getting some life-saving hot liquid into me, despite my protestations, then made me ready for the airlift. He also tried to put his spare gloves on my bare hands, but they were frozen solid and the gloves wouldn't go over.

Once the rescue harness was in place, Iglesis radioed the helicopter to come in with the winch line, extended with a climbing rope to 90 metres. The timing of this manoeuvre would be crucial. There was still too much updraft for the aircraft to hover over the *brèche* so they would have to make a fly-past, trailing the line underneath them. Truchet was such a precise pilot, he could land the end of his winch line on a sixpence, but in those unpredictable conditions it was going to be difficult.

Truchet circled round and made the pass. True to form, he swung the winch line straight into Iglesis's outstretched hand. Iglesis snapped the karabiner onto the rescue harness and I was lifted off the mountain.

Truchet flew back down to the Lognan Station and set me down into the waiting hands of Pouts and Dr Moracchioli. While Moracchioli gave me immediate treatment, Pouts got me strapped onto a stretcher and loaded into the Alouette. Without further delay the

Alouette flew me directly to the helipad at Chamonix Hospital where the full emergency staff were waiting.

Meanwhile, the Lama returned to Les Droites and repeated the fly-past manoeuvre to pick up the other climber. Iglesis then retraced his steps to the west summit and was himself lifted to safety and carried down to the dropping zone where Agresti was already facing a barrage of journalists, photographers and film crews. Iglesis, as he jumped out of the helicopter onto the tarmac, had tears running down his face.

It had been one of the most difficult rescues in the history of the Alps. Many in the team were understandably disappointed with its outcome, but to label the mission a failure would be to do a great disservice to the skill, courage, commitment and determination of all those who participated, both police and civilians. For my part, I owe my life to the PGHM, and for that I am eternally grateful. Iglesis was given a medal in recognition of his role in the rescue, although he insisted that Philippe Pouts, or any of his fellow *securistes*, would have done the same had it been their turn to go in.

CHAPTER SEVENTEEN

Nadir

IT WAS ON MONDAY, my eighth day in hospital, that things took a turn for the worst. I had been feeling nauseous and feverish all morning. Sometime in the early afternoon I recall a sudden shiver running down my spine. A few seconds later the shiver returned and before I knew what was happening my whole body was trembling uncontrollably. I managed to shout for a nurse who came running quickly and the last thing I remember is people rushing all around me, and an oxygen mask coming down over my face.

My breathing felt strange. I realised that I didn't have any control of it. My lungs seemed to be rising and falling on their own accord. I became aware of the tubes running through my nostrils and down my throat. A machine was breathing for me.

I opened my eyes and looked about but couldn't quite work out what was happening. I hadn't moved, but sitting beside my bed with tears in her eyes was my mother. Behind her, looking awkward, stood my friends John Irving and Finlay Bennet. Something was odd. It was their hair. Normally they both had brown hair, but now it was a bizarre shade of yellowy orange. It didn't make any sense. I felt groggy as hell.

I opened my mouth to speak but no sound came out. I was prevented from speaking by the tubes in my throat.

My mother was saying, 'We love you so much, Jamie, we love you so much.'

Then I looked down at my arms sticking out of the bedclothes. To my horror I realised that where my hands had been, in their large loose dressings, there were now only neatly bandaged stumps. So it had happened. It was all over. I looked down at the bottom of the bed and judged by the lack of any bump that my right foot had gone too. I didn't feel any grief, or any shock – only relief. It was all over. Look Mum, no hands. Sleep dragged me under again.

When I came round again, my dad, my mum and Anna were sitting round the bed. I allowed myself to regain consciousness slowly, during which time I decided that having those horrible tubes stuck in my windpipe was the most intolerably unpleasant torment imaginable. My left arm was trussed to various drips and machinery, but my right arm was relatively free, and when I felt strong enough to move, I waved it frantically at my uncomprehending visitors.

'What is it? What's wrong?' asked my dad in concern.

I pointed the stump in the direction of my nose and made an expression which I hoped said, 'Take these horrible tubes out of me!'

'Don't worry about the tubes,' said my dad, 'they're there to help you breathe.'

I continued to wave the stump, attempting to mime a pulling-out motion. Eventually Dad cottoned on.

'You want them out? I'll see if I can find a doctor.'

He returned shortly with Dr Marsigny who looked pleased to see me awake and active.

'We will have to keep you intubated today,' explained Marsigny, 'but we will monitor you and hopefully we can take you off the ventilator tomorrow morning. We have to be sure that your lungs are strong enough.'

As Marsigny left I realised that I had no idea what time it was. How long was it until tomorrow morning? Hopefully it was now later on in the day and tomorrow wasn't far away. I desperately wanted to know how long I would have to wait, but there was no clock on the wall and I couldn't see anyone's wristwatch. The snow falling past the window gave no clue of the time, so I returned to waving my arm about.

I tried to point to my wrist but found there wasn't really a wrist there any more. Dad thought I was asking what had happened to my hands and began to explain that they'd had to be amputated. I attempted to draw a clock in the air but no one could make any sense of it. Dad wrote out the letters of the alphabet on a piece of paper for me to spell out what I wanted, but the letters were far too small for my bandaged stump to point to with accuracy and more exasperating confusion followed. Eventually we returned to the ridiculous game of charades and I somehow conveyed the concept of time to the players by making a pendulum motion with my arm.

'Oh, the time! You want to know what time it is! It's almost four o'clock.'

I sank back exhausted. At least it wasn't too long till tomorrow. It then occurred to me that I wasn't sure what day tomorrow was, but I decided to let it pass for the moment. I'd kind of lost track of the days lately anyway.

It wasn't for some time that I learnt how many days I'd actually lost and what great danger I had been in. I had passed out on Monday and I woke up on Friday – I had been under heavy sedation for four days. Later on I was filled in on the events of those missing four days.

By the Monday morning I was being given just about every antibiotic known to man in the attempt to control my septicaemia. The uncontrollable shivering, or rigor, that had overtaken my body was an immune reaction caused by my fever. The additional strain proved too much for my sorely weakened system and I started to fall into septic shock, an extremely dangerous condition which is often fatal. To make matters worse I developed pulmonary oedema. My lungs began to fill with fluid and quickly became incapable of drawing breath.

The doctors had very little time in which to stabilise my condition and they had to act fast to save my life. They sedated me in order to take over control of my vital functions, and intubated me so that a ventilator could breathe for me.

Anna, already in a state of severe distress, found this latest turn of events almost too much to deal with. She had had to be so strong for so long, and now things were only getting worse. She didn't feel that she could cope any more. Fortunately she was saved from breaking down completely by her mother, Sinikka, who flew out to take care of her. My mother and father, who were also distraught when they heard about my downturn, came out to Chamonix the next day. Meanwhile, Chris, Jane and Judith had returned to Edinburgh, unable to say goodbye to me.

Flo had the sensible idea of renting an apartment in the centre of town so that everyone could stay together in comfort, and all my visitors, coming and going, could have somewhere to sleep. She was also then able to take charge of cooking operations, making it easier for everyone to eat.

Meanwhile at the hospital I remained unconscious, in a critical condition. Eventually, on Tuesday, the decision was taken to operate. It was the only way to decrease the amount of toxic material that was entering my bloodstream. The surgeons Rik Verhellen and Guy Allamel deliberated for hours before ultimately admitting that complete removal of both hands and the remaining foot was the only way of saving my life. Finally, they operated. If it was any consolation, when the hands and the foot were cut open and examined they were all found to be completely dead.

Everyone involved in my case was severely disappointed. Ever since I had been brought in after my miraculous rescue, half frozen to death, they had fought hard to save what they could of my hands and feet, but in the end had lost everything. Not being able to conceive how an active person could enjoy a life without hands and feet, some felt that they had failed me. At least one person thought I would be better off dead.

To make matters worse, the exhausted surgical team had barely finished stitching up my stumps when a disaster occurred which was to require their expertise throughout the rest of the night and the next morning.

Far up the valley, at the little village of Le Tour where we had been snowboarding on the first day of our trip, snow had been falling on the slopes for days and weeks now, building up into a vast unstable pack. Finally the pack slipped under its own weight causing a monstrous avalanche that swept down the hillside. The avalanche was far greater than any that had occurred at that spot before and nothing stood in its way. Trees were brushed aside like matchsticks and when it struck the outskirts of the village, all buildings in its path were totally flattened. Thirty-five people were killed and dozens more were injured. At Le Tour, all the rescue services in the valley spent the night and the whole of the next day digging for survivors. At Chamonix Hospital, the emergency department and surgery teams were treating the injured for shock, hypothermia and broken bones. It was a bad time for the people of Chamonix. Anna, who saw some of the doctors and surgeons on Thursday morning, said that they looked absolutely shattered.

All this time, I slept on regardless. The other major event that I slept through was Jamie's funeral. Stu had arranged for Jamie's body to be taken home to Oxfordshire and the service was held in a crematorium on the outskirts of Oxford. The building was packed and overspilled with Jamie's friends and relations. There were more people outside than inside. Afterwards a huge party was held in Jamie's honour.

The next day, John Irving and Finlay Bennet flew out to see me. With them was Alice Brockington, Jamie's girlfriend. She wanted to come to Chamonix, not just to see me, but to see the mountain that had taken Jamie away from her, to understand better what had happened.

Before they flew out John phoned Anna and asked if there was anything they could bring with them. Anna, who was in a state of extreme stress, could think of nothing to say, but suddenly remembered how I'd enjoyed the snacks that Chris had brought me.

'I don't know ... some cheese and onion crisps and Irn Bru,' she blurted out.

So John, who is a master of largesse and would never do anything by halves, brought out a large catering box of crisps and a whole case of Irn Bru. After I was revived from sedation, I was presented with these gifts but by then I was way too ill to face the thought of crisps and fizzy drinks and so they sat under the sink in my room for the rest of my stay in Chamonix, while I tried to encourage my visitors to take some away with them.

Every day, while I lay unconscious, Anna would spend hours sitting by my bed, willing me to get better. And I did begin to improve very quickly after my amputations. The infections died back and my wounds began to heal. By Thursday evening the doctors agreed that my body was almost strong enough to take care of itself. On Friday morning I was taken off the drugs which were holding me under sedation.

Also on Friday morning, Alice and Anna took the *téléférique* up to the Aiguille du Midi from where they could see in the distance Les Droites, an insignificant peak among the chains of mountains all around. It was the first clear day since I was rescued and at that altitude it was very cold. Anna was shocked by the biting air and tried to imagine what it had been like for Jamie and me, trapped on that distant mountain ridge, in such inconceivably harsh conditions. The two girls stood for a while, looking out at the remorseless mountains, before turning and getting into the cable car which took them back down to the valley.

When they arrived back at the apartment, they learnt that I was waking up.

I spent a miserable night waiting for the morning to come. Without the assistance of the sedatives I couldn't sleep much and without my voice I was unable to call for a nurse to shift my position. The pain in my stumps and in my back was constant.

When the dawn finally crept through the window of my room, and the morning staff arrived, I immediately started signalling for my tubes to be removed. After what seemed like an age, a doctor arrived – Dr Guy Bouvier, a strange man who was usually bare-chested under his medical coat and who I was told disliked the English. Scots were all right though. He made a thorough check of my various charts and readouts and then consented to remove me from the ventilator.

The removal of the tubes from my trachea was a very unpleasant experience. As they were pulled out of my nose I gagged repeatedly but as soon as they were out I felt like I'd been freed from a strait jacket. I coughed and spluttered a bit, then took deep breaths, savouring the rise and fall of my chest under my own volition. Dr

Bouvier insisted I have an oxygen line taped under my nose, but it was little inconvenience after having those terrible tubes up my nostrils. I tried to speak but my throat felt like cardboard and I croaked like a frog. I was given a drink of water and started to feel a little better.

Dr Bouvier left me and I spent the rest of the morning in contemplation. Over the next few days I spent a lot of time lost in thought, trying to rationalise and make some sort of sense out of what had happened.

So this was it. After all the uncertainty, this was the nature of my fate. I was to spend the rest of my life with no hands and no feet. No hands and no feet. Jesus Christ. I almost felt like laughing at the ridiculousness of it. My hands and feet, all gone. I mean, losing fingers or toes is a common hazard of mountaineering. It's something that you know can happen. I'd even heard of climbers who'd lost a whole hand or a foot to frostbite, but to lose all four just seemed beyond belief.

I had paid a high price for my rescue from the mountain. You could say it cost me an arm and a leg – and I paid twice. Fortunately, even in that dark hour my sense of humour hadn't entirely deserted me. I found myself paraphrasing Oscar Wilde: to lose one hand, Mr Andrew, may be regarded as a misfortune; to lose both looks like carelessness.

So there I was, stuck in a hospital bed, my body mutilated out of recognition, and I just wasn't prepared for it. I'd had no prophecy of all this. Had the clouds of menace been gathering in the sky, plain for me to see and I'd ignored them? Had I been walking on thin ice, asking for this to happen?

I hadn't even conceived of it as a possibility. I mean, to die yes, that's always a lurking fear, but you just don't think to yourself, 'I'd better be careful or I might end up losing my hands and feet.' It simply isn't on the normal list of possible perils.

What had I done to myself? What had I become? What word did they have for people like me? Were there any other people like me?

Disabled. I didn't know if that was the current socially acceptable term. Or crippled, or handicapped, or physically challenged.

Challenged all right. This was going to be the biggest bloody challenge ever. None of these terms applied to me though. Not me. Disabled means people you see being pushed round shopping centres, blankets covering their frail legs. Not me. Handicapped means people who arrive in special buses, with strange expressions on their faces and saliva on their chins. Not me. I was young, active and super-fit. I could run up and down steep mountains, walk across rough terrain for days on end, and climb sheer overhanging rock faces without fear. I couldn't be disabled.

It was clear I had a lot of readjustment to achieve if I was to adapt to my new situation. I thought too about the physical adaptations I would have to make. I realised that apart from being able to spell prosthetics, and even pronounce it in one out of two attempts, I knew nothing about modern artificial limbs. I guessed that current technology lay somewhere between Long John Silver and the Bionic Man, but really I had no personal experience whatsoever.

Wracking my brains I remembered my friend Pete Jennings. His girlfriend Juliette Snow, who I'd met a few times, had an artificial leg. I'd seen her rock climbing once and had thought, wow, that's impressive, but the leg had been hidden beneath her trousers. At least it must be possible to lead an active life with one artificial leg. With two though, would it be possible to even walk? I didn't know. What about arms? In the past I'd seen various television items and newspaper articles about the latest in ultra-high-technology bionic arms but had never paid much attention. Was that kind of thing actually possible now? Could you touch and feel with a prosthetic hand? Were they available to anyone but the richest of amputees, or the lucky few guinea pigs? Would I have to pay for my artificial limbs? How were they attached? Were they fixed directly to the bones, or could you take them off at night?

So many questions. For now I had no answers, and no one in Chamonix Hospital seemed to have any answers either. None of the doctors had had any experience of prosthetic treatment and certainly none had an idea what might be done in a case as extreme as mine. Nor were any of my visitors able to provide many concrete facts, apart from oddments of anecdotal information, about a friend of a friend whose uncle had lost a leg in the war and suchlike. In fairness, all the stories that I was told about other amputees were very encouraging. The more I heard, the more I realised that there were other people out there like me, maybe not exactly like me, but with similar problems, who coped well, were active, and led as full a life as anybody else.

To add to all the doubt I was going through I was also struggling with my grief for the loss of Jamie and the difficult emotion of guilt. Guilt at having survived when Jamie was dead. Guilt at having the opportunity to go on, to carry on living life and loving and being loved. Guilt at being ungrateful enough to doubt whether it was an opportunity worth having, given my new circumstances.

So I made a resolution to myself. I'd like to be able to say I made the resolution that Saturday morning, straight away after being extubated, but really it was a resolution that formed itself gradually over the coming days, even weeks, while I struggled through the varied and unpredictable emotions that washed constantly over me.

I acknowledged that whatever happened to me from then on, whatever further bizarre twists and turns my life might take, and whatever difficulties I might face, the main thing was that I was alive. If nothing else, the loss of Jamie would teach me that. I was alive and it felt good. In fact, it felt wonderful. Jamie, I knew, would have felt the same way. Any trivial concerns such as the loss of my hands and feet were really insignificant when one considered the alternative.

I resolved to get on with my life and live it to the full, free from negative influences such as regret and guilt. I wasn't so headstrong as to set myself unattainable targets like running a marathon or climbing mountains, but I resolved that that day, when the tubes were pulled from my nose, must be the low point. From then on I would begin to get better, to improve in some way every day, and to slowly start the business of rebuilding the life that I had lost.

First, though, I had a lot of visitors to see and I suddenly felt very, very tired. Alice came to see me that Saturday afternoon. She came with Anna and sat on the edge of my bed for a while, the tears streaming down her face. I knew how bad I felt about Jamie, but I couldn't even begin to imagine how she felt. Right now, I was unable to talk to her about what had happened up there on the mountain. The very thought of forming the words seemed to drain all the energy out of my body. Alice realised it was too soon to talk too and after a while, with a big hug, she left me.

My next visitor was Alain Iglesis. This time he wasn't paying a social call, but was wearing his policeman's hat. He immediately began to interview me in a very official manner. Because there had been a fatality, there had to be a full report on the accident and Iglesis needed to know every last detail of our climb: when we started, how fast we climbed, where exactly we slept on each night, what we ate and when, what clothes we had, why we made the decisions we did. These questions were fired at me one after another and I felt like I was being bombarded. I could picture answers to all of the questions in my head, but I just couldn't make the words. I opened my mouth to speak but nothing would come out. I was too tired. After I'd stumbled through a few questions and completely failed to answer a few more, Iglesis realised how exhausted I was and gave up. In the hospital waiting room my dad sat with him and answered some of his questions as best he could. For those he couldn't answer, Dad came into my room and coaxed the information out of me. In the end Iglesis left satisfied.

I had two further visitors in the afternoon. Finlay and John shuffled into the room with broad grins on their faces, looking more than faintly ridiculous in their matching thatches of yellowy-orange hair. So it hadn't been a dream. They'd attempted to bleach themselves blond as a mark of respect for the two Jamies, they told me, but it hadn't come out too well.

I smiled, then realising I could no longer keep my eyes open, I mumbled, 'Thanks for coming to see me, guys. I'm really sorry but I'm too tired to talk any more.'

They understood and left me to sleep. They were returning to Scotland that evening, along with Alice, so I never even got a chance to chat to them.

CHAPTER EIGHTEEN

A Jet Plane

I HAD PROMISED MYSELF that I had now reached rock bottom – that from then on I would only get better – and indeed over the coming days I did start to get better. The sources of blood poisoning, my hands and feet, had now gone and the infections receded. The aching in my freshly cut bones gradually died away, and the pain in my back lifted as if a weight had been removed. Above all my mood improved and I began to feel that I did still have a life that was worth living.

I started to eat solid food again, although sometimes I had a little difficulty holding the food down. On one occasion, when Anna had just finished feeding me a bowl of courgette soup, I suddenly realised that the soup was on its way back up. I shouted for a receptacle and just in time Anna grabbed a bowl and came running. However, it was a kidney bowl and when the inevitable stream of green liquid came shooting out of my mouth, it didn't stop in the bowl but ricocheted round the curved sides and sprayed all over Anna. It was a testament to Anna's patience that I wasn't lynched on the spot.

By Monday I was de-catheterised and free from all drips and tubes. In the daytime, the nurses would lift me into an armchair so that I could sit upright which was a great freedom after a fortnight of recumbence.

I realised that I would be in hospital for a long time and I resigned myself to an institutional life, for the short term anyway. I might as well make the most of it. Cards and letters were still flooding in. One brief note of condolence, from my mate Sez, read: 'I don't know if jokes are in order, but let's get legless!' My walls were now covered with pictures, and flowers, which were unfortunately not allowed in the intensive care rooms, were amassing on a table in the corridor where I could see them through the internal window.

My dad bought me a cassette player and people brought or sent me talking books to listen to. Some of the nurses gave me music tapes to play. Obviously I couldn't operate the cassette player, and had to get someone else to put the tape in and press play, but I found I could stop the player at will by giving the row of buttons a clout with my stump, which pleased me greatly.

More welcome visitors continued to arrive. A rope access work colleague, Ali Robertson, who was teaching schoolkids to ski at a resort nearby in Italy, appeared out of the blue. He told me about a mate of his who'd lost one of his legs above the knee, and 'it didn't seem to bother him, like'.

Anna bumped into an old Edinburgh friend, Mark Ryle, who was working in a ski shop in Chamonix. Mark had, not so long ago, tragically lost his twin brother in a climbing accident and his strength of will to go on was an inspiration.

Doug Shephard and Sarah Hill, who had cut short a trip to New Zealand to attend Jamie's funeral and to come and see me, arrived with Andy Forrest, who lived in Geneva.

Everyone has their own favourite remedies – those little things that always make life's woes seem not so bad. For some it might be chocolate, or a cup of tea. For others, cream cakes or home-made lemonade. For Doug it was meat pies and beer. A nurse assistant heated up one of the pies he had brought me and I diligently nibbled at it, but my stomach wasn't really ready for such heavy fare so I let Doug eat the rest of them while I watched. He washed the pies down with a can of the beer and left the rest of the six-pack under the sink with the Irn Bru, for later. I was glad that my friends could behave as normal when they visited.

I wondered what it was like for my visitors to come and see me. To step in out of the blizzards that swept the streets of Chamonix, and to sit stiffly in my warm, clean, clinical room, the snow melting from their clothes and boots and forming puddles on the floor. I wondered how it felt for them to see me lying there, once so tall and proud, and now so small, helpless and incapacitated. I knew how emaciated and weak I was looking. I knew that the weeks of physical strain had taken it out on the remains of my body. My muscles had wasted away, my ribs were showing and my eyes were sunk deep into my drawn face. Not to mention my lopsided sideburns. I must have been a pathetic sight. I wondered what my guests said to each other after they'd left, back at the apartment.

I found myself envying them their world. I could smell the things they'd been doing, my sense of smell intensified by the lack of stimulus in my sterile environment. I could smell their sweat if they'd been out skiing, the chlorine in their hair if they'd been to the pool, smoke in their clothes and alcohol on their breath if they'd been in the bars or cafés.

I felt excluded from the normal, fun, happy world to which they returned the moment they left my room. I longed to be able to go skiing with them, to play in the flumes at the swimming pool, and to go out with them for a large drunken meal in a restaurant in town. One day I would, I promised myself, but right now I had to be patient.

During the night, the sound of a small boy crying drifted through from the room next door to mine. The crying went on and on, relentlessly, until eventually I asked a nurse what was wrong with the boy. He had a broken leg, the nurse replied, but that wasn't why he was crying. He was crying because his parents were dead. His entire family had been buried in the big avalanche up at Le Tour and he was the only survivor. Suddenly my own problems seemed quite trivial.

On Tuesday Anna burst into my room looking very stressed and said, 'Right! Forget your concerns today. Today you have to give me your sympathy.'

I looked at her with a dropping jaw. 'What is it? What's happened?'

It seemed the unfortunate little town of Chamonix had suffered another catastrophe. After the weeks of snow, and several huge avalanches, one of which had been tragic, it had now suffered a major fire.

Late in the evening, Anna, my parents, Doug, Sarah and Flo had arrived back at the apartment after a meal in a nearby bistro. As they came through the main building door, Anna had caught a whiff of smoke, but it had vanished and she thought nothing of it. Up in their apartment she smelt more smoke and immediately went through to the kitchen to investigate. Finding nothing, she looked out of the window. On the street below, outside the Michel Croz Building, which was a local museum adjoining the apartment block, she noticed a small fire brigade vehicle with a flashing blue light, a solitary fireman standing next to it. A minute later the fire alarm went off in the apartment and the word came from the concierge to evacuate the building.

Everyone grabbed some warm clothes and their passports and rushed downstairs and out of the building. Flames were now leaping from the windows of the Michel Croz Building and fire engines were squeezing down the narrow street. Anna and the others watched in horror as the fire licked through the roof of the building and climbed high into the sky, gradually creeping closer and closer to their apartment.

Anna didn't know whether to panic, cry or give up completely. Instead she asked herself what I would do in that situation, unflappable as I generally was, and guessed that probably I would take photographs. So Anna kept herself calm by concentrating on getting some good photos of the fire. As she was snapping away something exploded inside the building and part of the roof collapsed. Gradually it became apparent that the firemen could do little to save the building, but fortunately they did manage to prevent the fire from spreading to the neighbouring buildings and the apartment building was saved.

Eventually the word came round that all evacuated people should go to the town hall, so they made their way there as the fire destroyed the remnants of the Michel Croz Building. After a while waiting in a dusty boardroom, they were told that a nearby hotel had kindly agreed to give them all beds for the night, so eventually they were able to get some sleep.

In the morning they were allowed to re-enter the apartment. The Michel Croz Building was now a smouldering ruin but happily the apartment building and its contents were undamaged, if a little smoky.

I listened to Anna's story with a mixture of disbelief, concern and amusement. It all seemed too ridiculous that she should have to deal with this additional, unexpected worry. Together we just had to laugh about it.

'OK,' I said, 'today you get all the sympathy.'

On Tuesday I received an unexpected postcard. It began, 'We are the ladies of the Maison des Hautes Montagnes, Patricia Lurati and Françoise Mantel.' The Maison des Hautes Montagnes is an information centre for mountain users in Chamonix. It provides walking information, details of climbing routes, weather forecasts, and is a base for the guides. The ladies went on to offer me their sincere condolences and asked if it would be all right for them to visit me. I passed a message to them via the nurse who had brought the card that I would be delighted to see them and on Wednesday afternoon they came.

They were both tall, beautiful women, in their mid to late thirties. I wondered why they had been particularly concerned to see me, but then Patricia explained. She had first come to Chamonix more than a decade before, with her boyfriend. She wasn't a climber, but her boyfriend was, and one day, he and a climbing partner had set out to climb the North Face of Les Droites, just like Jamie and I. They had never come back. She had lived in Chamonix ever since, knowing that her lover was still up there, somewhere in the cold mountains.

Patricia and Françoise were both very kind and sympathetic to me and came to visit again, bringing me presents and games to keep me occupied.

On Thursday I had to have another operation, to attempt to close up the ends of my two left stumps. The surgeons had left the bones as long as they could and consequently the remaining skin wouldn't quite close over. I might have to have plastic surgery, they said. I was impatient to get the stumps all sewn up so that my body could get on with the process of healing. I felt that I had reached a stage now where, although I perhaps hadn't come to terms with what had happened to me, I had at least admitted it and I felt ready to accept the challenge that lay ahead. Until the wounds were closed, though, I was still in limbo. On the other hand I realised that my wait could have been very much longer. In that respect, I felt fortunate that I'd had to have everything cut off. If the surgeons had attempted to save parts of my hands and feet I would no doubt have had to endure a very long period of uncertainty. It would have meant months, even years, of constant treatment and regular surgery, the outcome of which would be by no means certain. At least this way was short and simple.

I remember the first time I actually saw my stumps, in the flesh as it were, while I was having my dressings changed. Wrapped in bandages, as they were most of the time, it was easy for me to convince myself that nothing much had changed at the ends of my four limbs. I even used to imagine that my hands were actually still there after all, tightly bound inside layers of crêpe. When the bandages were removed, and I was able to see for myself my four, truncated, round-ended limbs, each closed off with a neatly stitched seam, it brought home to me how very real my disability was.

I spent many of my waking hours mulling over all the ways in which my new disability would change my life, and could come up with no aspects that might remain unaffected. On a very basic level, I was entirely reliant on other people for even my most simple human needs: eating, drinking, washing, going to the toilet. It seemed reasonable to assume that in the fullness of time I would become capable of some or all of these tasks, but at the moment I had no idea how, and I was frightened by the enormity of it all. On the next level were all the normal activities I might undertake daily: mobility would be a problem. Would I ever walk again, or would I perhaps be confined to an electric wheelchair? What about my flat? It was on the second floor. Would I have to sell it and move to a specially equipped ground-floor flat? Writing, cooking, laundry, playing games, driving, shopping, DIY – I had no idea if I would be able to do any of these everyday things again. What about earning a living? My job as a rope access technician and instructor was entirely practical and physically based. I was certain I wouldn't be able to do it any more. Would I be able to get another job? Anna might be able to support us, but what if she needed to be at home to take care of me? Dozens of problems presented themselves.

Then there was the greater question still of quality of life. It would be all very well to be able to take care of myself and survive on a day-to-day basis, but would I be able to make my life actually worth living? I have always been a very active person and I really didn't know whether I'd be able to cope without being able to do all those things that I loved to do – running, hill-walking, skiing, sailing, climbing. Most of all climbing. I just couldn't believe that my climbing career had been so suddenly, so comprehensively, brought to an end. I had been climbing for thirteen years – it had defined the second half of my life. I had so many plans, so many things still to do. Every day I would remember with disappointment mountains and routes that I had always intended to climb and always assumed I would eventually get around to climbing. Now I never would.

I thought about my favourite rock climbs – the golden sandstone of Northumberland, for example. I've no idea how many times I've soloed up the wonderful flake crack of Lorraine at Bowden Doors – over a hundred probably. I tried to imagine making that delicate and awkward series of moves one more time, this time with artificial legs and arms. It didn't seem likely.

I spent a lot of time pondering these and many other issues, until my case just seemed too desperate. So I decided that trying to disassemble my life into all its fundamental parts, and reconstructing myself piece by piece, was too great a task. Instead I had to throw out my old life and start again. Physically I was effectively like a newborn baby, unable to do anything for myself. Mentally, in many respects, I had to be reborn also. All my preconceptions about myself, who I am, and what I do, would have to be chucked out of the window. All my hopes, dreams and ambitions would have to be discarded and replaced. It would have to be a brand-new start.

Of course you can't really make a completely fresh start. You can't just press a reset button and begin again as if your life so far had never happened. It would be more an action of mourning the passing of my old life, as I was mourning the passing of Jamie, before building my new life on the ruins of the old. In this process of rebuilding, I would have the assistance my friends, my family and Anna, my relationships with whom would provide the thread of continuity from the old me to the new.

I tried to forget about problems like, would I ever climb again, or would I ever walk again, and concentrated on more achievable goals like turning the pages of a newspaper. This I found I could manage with a bit of patience and a lot of clumsy fumbling with my stumps. I couldn't, however, sit up in the bed to read the paper, until I discovered I could push the electronic controls for the bed with a corner of my bandages. For the first time since my arrival in hospital three weeks previously, I felt like I was doing something for myself, and it felt good. From now on, life was going to be a series of little challenges like this, and I resolved to draw as much satisfaction as possible from achieving each one.

I also set myself a few more long-term goals. On my wall was a picture that someone had sent of Anna and me at a wedding the previous year. We had received invites to a couple more weddings in the coming summer and I determined to be able to go to those weddings and hold my own drink and eat my food myself. I spent a long time gazing at that photo. We looked so happy together.

Dr Marsigny was aware that I was anxious to go home to Scotland and on Friday he declared that I was fit enough to travel. Arrangements were made for my repatriation. My insurance company sorted out all the travel arrangements. Judith Lane, one of the friends who had come over to see Anna and me, worked in the Princess Margaret Rose Hospital in Edinburgh. The PMR Hospital was, I was told, one of the best institutions in the UK for orthopaedics and prosthetics and it was arranged for me to go there. Judith pulled some strings to get me a private room. My flight home was booked for the following Tuesday.

I looked forward to going home, but I realised I was going to miss Chamonix Hospital. I had only been there for three and a half weeks, but I had been through so much there that it felt very much a part of me – in a way the birthplace of the new me. Everyone there was so friendly to me and I had become close to many of the staff.

That day Dr Manu Cauchy had a birthday party in the intensive care staff room. He brought Anna and me a piece of cake and a glass of something alcoholic. I took a sip from the glass and my eyes just about popped out of my head.

'What is it?' asked Anna.

'I don't know,' I said. 'I think it's a really strong spirit of some sort.'

Anna tried the drink. 'No it's not,' she said mockingly, 'it's very weak diluted wine!' I had obviously completely lost my capacity to tolerate alcohol.

Later on in the morning one of the nurses, Pascale, arrived looking pleased with herself.

'Last night I was a Bond girl!' she said posing dramatically with an imaginary gun in the doorway. I imagined her skiing at breakneck speed next to Pierce Brosnan while being chased by evil, machine-gun-firing henchmen. She was certainly beautiful enough to be a Bond girl, but it turned out she had been providing medical cover for the filming of the skiing stunts in *The World is Not Enough*.

The last few days at Chamonix dragged on a bit as I was really only waiting to go home. On Monday, the day before we were leaving, Anna and I said our goodbyes to our new friends as they went off shift. Everyone insisted that I should come back the next year, so that they could see how I was getting on. I made a promise to Dr Marsigny that I would return. This time, I said, I would walk into his hospital and shake him by the hand. He gave me a bundle of medical notes, a summary of which he had translated into English, 'in case some of your Scottish doctors can't understand French,' he said with a wicked smile.

The nurses bought me a T-shirt as a souvenir of my stay in Chamonix, and Anna got them some chocolates and a card, bullying me into writing the card myself. First I tried holding the pen in my mouth but that seemed hopeless. Then, gripping the pen carefully between my two stumps I slowly managed to scrawl, 'Merci pour tout. Grosses bisses, Jamie.'

* * *

154

Tuesday morning, the day of my departure, finally arrived. Anna came to the hospital with our baggage first thing. My dad was staying on for one day to clean up the apartment, and everyone else had already returned to the UK.

The travel was being handled by a private company with the rather fantastic name of International Rescue and we were picked up at 8.00 a.m. by a neat little estate-car-style ambulance, manned by a couple of smart young paramedics. Once again I felt the unfamiliar sting of cold air on my cheeks as I was loaded into the back of the vehicle. Francine was the nurse on duty that morning. As she waved us off she had tears in her eyes.

We made fast progress down the great hill that leads out of the Arve Valley, while outside the ceaseless snow still fell. Before long we were pulling into a rear entrance to Geneva airport where an impossibly small, sleek jet was waiting for us on the runway. Beside it stood two German pilots, immaculate in their smart uniforms. Also waiting for us were a German female doctor and a paramedic, dressed rather scarily in all-white casuals, who fussed over me with Teutonic efficiency.

After I had had my stretcher searched by security officials, I was lifted into the little aircraft and strapped down. The others all got in and we were soon taxiing down the runway and accelerating up into the sky.

The flight to Edinburgh took a mere two hours, during which time Anna, who is a nervous flyer, had plenty of time to get anxious about the airworthiness of such a tiny plane.

'Do you think it's safe?' she whispered.

I looked about for clues: uniformed pilots, plush leather upholstery in the cabin, drinks dispensers built into walnut panelling. 'I think this is a very expensive little aeroplane,' I replied.

Later on when we got a chance to speak to the pilot he explained. 'Zis is ze Leer Jet,' he said proudly. 'When it is not being used as an air ambulance, it is used to fly celebrities all round ze world.' He then went on to list the names of people who had previously sat in Anna's seat: Pierce Brosnan, Claudia Schiffer, Boris Becker, King Juan Carlos of Spain.

I shuddered at the thought of how much this flight was costing.

The final, British link in this efficient chain of transport was to be an ambulance. Predictably, when we landed at a dank and drizzly Edinburgh airport, the ambulance was nowhere to be seen.

'Usually ze ambulance waits for us,' said our pilot, genuinely mystified. Eventually, after a couple of phone calls, a battered old patient transfer wagon rolled up and carted us all off round the by-pass towards the Princess Margaret Rose Hospital. As we drew up alongside the hospital's rather dingy entrance, paint peeling from the walls, my medical escorts looked horrified.

'This is not a hospital, this is a farm!' the doctor protested.

I must admit, having come from the brand-new, super-modern Chamonix Hospital, I shared her apprehension. Fortunately the PMR belies its outward appearance and is actually a centre of excellence in the fields of orthopaedics and prosthetics. The German medics left me in the robust hands of some good old Scottish nurses and I began my new life in my home country, relieved to be released from the land of constant snow.

CHAPTER NINETEEN

New Beginnings

THE PMR HAD the atmosphere of a hospital in decline. It was originally built in the 1930s as a TB hospital, in a fine location looking out towards the Pentland Hills to the south of Edinburgh. Thankfully the wards, which were originally open to the elements at one end, now had walls on all four sides. Several of the wards were already closed and the rest were due to be relocated to Edinburgh's new super hospital at Little France in two years' time. The remaining in-patients were mostly elderly people having hip and knee operations.

Nowadays most amputees are treated at the Astley Ainsley Hospital but because of the severity of my case I was to remain at the PMR, which had the advantage of having Edinburgh's prosthetic service on site. Besides, I got the impression there was a bit of rivalry between the PMR and the Astley Ainsley and that as a high-profile and unique case I was quite a catch for the PMR. 'To us, you're manna from heaven,' as one of my consultants put it.

I was to spend my first day at the PMR in an open ward until the room I was to be allocated became free. I passed the early afternoon with Anna, settling in, having some food, and being introduced to all the nurses. Fortunately the ward was almost empty because later in the afternoon visitors started arriving. Before long there were about fifteen or twenty people gathered round my bed.

Happily this was a trend that was to continue for many weeks as, every day, upwards of a dozen people would squeeze into my room to see how I was getting on. I was delighted to be the centre of so much attention and it cheered me up no end. My friends, many of whom had been nervous about coming to see me, were generally relieved to see me so happy, which cheered them up too. My visiting hours became established as a regular social event where people would come, not just to see me but also to meet and chat and catch up with other friends.

For a while, my hospital bed was the hub of all gossip among the various circles of people who knew me, and consequently I would often find out about various liaisons, engagements and pregnancies before anyone else. Having previously existed in a kind of gossip siding, up which only occasional snippets of information would be shunted, I found this new situation quite novel. Considering myself too ill to apply much effort to keeping secrets, I more than once caused upset by letting the cat out of the bag about some piece of news before the appropriate announcement had been made. Perhaps fortunately, I lost my position as social epicentre when I left the hospital and am now safely returned to my quiet siding.

Visiting time was always good fun and I never knew who might drop in. Over a period of a few weeks almost every person I knew made the effort to come and see me, making me realise just how many friends I had and how important they all were to me.

That evening, with the excitement of the day over, an hour or so before lights out, I was visited by a lady called Pat who arrived in an electric wheelchair from the next door ward. As a child she had contracted polio, and it had left her crippled for the rest of her life. At first I assumed she must be a long-term resident of the hospital, but she explained that she was just in for a minor operation on her hand. She lived in her own house, cooked, cleaned and shopped for herself, and drove her own specially converted car. She had read my story in the newspapers, and when she had heard that I was in the hospital, she had wanted to come and see me to reassure me that it was possible to be disabled and to lead a fulfilling life. Pat was the first, but since meeting her, my path has crossed those of dozens of disabled people who set similarly inspiring examples.

I lay awake for a while on my first night, but eventually got to sleep through the snores and sleep-talking of a couple of young lads who were in to have their football-injured knees repaired.

In the morning I was to have a treat. Since coming down from the mountain I had only had bed baths and so one of the nurses, a colourful character called Elaine who always had a trick or two up her sleeve, gave me a shower. I was helped into a bath chair and wheeled into the shower room where Elaine carefully taped plastic bags over each of my stumps to keep the water out of the bandages. For fifteen glorious minutes I basked in the spray of warm water, feeling that I'd never had such a wonderful experience in my life. All too soon, I was dried off, put into a pair of hospital pyjamas and taken back to my bed to begin a busy day meeting some of the people who would be involved in my treatment.

There were two consultants who would be looking after me, both orthopaedic surgeons.

Mr Colin Howie, a tweed-clad Scot with a bushy moustache, was the man who had arranged for me to come to the PMR. He was to provide general help and advice for me, in the style of a sort of mentor, but took little active role in my treatment. On that first morning he looked with me out of the ward window at the Pentland Hills on the skyline and promised me that, with a little determination, I could be back up there by the summer. I doubted it.

He also took a look at my medication list. 'I see you've been taking a sleeping pill,' he said. 'Don't you think that perhaps a draught of whisky would better do the trick? And I think that once you're up and about a bit more, a trip or two down to the pub would help things feel a little bit more normal.'

I readily agreed to these ideas and Mr Howie wrote me a prescription for a nightly dose of whisky. In my mind I conjured up a romantic image of stretching out in a large leather armchair by an open fire, sipping from my glass of twelve-year-old malt. That night, when the nurse fed me the full 60ml prescription dose of cheap whisky from a plastic medicine cup, my dream was shattered and the rough alcohol just about floored me in my weakened state. At least I began to sleep well after that.

Mr Roddy MacDonald was to be more directly involved in my treatment. He had spent many years working as an army surgeon and had a lot of experience with amputees. He had a close look at my stumps. The two right stumps, arm and leg, were healing up nicely. The two left stumps still hadn't been closed. Mr MacDonald explained that I had the option of having the bones trimmed back further, or to have plastic surgery. He was in favour of trimming the stumps as, in his opinion, they would still easily be long enough for the successful fitting of prostheses, and besides, skin grafts were likely to break down under the pressure of prostheses.

I was anxious for my stumps to heal as quickly as possible so I was happy to go along with Mr MacDonald's suggestion. A date later on that week was set for the revision of my left stumps.

Various prosthetists came to see me that first day, but really just to introduce themselves as it would be a while before I could begin to have artificial limbs made. Mr MacDonald reckoned on a minimum of six weeks from the final operation to the first fitting of prosthetic legs – six weeks that I was very impatient to see swiftly through.

Other people who arrived at the foot of my bed were of more immediate assistance.

Doreen Falls was a friendly but often frighteningly strict lady, and she was to oversee the various issues regarding my mobility. As an experienced physiotherapy assistant, Doreen effectively ruled the physiotherapy department in the hospital, despite what the physiotherapists might tell you. Later on she would help me learn to walk on my prosthetic legs. At this stage, however, she taught me to get about on my bum. So far, I had mostly lain or sat in whatever position the nurses put me, helpless as a rag doll, unable to shift my body myself. Doreen showed me how I could 'walk' on my bottom, most easily backwards, by shifting first one cheek then the other. I soon became an expert at this bum-walking and could manoeuvre myself around my bed with ease. She also showed me how to bum-walk backwards off my bed into a wheelchair. This gave me a great deal of freedom as it meant I no longer had to be lifted about by the nurses.

However, the person who was able to give me the greatest amount of freedom on my first day at the PMR was my occupational therapist, Helen Scott. I must admit that at that point I had no idea what an occupational therapist was, thinking vaguely that they mainly did art classes in hospitals. In actual fact, for a new amputee, especially an upper-limb one, an occupational therapist may in many ways be more important than the prosthetist, helping the patient to relearn all those everyday life skills and functions such as feeding, dressing, washing, etc.

Helen was a tall, thin, nervous lady whose slightly scatty nature gave little indication of the vast amount of experience she had in helping people with upper-limb deficiencies. At that stage I didn't know what Helen would be able to do for me, but when she asked what it was I wanted to do for myself the most, I had no hesitation in replying, 'Feed myself.'

Helen took a measurement of my right stump, bandage and all, and went off to her sewing machine. She came back a couple of hours later, at dinner time, with a small nylon strap, like a watch strap. It fastened with Velcro and had a sleeve into which the handle of a spoon could be inserted. Helen fastened the strap round my forearm and slotted in a spoon. With a little practice I found I could scoop up a spoonful of soup, and bring it to my mouth. I was absolutely delighted with this achievement and, unassisted, I slurped my way through the rest of the soup with rekindled pleasure.

Over the coming days I practised my strap technique. Using my left stump, I found I could fiddle the strap into position on my right arm. With my teeth, I could then fasten the Velcro. Holding the bowl of the spoon with my left stump, I eventually managed to push the handle into the sleeve on the strap. I discovered the strap worked equally well with a fork. It was rather clumsy at first, but if I used my left stump to further control the fork, I found I could manipulate my food quite effectively.

Soon I was eating all my food by myself, only getting help to have it cut up, and consequently I began to eat a lot more. The only disadvantage was for my nurses, who frequently had to change my soup or curry-stained bandages.

I was impressed with my strap, although I naively considered it to be a stopgap method of feeding myself before I got my new hands.

To this day though, I still eat with one of Helen's straps which I always carry with me in my pocket. It's small, it's reliable, it doesn't run on batteries, and if I forget it I can always use one of Anna's hairbands or an elastic band.

The problem of drinking without assistance was solved simply by using straws, although drinking hot tea through a straw took a lot of getting used to.

Later on that day, I was moved into my own room. The room was a generous size, contained a bed, a couple of tables and a chest of drawers, had an en-suite bathroom, and was to be my home for the next three months. It was an absolute blessing having my own room, particularly later on when it became a sort of practice apartment in which I gradually learnt to live and take care of myself. In the early days it was good to have a private facility in which to entertain my greater than regulation number of visitors, to which the nurses kindly turned a blind eye.

The room also had a window looking out on the Pentlands and a door leading onto a small patio. All in all, it wasn't at all bad for a hospital room.

My mailbag was still bursting every day and I soon had cards and pictures covering every available space on the walls. Vases of flowers were scattered over every surface, along with boxes of chocolates and a few furry toys. My tape player from Chamonix was re-installed, a television set appeared from somewhere in the hospital and a friend brought in a video recorder. As if to complete the sense of homeliness in my little room, a couple of room-mates showed up in the form of a pair of Furbies, robotic cuddly toys, which would jiggle and blink and talk to each other all day. The nurses were complete suckers for these two characters and were always coming in and fussing over them, completely ignoring me.

Gradually I began to settle in to life in the hospital. It was a pretty easy life, my every need being taken care of, and I could see how I might become over-accustomed to it. It was not a fulfilling life though, and while I could easily have filled my days with books, television and videos, I was keen to get on with the business of learning how to live all over again.

* * *

I had the operation to trim back my two left limbs on Friday, 25 February. Beforehand, a young female doctor came to give me my preoperative anaesthetic.

'I'm your anaesthetist,' she said. 'I'm here to see that you sleep through the operation, but I also do a sideline in pain management. When you wake up from the op you'll be on morphine. The flow of the drug is controlled by a patient demand machine which delivers a dose each time you press a button, so we need to figure out a way for you to push the button.'

Together we examined the several different operating mechanisms which could be attached to the machine. The one we judged would be best for me was a rubber bulb which I could squeeze between my two stumps, so we agreed that after the operation the bulb should be suspended above my head, ready for me to squeeze when I came round.

All very well in theory and when I struggled woozily into consciousness after the operation, I saw the bulb hanging over me as arranged. The only trouble was that my left arm was hooked up to the drip and I couldn't move it. As the pain in my limbs grew, all I could do was bat at the bulb forlornly with my right stump a few times before shouting for a nurse.

CHAPTER TWENTY

Memories

I WAS STILL STRUGGLING to deal with what had happened to me, and what had happened to Jamie. A dark pall hung over my heavier moments. It still didn't make sense. In my heart, though, I knew what I had to do. If I wanted to keep Jamie alive, bring him back and make him live for ever, then I could. So could everyone else who loved him. In our thoughts and recollections, our memories of happy days, Jamie would always be there, climbing on sun-kissed rock into eternity, always young while the rest of us grew old.

My own lost life, for which I mourned, was still there also. Complete with hands and feet I could always return to my favourite climbs, and feel once more the rasp of rough rock on skin, the ripple of strain down fingers and forearms, and the squeeze of tight boots on sore toes. All I had to do was close my eyes, and the rock was there in front of me. White limestone, baking in the sun. Warm mellow sandstone, glowing in shades of yellow and orange. Or hard black basalt, riven with angular cracks. I could imagine the smell of rubber and chalk, sweat and lichen as if I was there, balancing myself carefully on small holds, high above the ground, walking on air.

Lying in my hospital bed, trying to ignore the constant pain in my stumps, I allowed my mind to drift back a couple of years, to one of the happiest days I remember spending with Jamie.

* * *

Friday dawned, another golden morning. Jamie as usual was up first, rattling pans. I dragged myself out of my pit and the tent, onto the grass, and lay there for a while, soaking up the first rays of sunshine. However, we had a big day ahead, six climbs on three different hills, so I heaved myself upright and searched about our shambolic camp for the muesli.

It was the third day of the Lake District section of Jamie's Classic Rock Challenge. Jamie had set off a few weeks earlier on this mad-cap mission to climb every route in the climbers' bible, Ken Wilson's Classic Rock – a selection of ninety of the best British rock climbs in the lower grades, from Cornwall to the Hebrides. As if this wasn't a challenge enough, he was doing the whole journey by bicycle. He was also raising money as he went for a children's charity.

Despite the apparently haphazard nature of his planning, Jamie had so far successfully managed all the climbs in the south of England, including Lundy Isle, the Welsh section, the Peak District and Yorkshire. I had agreed to accompany him on all the climbs in the Lakes, so here we were at Seathwaite in Borrowdale.

By the time we set off, it was already getting hot. We crossed the river where Jamie had spent an hour the previous afternoon 'guddling for trout' – a skill he swore he had mastered as a boy, but if you asked me was the imaginings of a romanticised childhood. Certainly he caught no fish on that occasion.

On the way up to Gillercombe Buttress we escaped the sun in the narrow ravine of Sourmilk Gill, taking delight in scrambling up the slabby water-worn rocks. Cool clean water splashed all around and the gully walls were adorned with ferns, mosses and delicate flowers. We wasted some time swimming in pools and playing on water-slides, then hurried on upwards through the boggy Gillercombe to the foot of the first climb.

We soloed quickly and confidently up the rough clean rock of Gillercombe Buttress and before we knew it were on top of Bran-dreth, changing back from rock boots to walking shoes.

A long walk this time took us on a great traverse round the northern flanks of Green Gable, Great Gable, Kirk Fell and eventually Pillar Mountain, where the great dark hulk of Pillar Rock loomed. Today, for once, a little sunshine was slanting down the usually dank west face of the rock. We left our sacks at the bottom and soloed up New West Climb, a nice easy romp on good rock when not in its usual damp greasy condition. We scrambled back down to the sacks and stopped for a bite to eat before getting the rope out for the more difficult, but equally enjoyable, Rib and Slab Climb.

The rock seemed to be flowing from our hands and feet, like water, falling beneath us in a cascade as we climbed ever upwards. We were unstoppable and the grey rock passed in a blur, the details instantly forgotten. The moment was everything, and we savoured the passing of every one.

Back at the sacks, we packed away the climbing gear and set off once again, reversing the traverse beneath Pillar and Kirk Fell, before sneaking through the gap between Kirk Fell and Great Gable, and traversing the rattling scree slopes on the south side of Great Gable to find the iconic pinnacle of Napes Needle rising like a monument from the screes. Its smooth rock, polished like marble by the boots of generations of climbers, succumbed to some awkward, slippery climbing, and we sat side by side on the tiny summit block and paused for a while, gazing down into distant Wasdale.

Rising from the foot of the needle, the spiky dinosaur back of Needle Ridge gave an easy climb up into the confusing terrain of scree and rocks at the top of the Napes. We spent a while searching for the top of the descent gully which, when we eventually found it, took us to the foot of Tophet Wall. The sun only visits this imposing bastion of rock in the morning and our route, the last and hardest of the day, looked cold and intimidating. A pair of climbers, the first we'd seen all day, had just finished the first pitch but they kindly offered to let us pass, so we soloed the first two pitches before roping up for the difficult and spectacular overhang. Jamie pulled through this with apparent ease and I struggled on behind him.

After completing the climb, we went down for the sacks, then descended to indulge in another swim in the inky waters of Styhead Tarn. The sun was sinking now and we had to get moving quickly to warm up. Before long we were plodding wearily through the bracken slopes of Grains Gill, back to the tent, where the beer waited, chilling in the river.

* * *

I knew how lucky I was. I was armed with a multitude of fond and vivid memories, more than many probably, and would always have them for when I needed them most. I had already had a pretty good run for my money. If I had died up there on the mountain alongside Jamie, as I still thought I should have, I would have died having had a good life. You can't ask for more than that. Anything that happened from now on was a bonus. How could I possibly feel miserable about my amputations? They were a small price to pay for my stay of execution.

A friend who has a dry sense of humour once reassured me that my arms and legs would be waiting for me in heaven. A playful remark, but one of genuine philosophical interest. I've never been a religious person, nor am I an atheist, preferring to sit on the fence of agnosticism. Many people have asked me whether my experience up there on the mountain changed me spiritually. Of course my brush with death caused me to re-examine the way I felt about God, faith and religion, but the more I thought about it, the less I felt like anything in me had changed. I had been to the very brink of death and peered into the darkness beyond, yet I hadn't found myself looking into the face of God, nor received any other revelation. I had come away from the episode feeling small and confused, been given no answers, only more questions. More than ever I felt like a helpless piece of flotsam, adrift without explanation on a sea of uncertainty.

In a strange way, however, I did now feel spiritually more secure. I felt that it didn't matter to me any more whether there was a God, an afterlife, or a reason for being on this Earth. I'd come as close as I could to finding an answer to these questions and there hadn't been one. There would be no solution to these problems and it was pointless to pursue them. What was important was life. I was still alive, and that was all that really mattered. All I could do was to get on with the business of living it as best I could, for myself and for others. A benevolent creator, if he exists, would I'm sure understand this and forgive me my lack of faith.

Before too long I was once again free from all drips and machines. The pain in my stumps gradually faded and I soon became quite mobile. The hospital supplied me with an electric wheelchair and my horizons expanded to include the whole of the hospital, although I quickly discovered that there wasn't much to see: the canteen, the Women's Royal Voluntary Service, a couple of dingy wards, and 100 metres or so of corridors, their walls brightened by the occasional painting. Still, it was nice to be moving about once again. I also had a conventional wheelchair in which Anna or other friends would sometimes take me on a tour of the outside of the hospital, but once again there was little to see, unless you're interested in passing traffic on busy roads.

Another benefit of my increased mobility was that I could begin doing physio. My body was by now shockingly feeble and emaciated, my muscles withered away to almost nothing, and I was going to have to work hard if I was to ever get fit again. To begin with I felt weak and lethargic, but my physiotherapist, a tall, attractive girl called Joy, did her best to motivate and encourage me.

At first, bed bound, there were few exercises I could do, but there were some. Joy got me to lie on my back and push down hard with my knees into the mattress, or into a rolled-up towel, in order to get my quads used to working again. That and a few other static exercises, such as buttock clenches, I could do on my own. Other dynamic exercises I could only do during my daily physio sessions. Joy was quite inventive about finding ways for me to exercise my various important muscle groups. As soon as my stumps were well enough to take a little rough treatment, she would strap physio weights (nylon bags filled with lead shot which attach to the arms or legs) to my stumps. To stop them falling off the ends of my stumps, she would wrap yards of crêpe bandaging round them. I could then do various arm and leg-raising exercises although more often than not each set of exercises would end prematurely when the weights slipped off my stumps and dropped with a thud to the floor. Patiently, Joy would replace them and carefully wind on the crêpe bandages again.

Other exercises, such as pectoral presses, we did with an elastic physio band. Joy attached one end of the elastic to the end of my bed and the other end to my stumps. I could then pull against the stretch of the elastic. Later on, Helen made me some neoprene elbow slings that could be attached to physio springs so that I could work my arms harder.

At first I found this light physio work quite exhausting and my poor muscles, what was left of them, would be left quivering after each session. After a while, however, I got used to it and I looked forward to my daily workouts with Joy.

When I was mobile enough to get into the wheelchair, we had the sessions in the physio room which was much more satisfactory than attempting to exercise on my bed. I also found that by rolling onto my stomach I could slither off my chair, or off the physio bed, and onto the floor. Once on the floor I could crawl about on my knees and elbows a little, although it quickly became painful in my stumps. Now that I could get onto the floor, there were many floor exercises that could be done. We did lots of ball-rolling and throwing games to improve my upper body strength and coordination. I soon learnt to catch the balls between my two stumps. One of my favourite exercises was the wobble board. A wobble board is a circular board, supported by a half ball underneath. The idea is to stand or kneel on the board and gently rock back and forth. All the muscles in your legs, abdomen and lower back have to work together as you struggle to find your balance. With practice you can balance on the board without letting the edges touch the floor. At first I just sat on the wobble board, but as my stumps healed I managed to stand up on my knees. Then Joy would throw balls for me to catch while I tried to remain in balance on the board, feeling like a performing seal.

I was never going to get super fit doing this physio work, but hopefully it would prepare me for the day when I first attempted to stand on prosthetic legs.

On the whole, I quite enjoyed life at the PMR. All the nurses and medical staff were really friendly to me and I got on well with them. My room was pleasant and very comfortable and my visitors were able to come and go as they pleased. However, the one aspect of hospital life I didn't take to was the food.

I suppose the food was OK. I mean it was perfectly fit for human consumption and I never got ill from it. It was fine for a day or two but soon I just got sick of it – bland, mass-produced, institutional food, which had generally been left to sit in a heated trolley for an hour. Also the menus from which I had to select the day before could often not be relied on to provide accurate descriptions of what would arrive the next day. Fresh fruit salad, for instance, turned out to be from a tin. Chocolate mousse was in fact some kind of instant whip.

To make matters worse I was visited by a dietician who poked and prodded and took various measurements of my body and told me that I was dangerously underweight. I protested that I had always been really skinny but she insisted.

'I want you to eat as much fatty food as possible,' she said. 'Eat all the chocolate you can. And I'm going to give you a carton of cream every day to put on your breakfast cereal and puddings. And what about a cooked breakfast? Do you think you can manage a cooked breakfast?'

Every slimmer's dream, I thought, to be given these kinds of instructions by a qualified dietician, but I just couldn't work up the appetite for it.

I tried to eat as much chocolate as I could, but forcing the cream down made me feel sick and I almost went off cream for ever. The cooked breakfasts were even more of a disaster. The hospital kitchen's idea of a cooked breakfast consisted of two Lorne sausages, two link sausages and three bits of bacon. No egg, no tomato, no mushrooms, no beans. Not even a piece of toast. Just solid meat.

I politely protested and the next day the meat fest was accompanied by a bread roll and a mound of reconstituted scrambled egg that silently oozed water onto my plate.

The dietician, poor lady (she was very nice and only wanted to help me out), also wanted to add build-up drinks to my diet – three a day. I detested these milkshake-like drinks and after trying them for a while I rebelled completely and stopped eating all of my food supplements.

Fortunately, Anna came to the rescue. Our flat was only ten minutes drive away, so a couple of times a week, she would cook me a fantastic meal at home, then drive it to the hospital in an insulated bag. Everyone in the ward, including the staff, were soon very envious of my new improved diet. Anna's meals on wheels, plus the occasional takeaway pizza, helped supplement the regular hospital food and I slowly began to gain weight again.

CHAPTER TWENTY-ONE

Occupational Therapy

Now that my arms and legs had been trimmed to their final size, the only injured part of my body that remained unresolved was my right ear. The frostbite in this ear had behaved in the way in which the French doctors had hoped my hands and feet would. The dead or necrotic tissue in the ear had shrivelled and dried and separated from the live tissue. The doctors left the necrotic tissue to progress with this on its own accord and I now had a mostly healthy-looking ear with an almost detached upper section that was black and shrivelled. My friend Andy reckoned that it looked like I had a piece of dried banana behind my ear, saved for a peckish moment.

A plastic surgeon had come to see me, mainly to examine my stumps to see if he could help with skin coverage, but he also offered to rebuild my ear with cartilage taken from my ribs and skin scavenged from elsewhere on my body. I was revolted at the thought of having my chest unnecessarily cut open as well as everything else, and decided that a small section missing from my ear was a trivial disfigurement compared to having no hands and feet. It was something I could quite easily live with.

A couple of weeks after arriving at the PMR the doctors decided that it was time to trim the necrotic material off the ear. I was taken to another hospital in nearby Livingston and had the minor operation to tidy the ear up. I had hoped that the piece of dried banana would fall off of its own accord and I could keep it as a souvenir in a matchbox to frighten small children with. Perhaps if I'd still had idle fingers with which to pick this giant scab it might have accidentally dropped off, but in the end it was destroyed in the operation.

It took a further few weeks for the remaining ear to heal over and meanwhile I had to wear a bandage on my head. With bandages on each limb and one on my head I now looked like an unfortunate First World War victim, or a comedy patient in a Carry On film.

I hated wearing the bandage on my head and always felt hot and uncomfortable. I begged the nurses to contrive some other way of attaching the dressing to my ear. Elaine gave me a knowing smile and said she knew just the thing. She disappeared to have a rummage through the ward store cupboard. When she returned, accompanied by a giggling colleague, she held an unidentified, frilly, elasticated object. When fitted over my head, like a headband, it held the ear dressing gently in place, without squeezing my head or heating me up too much.

'What is it?' I asked.

'Oh it doesn't matter what it is, as long as it does the job,' she replied with a smirk, while the other nurse tried to suppress a snigger.

'No, I want to know,' I insisted, realising that something was afoot.

'Well,' said Elaine, 'if you must know, it's a pair of disposable knickers, with the crotch cut out.' This time the junior nurse couldn't contain herself and ran from the room, her hands over her face.

'Knickers?' I asked incredulously.

'Disposable ones,' Elaine reassured me, 'with the crotch cut out. Don't worry, dear, you can't tell. No one will know.' And with that she left me with my knickers on my head.

As it happened, the knickers were very successful as a comfortable bandage and I carried on wearing them on my head until my ear was fully healed.

Nowadays my ear looks unremarkably damaged, as if part of it has been bitten or torn off and, despite the occasional comparison to Van Gogh and Evander Holyfield, most people never even notice. I think of it fondly as my fifth stump and I'm certainly glad I never bothered having it rebuilt with plastic surgery.

In the early days, one of the major limitations to my rehabilitation was the fact that my limbs were swaddled in bandages, making any manipulation of objects difficult and insecure. However, I could broadly push things about, and even accomplish more fine control tasks such as turning the pages of a newspaper, although not usually without a good deal of frustration.

Most task learning was driven by simple necessity. If I wanted my drink moved closer or my pillows rearranged and there was no nurse available, I would just have to do it myself. I found I could hold things OK between my two stumps although the bandages often caused them to slip. Pushing things away from me and pulling them towards me wasn't too difficult either, but I had to be careful with anything that might spill. I had my meals on a small tray-top table next to my bed. I would sit up on the bed and shuffle round until I was sitting on the edge, then the nurse would push the table up to me, so that I could manoeuvre my various plates, bowls and cups about as necessary, trying not to slop too much soup into my custard.

I also found I could operate the remote control for the television. The buttons were very small and fiddly but a few carefully aimed stabs with a folded corner of my bandage would usually produce the desired audio-visual adjustments, give or take the occasional unexpected and spectacular volume increase.

All these gradually mastered skills were a great help to me in the course of each passing day, but it was abundantly clear that things could only start properly once the bandages came off.

Fortunately I was a fast healer, I was told, and my scars quickly began to seal up. One by one, my stumps each had their stitches removed. As the nurse nonchalantly whipped them out with a few deft flicks of a scalpel, my missing toes curled in revulsion. After the stitches had gone my bandages were reduced to small dressings over the wounds and I began the process of becoming accustomed to my new arms.

Helen was also intent on seeing that my new arms became accustomed to me, and to whatever I might do with them. This, she explained, was called desensitisation and was very important for me to be able to use my stumps effectively.

She began with a piece of cotton wool and started to rub it gently over the end of one of my stumps. I pulled my arm back, cringing as every nerve in my arm fired in confusion, not knowing where the signals were coming from. Strange electrical tingling pulses shot down my forearm, sending a shiver down my back. Helen grabbed my arm back, like I was a naughty schoolboy flinching at corporal punishment, and continued with her bizarre torture. I felt like fingernails were being scraped down a dozen blackboards all at once and the combined spine-shuddering feeling was being concentrated into my arm.

Eventually Helen put away the cotton wool and produced a small rubber mallet. She then proceeded to rap the most sensitive part of my stump with the little hammer, in short sharp blows. Shockwaves of cringing, blackboard-scraping feeling pulsed down my arm, sending it jerking about uncontrollably. Just when she knew I could take no more, Helen dropped my arm and moved across to the other one. Only when she had finished me off completely, leaving me a quivering wreck, did she relent and pack away her instruments of torture.

As a parting shot she set me some homework. 'Whenever you're not doing anything else,' she said, 'I want you to rub your stumps on any surface that's available, to toughen them up. Your bedclothes, the edge of your table, anything to help them get used to everyday life. I'll see you tomorrow. By the way, isn't that a pair of knickers on your head?'

Helen kept her word and arrived with her little box of toys the next day, and the day after that. Gradually the sensations in my stumps grew less, although Helen soon graduated from cotton wool to towelling to dimpled rubber, until she was eventually rubbing sandpaper on my unfortunate limbs.

It took a long time, but nowadays I feel little unwanted sensation at all and my stumps are as tough as my elbows, although an accidental blow can still send me howling round the room in agony.

Now that my stumps were free from bandages, I was able to try a greater variety of tasks. Every day, apart from torturing me with cotton wool, Helen would encourage me to attempt a wide range of activities. Sometimes we would operate from my bed. More often, Helen would help me into my wheelchair and we would roam the hospital in search of everyday tasks.

Sitting next to me on my bed, Helen got me to pick up a jug from the table and pour out a glass of water. This I did, carefully clasping the jug between my shaking stumps. As I set the jug down, Helen tipped the water back into it and said, 'Again!'

I obligingly repeated the feat.

'Again!' said Helen, like a child demanding the repetition of a simple game.

The water-pouring continued for a while until Helen was finally satisfied that I had mastered that particular trick, then we moved on to the next task.

In this manner we continued through all the items that came to hand in my room: cups, books, boxes of chocolates, letters, cutlery, even the Furbies, who were more than happy to join in the fun. All were endlessly picked up, put down, turned around, opened, closed, pushed and pulled as part of my manipulation practice. Helen also brought me various games. Ancient jigsaw puzzles and card games that looked like they'd passed through the hands of a dozen less-than-careful owners before finally washing up in the hospital occupational therapy department. These were useful to me more for the physical challenge than the originally intended mental diversion, but they were fun nonetheless.

At the same time, I tried dressing myself. It didn't take an inordinate amount of practice before I was able to pull on simple loose-fitting clothes like T-shirts, boxer shorts and jogging bottoms, although the latter two required a great amount of wriggling on my back. As soon as I was able to dress myself, I sacked the nurses from this particular task, pleased to be able to lessen my burden on the NHS in a small way and even more pleased to have taken another small step on the road to self-sufficiency.

Helen wheeled me into the bathroom to have a look at the challenges that faced me there. At first I was unable to even attempt much as my wounds hadn't entirely closed over and there was therefore a risk of infection. We did, however, do a dry run, as it were, in order to assess how I might achieve the various necessary tasks. As the weeks passed and my scabs dried up, I was able to attempt these tasks for real.

For brushing my teeth, an electric toothbrush seemed like the most obvious solution. I didn't have an electric toothbrush, so I thought I might as well try using my manual version. At first it seemed pretty much impossible to grip the small plastic handle between my stumps and vibrate it in a satisfactorily vigorous manner. I wanted to give up until an electric brush was acquired but Helen encouraged me to continue. I found that with a bit of fumbling I could bring the toothbrush to more or less any desired angle and hold it fairly steadily between my stumps. Then, by shaking my head up and down and from side to side, I managed to give my teeth a slow but rigorous scrub. It seemed an unworkably awkward solution at first, but after several attempts, toothpaste spreading its way all over the place, I began to feel that I was getting the hang of it. Pleased with myself, I sacked the nurses from this task too. To begin with, the entire business of brushing my teeth, including carefully unscrewing the toothpaste cap, squeezing the paste onto my brush, which I held by the handle in my mouth, replacing the cap, brushing, rinsing, etc., would take over ten minutes. Every day though, the task became a fraction easier and a tiny bit quicker, until one day I realised that I no longer found brushing my teeth difficult and that it took me no more time than it takes anyone else.

Flush with the success of the toothbrush, Helen and I turned our attention to shaving. Helen suggested an electric shaver, but I much prefer to wet shave and was determined to learn to do it again. We thought at first that I might be able to manage a normal razor like I did the toothbrush, but soon found that I couldn't manoeuvre it to all areas of my face at the correct angle for shaving. We tried using a specially extended razor but still it was just too awkward, and became even more so when hot water and soap were added to the equation.

Helen arrived the next day with one of her many catalogues. This one mostly contained products designed for people with reduced limb function: arthritis sufferers, stroke victims and such like. The item she had found was a razor for people who had limited use of their fingers – a normal razor mounted onto a universal joint that strapped into the user's palm. If it could be adapted to strap onto my stump then it might be ideal for me. Helen ordered the device and a couple of days later it arrived. She removed the existing Velcro strap and replaced it with one that would fit my stump.

As with the toothbrush affair, the whole shaving thing seemed impossibly difficult at first. After a lot of fumbling about, I would get the blade into a particular position, shave a small patch of beard, only to find that none of the rest of my face was in reach. I'd then have to move the blade again, estimating the appropriate position as best I could before shaving another small patch. I got there eventually, however, and to my relief I finished with less cuts than I usually got when one of the nurses shaved me. So the nurses lost another job. Of course, as with the toothbrushing, the shaving soon got easier and faster until it too no longer seemed such a trial.

With learning to wash myself, apart from a few dry experiments, Helen pretty much left me to my own devices. Since I had been able to get into the shower chair, I had been having a shower every morning, the nurse who was on duty wheeling me into the shower and washing me in the chair. When I felt confident enough, I asked the nurses to put the soap, shampoo and flannel next to me on the chair, turn on the shower, and leave me alone. I would then have plenty of fun juggling with the soap and the slippery shampoo bottle, and trying to reach every part of my body with the flannel. I was soon managing quite well although I would often have to pull the alarm cord when some or all of my washing kit fell on the floor. I found I could reach most parts of my body with the flannel, apart from my upper back, which wasn't too important. I could reach my left armpit with my right stump, but frustratingly, not my right armpit with my shorter left stump, so I devised an alternative method. Holding the flannel in my teeth, I swung it into my armpit and clamped my arm over it. Still with my teeth, I would then pull the flannel out, giving the armpit a good wash on the way.

Once washed I would pull the cord and wait for the nurse to come and dry me down and return me to the bed. It wasn't long, though, before I learnt to dry myself as well.

It embarrasses me somewhat to write about going to the toilet, but I know that it's the forbidden question to which everyone who's curious about me wants to know the answer. On more than one occasion, people have whispered to Anna, 'How does he manage in the bathroom?' although few have ever asked me to my face.

Of course it's a good question, one to which I was understandably anxious to find an answer myself, not wanting to spend the rest of my life having my bum wiped for me by somebody else. Mr Mac-Donald and Mr Howie had both vaguely reassured me that there were 'ways round the problem', 'things which could be done', and had left it at that, leaving the nitty-gritty to the occupational therapists.

Helen, fortunately, wasn't so reserved. 'What about the bottom, Jamie?' she would earnestly enquire. 'Have you had a think about the bottom? Any progress with the bottom?'

There was, it seemed, all sorts of specially adapted toilets available that could wash the user's bottom automatically, or there was the simpler option of the old-fashioned bidet. I didn't want to be limited to going to the loo in my own home, though, so I strived to find a more universal solution. Luckily my right stump is long enough to reach the crucial area so it was simply a case of finding some way of attaching toilet paper or something similar to my stump, and being able to release it once finished.

First I tried disposable wet wipes in the hope that the wetness would provide enough friction to hold the wipe in place, but this wasn't too successful. I then had a go at wrapping a load of toilet paper round and round my stump, but couldn't quite get it to stay in place. Helen came up with the idea of using an elastic band. I would put an elastic band onto my wrist with my teeth. Then, holding the band out with my teeth, I'd push a corner of my length of toilet paper under it. This held the paper in place while I wrapped the rest of it round my stump. I could then wipe myself relatively easily, although I almost fell off the toilet a few times in the process. I then pulled the paper free from the elastic band, allowing it to drop into the pan, and disposed of the elastic band. Job done.

As time went by, I grew more adept at this particularly tricky task, and was eventually able to dispense with the elastic band, so that now I can use any loo without need of any special equipment.

It took many weeks to master all of these self-care issues, but once I had, I was almost completely independent in the bathroom. I just had to be wheeled into each position – shower, sink or toilet, passed the appropriate toiletries, and left to get on with it till I rung the bell for assistance. I began to feel for the first time that there was hope that I might eventually lead a relatively normal existence.

Helen would also often wheel me down to the occupational therapy department for our daily sessions. There we would experiment with the various weird and wonderful contraptions and adapted devices they had to help people with upper-limb deficiencies. There were kettles on gimbles that could be tipped up without lifting, chopping boards with spikes for holding vegetables, scissors mounted on stands that could be operated by a simple push, and a whole host of other variations on everyday tools and appliances, most of which I noted were quite low tech.

The gadget that impressed me most, although it had no relevance to my needs, was a foot-operated spoon. It was an enormous, Heath Robinson contraption with all sorts of cables, joints and pulleys, at the centre of which was a rather ignominious little spoon. The user would sit on the integral chair, and by means of two foot pedals, could manoeuvre the spoon from bowl to mouth. I never saw anyone operate the machine, but it looked as difficult to pilot as a jet plane.

Helen was keen to see that I would be able to manage all the little operations one comes across in a day-to-day household situation. Opening and closing doors was a great favourite. Cupboard doors, fridge doors, room doors, locked doors, all were opened and closed, opened and closed, ad nauseam. I found I could manage most door handles quite easily, so long as they weren't too stiff, and pulling the door open wasn't much of a problem either. Turning a key in a lock was a much more tricky action, which I could only manage if the key was quite big and the lock well oiled.

We also spent a lot of time in the department kitchen, trying to operate kettles and tin-openers, wash dishes, and that sort of thing. I must admit that I had less enthusiasm for learning to cope with this kind of chore than I had with the more immediate and personal bathroom chores, and I made less progress in the kitchen.

* * *

179

Throughout my stay at the PMR, while I was struggling with toilet paper and cupboard doors, Anna was struggling to adjust to the changes in her life, which had been turned on its head every bit as much as mine.

Before the accident, the three of us – Jamie, Anna and I – had all lived together. Now Anna was in the flat on her own, the door to Jamie's room firmly closed, his things lying as he had left them. The rest of the flat was cold and empty, and often Anna would go round to her parents' house, not wanting to sleep on her own. Pots and pans from the meals that Anna cooked me would pile up in the kitchen. Until only a few weeks before, Jamie and I used to squabble about whose turn it was to do the dishes. Neither of us was doing them now.

Anna worked for a software testing company in Edinburgh. After we returned from France she couldn't face the prospect of going back, and was excused from working by her doctor on grounds of stress. Eventually she did return, but only part-time, going in to work in the mornings, sorting out our lives and running errands after lunch, and coming to the hospital in the afternoons. She came to see me every day, which was fantastic as it gave us plenty of time to be together, to support one another, to re-evaluate our relationship with one another, and to care for each other through what were very trying times.

Every afternoon I would relate with alacrity any little achievements I had made that morning, and demonstrate any new skills I had mastered; on the days when I felt I was making no progress and that my whole existence was just a waste of time, Anna would always manage to cheer me up and make me feel a whole lot better. On the days when she felt that everything was black, I would try to do the same for her. Together we found we were stronger and life didn't seem quite so hard.

On top of all our other problems, we were also worried about financial difficulties. I obviously wasn't able to work, Anna was only working part-time, and of course we no longer received rent for the spare room. The bills still had to be paid, however, and the mortgage still came out of my bank account every month. We were both very relieved therefore, when my insurance company paid out a lump sum big enough to tide us over for a while.

My two bosses Gordon and Alan, who have always been friends foremost and employers second, also helped alleviate the situation. It was obvious that my career as a rope access worker had come to an abrupt and untimely end, but they were good enough to keep me on full office-rate pay for as long as I was in hospital and they assured me that there would always be a job available for me in the Web office. This was a great weight off our minds and Anna and I were able to concentrate more on practical matters and worry less about money.

CHAPTER TWENTY-TWO

Daytripping

A RED-LETTER DAY CAME one morning when my very own fold-up wheelchair arrived. The large and cumbersome hospital chair was too big to fit into Anna's car and too heavy for her to lift, but the new, smaller, lighter model was much more manageable, opening up the possibility of trips outside the hospital for me.

Getting from the chair into the car was the difficult bit. Anna would push the chair up into the open door and I would then have to wriggle onto the car seat, pushing with my elbows on the rim of the door, and trying not to fall out onto the street. Once I was in, Anna could then pack up the chair, stow it in the back, and we were off.

On our first trip out we decided to go to the Museum of Scotland, which had just recently opened. It felt strange driving through the streets of Edinburgh on a normal Saturday morning. I found myself staring out the window at all the ordinary people, wrapped up in woollens and heavy coats against a chilly March wind, as they went about their everyday business, and I felt very different from them all. It seemed as if I had left their world behind and gone to live in a very different and strange environment. It was as if I'd been away for many years on a long journey, finally returning home to find nothing altered, but discovering that it was myself that had changed beyond recognition.

In fact Anna and I were soon to discover that our familiar town of Edinburgh was a greatly changed place when viewed from our new perspective of wheelchair users. Frankly I was shocked, in this day and age, how poorly facilitated we are for something as fundamental as a wheelchair. Pavements are uneven and potholed, kerbs rise up from the roads like brick walls, public buildings are guarded by staircases, and disabled parking spaces are invariably taken by those who have no reason or right to.

Fortunately the new Museum of Scotland was an excellently provided modern building, and I thoroughly enjoyed whizzing round the polished concrete floors, being pushed by Anna and a couple of friends, pausing occasionally to look at the odd exhibit.

After the success of the museum trip, we made the effort to go on excursions every weekend and I slowly started to acclimatise myself to the outside world again.

I was surprised to discover that people in the street knew who I was, and the bolder would occasionally say so. One lad came up to me and said, 'Awright pal, you're that boy off the moontain an' that, int ye? You're doin' magic pal, magic!' before swaggering off with a gap-toothed grin and an encouraging thumbs-up gesture. A couple of little old ladies approached me in a café and whispered cryptically, 'We know what it's like, son. You stick at it.'

It was at this stage that I really started having to deal with the reactions of strangers to me. It was odd to think that before my accident, anyone who encountered me in the street would have no reason to look twice, but now I was likely to be the strangest-looking person they'd met all week. I noticed people staring at me, and though most adults were too sly to be caught, small children just couldn't take their eyes off me and would often embarrass their parents by asking in a loud voice, 'Mum, why's that man got no hands?'

'Shhhh!' the embarrassed mother would implore.

'But Mum, how does he . . .?'

'Be quiet!'

'But Mum, loooook!'

'Shut up, will you!' the by now absolutely mortified parent would snap.

People would often feel the need to say something, mumble their sympathy, or apologise unthinkingly. It's a strange reaction – I've done it myself in the past. You turn round in a busy shop and some-one's in the way. So you move round them. Then you turn round in the same shop and someone sitting in a wheelchair is in your way. You say, 'Oh, sorry!' and back hurriedly away feeling like you've violated the wheelchair's personal space. I became quite fed up with knee-jerk apologies from flustered passers-by.

Other people just wouldn't know how to react to me and instead would turn to Anna and ask if I needed any help, as if I wasn't there. I'd heard of this 'Does he take sugar?' reaction to disabled people, but was quite shocked by the reality of it. People genuinely seemed to assume that because I was in a wheelchair, I would be unable to speak for myself. So I came to the conclusion that there probably wasn't any point trying to take account of other people's reactions and prejudices, and that the best thing I could do was to just get on with it and try not to be embarrassed in public.

Despite a common awkwardness, and the occasional misunder-standing, I found people in general to be incredibly helpful, generous and encouraging to me. Folk would bend over backwards to help me out, and there was never a shortage of volunteers to assist Anna with getting the wheelchair up and down steps and through difficult door-ways. It was quite spiriting to receive all this support and it helped me to feel a little better about myself.

Now that I was more mobile, I thought back to what Mr Howie had said to me on my first day at the PMR about going to the pub. This sounded like a very attractive step on the road to normality, so Anna and I put the word round to all our friends that evening visiting time on Wednesdays would from then on be held at the new venue of the Steading. This was a runaway success and more people would come to visit me on Wednesdays than on any other day of the week. The Steading Inn didn't know what had hit it.

On my first visit to the pub, I was bought a pint and was immedi-ately confronted with the problem of how to drink it. Someone fetched a straw and I tried drinking the beer through that. Not enjoying being compared to a fifteen-year-old who'd heard you could get drunk quicker that way, and tiring of jokes about not being able to hold my drink, I quickly rejected the straw idea, and tried to pick the pint up between my stumps. It felt quite unsteady and I was terrified that the glass would slip at any moment, but I managed in an awkward manner to bring the pint to my lips, take a sip and place it carefully down again. I have been drinking beer like this ever since. It is of course a technique that requires plenty of regular practice.

My mate Jim Hayes, who advocates that every pint should be accompanied by a fag, wanted to see if I could roll a cigarette. Happy to accept a challenge, I took Jim's smoking kit and set to work. The net result of an industrious few minutes was a crumpled and beer-soaked pile of papers, and all of Jim's tobacco spread liberally over my lap, the table and the floor. Several weeks later, however, as much to my surprise as everyone else's, I produced my first stump-rolled cigarette, and have regularly rolled them as my favourite pub trick ever since.

I had all of two pints that first night and Anna delivered me back to the hospital feeling quite drunk. My drunkenness on Wednesday nights increased as I built up to three or even four pints in the evening. In my dishevelled state I was a great amusement to the night nurses, who were quite unaccustomed to hospital patients who absconded to the pub in the evening and rolled up long after lights out, demanding to be let in. Often Anna and I would arrive at the back entrance to the hospital, next to my ward, to find the doors locked. Propped up against the doors would be a pee bottle. The faint sounds of giggling drifted from the open window of the darkened staff room. When I had persuaded the joking ladies to let us in, Anna would help me get into bed and tuck me up for the night. On several occasions, on leaving the wheelchair, I failed to establish myself on the bed and toppled hopelessly onto the floor. Once, I managed to bring Anna down with me, just as one of the nurses walked into the room.

'What on earth is going on here?' she exclaimed, as she surveyed the two of us rolling on the floor in fits of laughter.

Two gentlemen knocked on my door one morning and introduced themselves as Rob Farley and Bill Douglas, biomechanical engineers. They were based at the PMR as part of the Rehabilitation Engineering

Services and it was their job, Rob explained, to modify, or design and build, any non-standard items of equipment that might be useful to me in my rehabilitation. They would, for example, make any wheelchair modifications that I might require, or make tools that could help me to use a computer.

This seemed to me to be a fantastic facility and I resolved to make every use of it. Over the coming weeks I kept Rob, Bill and their assistants busy making all sorts of gadgets for me.

I had been experimenting with pushing myself about in my wheelchair. I couldn't reach the wheel rims, with which a user would normally propel the chair, but I could get some purchase on the rubber tyres with the skin on my forearms, and very slowly wheel myself about. The trouble was, the skin on my arms would get quite raw and I needed something to protect them. Rob and Bill set to work with pieces of leather, straps and buckles and made me a pair of driving gloves that slipped over my stumps and fastened with good old Velcro.

My driving gloves extended my range in the wheelchair, causing me to get into big trouble with Doreen one day, when, late for an appointment down at the limb-fitting centre, and tired of waiting for the porter to come and collect me, I set off out of the building on my own. I was found rolling down the hill in the car park, steering along the side of a wall in an attempt to control my speed and avoid running into the back of an ambulance. I thought I'd done rather well in terms of gaining some independence, but Doreen gave me a grand dressing down.

'What if you'd been hurt? What if you'd run out of control? We can't just have patients wheeling all around the hospital grounds willy-nilly!' Still, at least the driving gloves were a success.

I was also keen to find a way of operating a computer so that I could get on with some correspondence. The solution was fairly simple in the end: Helen obligingly made a couple more Velcro straps for me, one for each stump, and the biomechanics made some rubber-tipped, steel-wire probes, which slotted into the straps and stuck out like index fingers. I could then manage two-fingered typing just as well as I ever had. I could operate a normal mouse reasonably easily with my stumps, the tracker-ball type even more so, and all of a sudden I was computer capable.

I was disappointed that hospital funds wouldn't run to providing me with a computer, along with the means to operate one, but luckily I was able to use an old laptop that had belonged to Jamie. Once Anna had installed this in my room, I began the huge task of writing letters of thanks to everyone who had written to me to express their condolences and well wishes, and who I hadn't yet been able to thank personally. This took quite a while but it kept me busy during the slack hours of the day.

Helen had been concerned that I was having difficulty turning keys in locks and had suggested that I get all my keys modified with an extra piece to provide more leverage. I didn't fancy the thought of having to cart around a bag full of giant keys, so devised the idea of a key lever. I described my idea to Rob and Bill and they made it for me out of stainless-steel wire. It's simply a small, lever-shaped object, with a slot in it, which can be fitted over the head of any key. You insert the key into the lock, put on the key lever, and push down on it to turn the key. When I received my key lever, Helen whisked me off on a tour of the hospital to unlock and relock every cupboard and storeroom we could find. Another success for the bio boys.

During this period, now that my arms were well enough healed, I first started receiving treatment from my upper-limb prosthetist, Malcolm Griffiths.

'Pleased to meet you,' said Malcolm, a tall, softly spoken and unassuming man in an all-white hospital outfit. 'I'm going to be taking care of your upper-limb prosthetic needs, so over the next few years you and I are going to get to know each other pretty well. Is that ladies' underwear you've got on your head?'

Malcolm, it turned out, was a keen hillwalker, so we had something in common, and he was very encouraging about my chances of getting back into the hills one day.

First things first, though, we began by looking at my more basic and immediate requirements. I had been expecting Malcolm to simply set about his black art and make me some fully functioning prosthetic hands and so was surprised when, as Helen, Rob and Bill had done before him, he looked to me to tell him what it was that I required.

Well, obviously I wanted a pair of top-of-the-range, state-of-the-art, computer-controlled, robotic arms, like the one Luke Skywalker gets in *The Empire Strikes Back*, but Malcolm was quick to rein in my science-fiction fantasies, and focus on realistic possibilities. Once the swelling in my left stump had gone down a bit, he said, he would make me a prosthetic arm for my left side, a simple mechanical one to start with. When I had mastered the mechanical arm, we could look at some of the more technological options that were available.

As for my right arm, it had been amputated just short of the wrist and is therefore quite a long stump. It would be perfectly possible to build a prosthetic arm for this stump, Malcolm said, but once all the mechanical components had been added on the prosthesis would end up being cumbersomely long and unwieldy. It would therefore be better to create something simpler for the right arm.

I was still getting to grips with feeding myself clumsily with my strap and a fork, and wondered if Malcolm could come up with a way for me to use a knife. He began work on my first prosthesis right away by taking a plaster cast mould of my right arm.

The next day he returned with a laminated plastic socket, moulded from the plaster cast, which fitted snugly over my arm. Together we then estimated the correct position and angle at which a knife should be fitted and Malcolm went away to add a further lamination into which was fitted a slot to accept a knife handle. He also fitted a perpendicular slot on the underside that would take a fork or a spoon. The bio boys ground down the handles of a set of cutlery to fit Malcolm's slots and the tool was ready.

I had thought that having my spoon or fork held more rigidly in the plastic socket would make them easier to use, but I immediately found that the increased rigidity also meant a decreased flexibility, and I could no longer rotate my arm to keep the cutlery level as I brought it to my mouth, so I continued using the strap. The knife worked well though, and with it I could awkwardly cut up meat or butter toast. I never got into the habit of using my cutlery knife much, the whole device being so much less portable than my little strap, but I did get a sharp kitchen knife ground to fit it, and still use it all the time for chopping vegetables.

* * *

Meanwhile, Helen had learnt that I was destined for a job in an office and was keen to develop my stationery-handling skills. Before I knew it, I was being whisked back to the OT department, this time to go through the office with a fine-tooth comb. Filing cabinets were opened and closed, papers were shuffled, folded, stapled and punched, ring binders were clicked open and clunked shut, and stamps were licked and stuck, until I began to think that perhaps I didn't fancy working in an office after all.

Helen seemed oddly interested in one task in particular. Again and again she asked me to fold a piece of paper and slip it into an envelope, and I began to grow suspicious. As she dropped me off back at my room she casually said, 'Oh, and I've got a wee bit of homework for you.' She produced a ream of paper and a large pile of envelopes and dropped them on my table. 'Departmental mail-out. There's only two hundred of them. If you could have them all stuffed for tomorrow afternoon I'd be very grateful.'

I have to admit that I cheated a bit and recruited Anna to help with the chore, but I was certainly very skilled at stuffing envelopes by the end.

Another everyday skill I had to remaster was handwriting. I say remaster but I wasn't exactly a beautiful calligrapher before the accident so I didn't have a very high standard to meet. Helen and I tried various possibilities, and soon found that my feeding strap could be usefully put to the purpose. I rotated it round my wrist slightly from the feeding position, and put a pen in the sleeve, preferably one with free-flowing ink. Then, by moving my arm across the paper, I could attempt to write. The results were fairly illegible at first but after Helen had made me write my lines a few hundred times I found I could produce a scrawl that was reasonably decipherable, at least to me.

The strange thing was that, as my scrawling improved, my handwriting took shape in exactly the same form as my pre-accident writing. Some people even reckoned that it was slightly improved. It just goes to show that handwriting style is a function of the brain, not of the hand.

CHAPTER TWENTY-THREE

Disabled Friends

I WAS NOW MAKING progress in leaps and bounds, far surpassing even my wildest expectations, in terms of relearning the countless everyday skills that so recently I was certain I'd lost for ever. Who would have believed that so soon after such a debilitating accident, I would once again be feeding myself, washing, dressing, shaving or even going to the pub? I still felt frustratingly immobile though, my movements being confined to riding in wheelchairs, shuffling on my bum and a bit of crawling on all fours. More than anything else I wanted to be able to stand up and walk again, and I began to get impatient for some action.

Mr MacDonald had told me that a minimum of six weeks should elapse between my final operations and the fitting of my first prosthetic legs, so six weeks to the day after I'd last gone on the slab, I caught him as he did his ward round and reminded him of his promise. He took a further look at my limbs and conceded that it was about time to begin work on my right leg. I got terrifically excited by this news and could barely wait for my appointment at the limb centre.

I'd already met my lower-limb prosthetist, Morag Marks, a bright, cheerful girl, no older than me, who threw herself with enthusiasm into the task of getting me back on my feet. With me,

190

Morag was faced not only with the usual difficulty of producing comfortable and functional legs, but with the additional problem of finding a way for me to put the legs on and take them off – contrary to my initial speculation back in Chamonix Hospital, it transpired that prosthetic limbs are not screwed directly into the bones, but are free to be attached and removed at will much like socks and shoes.

Morag had already had a think about the problem and reckoned that the Iceross system, manufactured by an Icelandic company called Össur, might do the trick.

The Iceross is a silicone rubber sleeve that fits tightly onto the stump. It is stored inside out and it is donned by rolling it onto the user's leg. Morag was hopeful that I would be able to roll the Icerosses onto and off of my legs with my arms.

Protruding from the bottom end of the Iceross sleeve is a two-inch ratchet pin and it is this pin that holds the main leg on. The leg consists of a pressure-moulded carbon-fibre socket that encloses the stump up to just below knee level, attached to the bottom of which are the various foot components. When the stump is pressed into the socket, the ratchet pin engages with a hole in the bottom of the socket, locking the whole assembly into place. The pin is released by depressing a small button on the outside of the socket.

At this stage Morag just wanted me to get used to the Iceross on its own. It is not easy for the body to tolerate being enclosed in silicone rubber, and many people's skin produces an allergic reaction. I was to start by wearing the sleeve for only an hour at a time and gradually build up until eventually I would hopefully be able to tolerate it all day.

Morag left me with my Iceross and Doreen took charge of seeing that I practised with it. At first I hadn't a chance of getting it on or off (my arms were still bandaged at this stage) and didn't hold out much hope of ever managing. Eventually, however, I found I could roll the sleeve on and off if Doreen got it started for me. Lubricating it with talc also helped. I got the bio boys to make me a special stand onto which I rolled the sleeve, holding it in position for the next time I donned it and this made the task slightly easier, but it was to be many months before I could completely don and doff my Icerosses by myself.

In the beginning, wearing the Iceross for as little as an hour was distinctly uncomfortable and when Doreen pulled it off, pools of sweat would trickle out. My skin would become red and irritated and Doreen stressed the importance of vigilant hygiene, always taking care to give my stump and the sleeve a good soapy wash afterwards. But my leg would still feel itchy and I began to feel quite depressed about the thought of having my legs wrapped in plastic every day for the rest of my life.

Gradually, however, by creeping degrees, the discomfort grew less, until I found I could wear my sleeve for hours at a time, forgetting it was there while I read or watched the television.

The next stage in getting me up and walking again was the use of early walking aids, or PPMM Aids as this particular type was called. The idea of an early walking aid is to get the patient upright and using their walking muscles as soon as possible after amputation, before the muscles atrophy and the sense of balance deteriorates. It is not really possible to walk on early walking aids, but at least they get you upright and moving about.

The PPMM Aid is a monstrous-looking device, consisting of a large inflatable rubber balloon-like sock that envelops the whole leg. As the sock is inflated round the leg, it also expands into a metal frame that gives the device its rigidity. On the base of the frame is a rocker acting as a simple foot.

For the first couple of sessions Doreen insisted that I just sit with the inflatable balloon on my right leg, while I got used to it. Then we put the complete device on my right leg and with just the balloon on my left leg, I would sit – itching to get moving but Doreen restrained me. Eventually I was allowed to attempt to stand up on the right leg.

Doreen got the tallest, widest Zimmer frame she could lay her hands on and fitted it with arm gutters. She jacked my bed up to its highest setting so I could place my stumps in the gutters, bound them in place with crêpe bandage and I was ready to stand up.

I took a deep breath and heaved. Doreen heaved too. It was a huge struggle getting me up, what with the cumbersome PPMM Aids preventing my knees from bending and my arms being strapped to the Zimmer frame, but suddenly I was upright and looking around my hospital room from a whole new perspective. After two months spent lying down or sitting, it felt very strange indeed to be standing. Even though I wasn't at my full original height, I still felt dizzyingly high up. If I'd had feet I'm sure the blood in my head would have rushed straight to them.

'Doreen, I had no idea how small you are,' I said, rather rudely.

'Well, I had no idea quite how tall you are,' Doreen retorted.

In fact, all of the ward staff who crowded in to see the spectacle of an upright Jamie were amazed to discover how tall I was. They were used to a skinny wee wretch who took up less than half the space in the bed, and had always assumed that I was quite a short person, but now I towered over all of them.

Soon, the pressure in my stump grew too much and I was forced to sit down again, and became once more the small person in the bed. The next day I managed a few short hops on the PPMM Aid, and the next again day I hobbled out into the ward, pushing my Zimmer in front of me, steadied by Doreen, and followed by a nurse with a tall stool in case I needed to sit down suddenly. This strangely regal procession was a regular sight in the ward over the next few days, and I was jubilant that I was actually starting to walk again, although I shuddered to think what people would think if I walked down the street wearing two of these giant inflatable legs, half human, half Michelin man.

At the same time as these developments, I began to discover another way of recovering my mobility. When I did physio with Joy, I often crawled about on the floor mats. The pain in my stumps was intense at first, but as it eased, and the general swelling went down, I found I could walk about on my knees quite effectively. This was all very well on the soft physio mats but I couldn't do it on the harder carpet and lino in my room. I needed to find a way of cushioning my knees.

Weeks before, Doreen had given me a pair of elbow muffs – blue and white fluffy things which I was supposed to have strapped onto my arms when transferring in and out of wheelchairs, to protect my elbows from damage. I hadn't bothered using them much and they were lying abandoned in the corner of my room. I got one of the nurses to strap them onto my knees, then carefully lowered myself off my bed onto the floor. Gingerly I took a couple of steps, and found the elbow muffs offered just enough cushioning to allow me to walk.

Suddenly I was a whole lot more mobile. I couldn't go far, as my knees soon began to hurt, and I was extremely conscious of how precious they were to me, but I could get about my room and my bathroom and felt a lot more independent, needing little help from the nurses now. I also discovered that I could go up and down stairs on my knees, which would be a great help to Anna and I on our excursions into the outside world.

One Sunday we visited Edinburgh's Dean Gallery, which had just opened its doors to the public. Unfortunately they hadn't yet opened their wheelchair access doors to the disabled minority. Determined not to be defeated, I swallowed my pride, slid out of the chair, and crawled up the half-dozen stairs on my knees, much to the shock of the extremely apologetic entrance staff.

I subsequently asked Rob and Bill if they could make me a more padded, heavy-duty version of my knee pads. They duly obliged, making them out of leather, closed-cell foam and fleece, and I was then able to cover even greater distances on my knees.

I was delighted one afternoon when Juliette Snow came to visit me. She was the only person I'd ever met who wore an artificial leg and I was very keen to get a look at it and share her experiences of what it was like using it. Juliette had lost her lower right leg to cancer when she was a teenager. She had been lucky to live and was ill for a long time. Consequently, she had been relatively inactive as an amputee for several years, and it wasn't until she moved to Edinburgh, where she was encouraged by the enthusiastic staff of the limb centre, that she had began to participate in sporting activities once again. By now she regularly went hillwalking, rock climbing, canoeing and sailing, to name but a few. I was particularly impressed with her hillwalking exploits as, to me at that stage, even the thought of walking to the far end of the ward made my knees feel weak. Of course having one artificial leg is a different thing entirely from having two, but at least Juliette demonstrated to me that the things could actually work, and gave me hope that Mr Howie's prediction might come true and that I might one day be able to walk in the Pentland Hills which I gazed long-ingly at every day from my window.

Juliette pulled up her jeans and showed me her leg and I was sur-prised how much it resembled a well-used piece of sporting equip-ment. Multi-coloured and decorated with stickers, its carbon-fibre, plastic and titanium components were covered in scuffs and scratches, the scars of the tough life through which Juliette obviously put it. I don't suppose I'd been expecting something which looked like the limb of a shopfitter's dummy, or the classic sawn-off table leg of a sea-faring pirate, but nor had I expected something which looked quite so cool.

Juliette came to see me regularly after that and followed with gen-uine excitement my progress as I learnt to walk again.

I received another surprise visitor one day, while I was sitting alone with Anna. I had recently written to Cyril Wire, the 82-year-old who had lost both his hands, to thank him for his letter and to let him know how I was getting on. He was so impressed he had got in his car and driven from Glasgow to meet me in person.

Cyril had lost both his arms in a railway accident when he was sixteen, one through the shoulder and one through the forearm, but this hadn't stopped him leading a full life. He was married with chil-dren, had studied painting at the Glasgow School of Art and had gone on to become an art teacher. He was certainly a strange-looking character. Tall, thin and smartly dressed in shirt and tie, he might have appeared like any other old man, were it not for the fact that his right arm was completely missing, and where his left hand should have been he had a fearsome-looking metal hook. With this one hook, Cyril managed every task in his life.

He was keen to show me how the hook worked and I was just as keen to learn as it was the same device which Malcolm proposed to build for me. Cyril's stump fitted up to the elbow into a leather and steel socket. Modern sockets would be made of laminated plastic. A rotating wrist mechanism was built into the end of the socket and the hook fixed into that.

The hook itself was split down its length into two halves, each with rubber on the inside for grip. One half of the hook was fixed and the other was hinged at the base to form a gripper that could be opened by means of a clever harness mechanism. A nylon wire, attached to the gripper, ran under Cyril's arm and onto the harness, which was secured to his opposite shoulder. To open the gripper, Cyril simply had to either move his right shoulder forward or his left arm forward, thereby pulling the nylon wire. When released, the hook was closed by strong elastic bands.

It sounds complicated, but by a subtle combination of movements of the shoulders and his arm, Cyril could open and close the split hook at will. Using his hook, and any number of cunning tricks of the trade, he could tie his shoelaces, button his shirt, hold a cup, paint, drive, and do all of the hundreds of other tasks that made up his life. All of these things he did with concentration yet consummate ease.

I was extremely impressed. The one thing he'd never accomplished, he confessed balefully, was to tie his own tie. I couldn't help thinking that for a man in his position that should be the last of his concerns, but I suppose for his generation being dressed smartly was a matter of much greater pride than it is now.

Before he left, Cyril showed me one or two other items he had which could be plugged into the same wrist unit: a larger carbon-fibre gripper, a pair of pliers, a clamp for holding tools. Apparently the same company made dozens of different attachments to fit, from snooker cue rests to fishing rods.

That night, as I went to sleep, I thought about Cyril, and about Juliette, and about myself. Cyril seemed to manage, I thought. No – more than manage, he did incredibly well for himself. He had significantly less functioning upper limb than me and yet he still got on with it and lived his life. And Juliette – she'd gone through an extremely difficult time, and now had to live with one artificial leg, but she didn't let that stop her.

I was just going to have to do the same as Cyril and Juliette. Everything I had to do was possible – they and hundreds of other amputees had already proved that. I just had the tricky task of putting it all together for myself, of learning to overcome all my difficulties at once. It would take time, I knew, but for the first time I felt truly confident that I could get there.

* * *

An old friend, Geoff Allan, had been to see me a couple of times. I'd heard that he'd been acting rather strangely lately, and indeed his behaviour did seem rather over-animated. He seemed to be planning many things at once, including a radical career change, buying property in the islands of Scotland and running the London Marathon, raising money on behalf of me, touchingly. Wherever he went, he carried shopping bags full of rubbish, or art material, and he frantically scribbled chaotic notes and drawings in two large hardback books. Jacqui Austin, his landlady and flatmate, was becoming worried that his increasingly erratic and forgetful behaviour was going to cause a fire in the flat. Several times he had left pans burning on the stove.

We had put this strange conduct down to growing eccentricity, but one day the news came that Geoff had been admitted to hospital. In fact he had been committed under section 26 of the Mental Health Act – sectioned. Geoff's behaviour had been growing stranger and stranger until one Sunday morning, Jacqui had telephoned John Irving in a panic, saying that Geoff had gone mad.

John arrived to find Geoff, red in the face, pontificating wildly about becoming the First Minister of Scotland, knowing about all the secret airbases, and finding hidden messages written in the fridge magnets. John realised that it had reached the stage where Geoff needed professional help, and managed to persuade Geoff to come with him and explain his ideas to a psychiatrist.

Geoff was absolutely furious when, after describing his revelations to the doctor, to his complete surprise, he was forcibly detained at the hospital until further notice, for his own safety. And there he remained, at the Royal Edinburgh Hospital, for many weeks.

In actual fact, Geoff had previously visited hospital with mental health problems. On that occasion he had been suffering from severe depression. Now he was diagnosed as being a manic-depressive, currently suffering an extreme manic episode.

Later on that week, Anna and a couple of friends took me to visit him. It felt odd, me going to visit someone else in hospital. The Royal Ed is another dismally rundown Scottish hospital, and on this particular dreary, foggy day in March, the collection of drab and dilapidated buildings through which we wended, looking for the correct door, seemed a wholly unsuitable setting in which to house people with mental health difficulties.

Inside, the occasional bright and valiantly cheerful painting struggled to lift the austere atmosphere of long, empty corridors along which rows of locked doors stood sentry. A graffiti-scrawled lift took us to the floor where Geoff was accommodated, and a couple of burly orderlies escorted us to his room.

Inside it was pandemonium. Geoff was standing on his bed preaching to John, who was sitting patiently on the room's only chair. On the floor were Geoff's bedclothes, all of his possessions, and dozens of newspapers and magazines, out of which hundreds of cuttings had been taken. On the walls were a huge map of Scotland, puzzlingly annotated and decorated with stickers, a selection of the press cuttings, seemingly chosen at random, and various sections of cereal boxes and chocolate wrappers. The sink was full of water, in which floated assorted model boats constructed from plastic bottles.

Geoff jumped down onto the floor to greet us. 'Ah good, you're here,' he said as if we were slightly late. 'You'll have to put your comments in the Comments Book before you go.' Then he jumped back onto the bed, and back down onto the floor again. He was dressed in socks, boxer shorts and a T-shirt, on which were stuck cartoon stickers and strips of surgical tape in rows. The tape was covered in writing, none of which was decipherable.

'Come in, come in, park yourself over there,' Geoff said to me.

'Where?' I queried.

'Find a spot. Pick a spot,' said Geoff waving vaguely. 'X marks the spot.' When I looked an X of surgical tape did indeed mark a spot in the middle of the floor.

Geoff gave us a whirlwind tour of his room, and his world. 'This is the map, you see. Because it's all to do with maps, isn't it? And that's my job, you see. Surveying. Maps. Surveying airports. But I can't do anything about that right now because I'm stuck in here. But look! Gorillas in the Mist!' Fog lapped against the window, in front of which a cuddly toy gorilla peeped out from behind a solitary pot plant. 'And then I realised that it's all about broadcasting. All the time we're broadcasting, messages and waves. That's what this is.' He pointed to the scribble-covered strips of tape on his shirt. 'I'm broadcasting the messages all the time. And these are Pingu stickers, but that's just an in-joke in the ward. And this is Alice Through the Looking Glass.' A plastic doll gazed through the cellophane window of an empty chocolate box. 'And so I've written a PhD. I wrote it in two days. It takes most people more than three years, but mine's so simple, I managed to write it in two days. In fact the main formula is on one page.' He rummaged around on the floor and eventually pro-duced a battered hardback book. I recognised it as one of the two he had been carrying around with him. 'Look, look.' Geoff rifled through the pages. 'Here. You see, it's remarkably simple.' Geoff showed me the well-thumbed page, covered in lines, arrows, a few figures, and some inky pictures, and hurriedly explained some of its salient features.

As he talked, he annotated his magnum opus with a few more doo-dles, and then became distracted by something else in the room, leav-ing me none the wiser. He was trying to get dressed, but couldn't concentrate long enough to get any clothes on. 'Pass my trousers, please John,' he instructed, and then came over to show me his sink. 'It's a model harbour,' he explained. 'It's an experiment to measure the spin of the earth.' Meanwhile John was struggling with the trousers. They were hanging on a coat-hanger, but the wire of the hanger passed through the belt loops of the trousers. To remove the trousers John had to unwind the coat-hanger. 'It's part of an experiment I'm running on John,' Geoff confided to me. 'He's not doing too bad.'

Being with Geoff was exhausting. He was utterly non-stop, and despite the fact his circumstances were so tragic, he was hugely entertaining. His constant rapid-fire wit had us all in stitches and he was obviously enjoying himself enormously. Carrying on like that, however, would certainly lead to an early death, by heart attack if nothing else, and the psychiatrists and doctors were trying to help Geoff to stabilise his moods.

The second hardback book, the Comments Book, surfaced from the shifting moraine of Geoff's belongings, and we took it in turns to add our thoughts, pictures, and well wishes. In my unsteady hand I simply wrote, 'Keep on going,' the only advice I felt able to give.

A couple of weeks later, assisted by a cocktail of strong drugs, Geoff's mood came crashing out of the sky and plunged him into the depths of depression. The depression too was controlled by drugs, and by Geoff's strength of will, until he was eventually well enough to leave hospital.

Geoff wasn't cured of his manic depression. He probably never will be, but he has learnt to cope with it and he has learnt to get on with his life and make the most of it, usually without the need for drugs. He describes dealing with his mental illness as a part-time job. The rest of his time he devotes to odd jobs, artwork, mountaineering, and his friends.

What struck me, as I learnt to get on with making the most of my life, was how similar our disabilities were, and yet how differently we were treated. Both of our afflictions meant that we were incapable of looking after ourselves, living a normal life and interacting on equal terms with other people. Both of us would suffer our disabilities for the rest of our lives and were having to fight mentally to come to terms with that fact. And both of us, at that time, were doing our utmost to be able to leave the hospitals (Ward 6, both of us – a very significant fact according to Geoff) in which we were imprisoned.

But whereas people were more than happy to come and visit me, all but Geoff's closest friends were reticent about going to see him, locked up in the 'loony bin', especially when he was down. I had support, congratulation and encouragement from everyone I met, complete strangers were writing to me with words of admiration, and the newspapers were just about breaking down the hospital doors to get my story. Geoff had nothing, save for the few dedicated staff in his forgotten corner of a forgotten hospital, and the company of a handful of lonely and confused patients.

When it came to claiming disability benefits, for me it was a mere formality. Geoff ended up having to go to tribunal to claim the financial assistance he needed.

People were always happy to talk about me and how I was getting on, what I'd achieved recently. With Geoff it was different. Nobody could see his illness; no one could measure his progress. His disability was invisible and so was the battle he was fighting. Yet we were fighting the same battle. And in the end Geoff came out on top of his battle, every bit as much as I did mine.

I reflected on how little I really had to complain about, how relatively trivial my disabilities were, compared to the difficulties so many thousands of others face daily and stoically cope with. I could be paraplegic, condemned never to walk again. Or blind, or suffering the insidious decline of some incurable degenerative disease. So many different and difficult handicaps that can afflict the human body and mind, and I merely had to cope with the loss of my hands and feet.

People seemed impressed with the way in which I had learnt to write on the computer. Jean-Dominique Bauby, the French editor of *Elle* magazine, completely paralysed by a stroke, wrote an entire book, *The Diving-Bell and the Butterfly*, by blinking one eyelid. What I had to do was easy.

CHAPTER TWENTY-FOUR

Picking Things Up

MALCOLM DECIDED IT WAS TIME for me to have my first mechanical arm. We got messy with the plaster of Paris one morning, and Malcolm went away with a perfect cast of my left arm. It took several fittings and adjustments of the plastic socket he'd made from the cast, but a week or so later I was presented with my very own arm, complete with super-shiny titanium split-hook. Eagerly, I tried it on. First a thin sock went over my stump, for a bit of comfort. Then the socket itself was pushed on. There are many ways in which a prosthetic arm may be secured, or suspended. My one was supercondylar, which means that the plastic socket snaps neatly over the knuckle of the elbow, staying in place whatever position the arm is in. Finally I had to don the shoulder harness that operates the hook. I found that by swinging the harness behind my back, after a couple of shots, I could catch the harness loop with my right stump and shrug it on like a jacket. Now I was ready to go.

At rest, the hook was closed, held in place by the elastic bands. If I pushed the arm forward, holding the opposite shoulder still, the hook opened. Holding the arm still and pushing the right shoulder forward also opened the hook. Relaxing allowed the hook to close again. With more complex combinations of movements of my arms, shoulders and back, I discovered I could open and close the hook at will, in any position of the arm, both static and moving. I'm unable to precisely describe the necessary movements, even if I wear the arm as I write, but the funny thing is, my body just knows what to do. The motion quickly becomes intuitive, like steering a bike or catching a ball. The body's information receptors, eyes and nerves, work together to control the muscles without the need for any input from the higher levels of the brain.

I was immediately able to complete simple operations like picking things up and putting them down. With a little more care I found I could manage more delicate tasks such as turning the pages of a book. Malcolm explained to me how the split-hook tool, barbaric as it appeared, had been developed over many years by generations of amputees, and was usually considered to be the most utilitarian and versatile device available. It was possible to fit similar devices which actually looked like human hands, but to begin with I would be better off with the hook. He left me to practise with my new arm.

Later that afternoon, Helen came to see me. If anything, she was more excited than me about my acquisition. She rushed into my room and immediately began gathering up assorted objects from my bedside tables, and scattered them over the bed and the floor. Diligently I retrieved the discarded books, tumblers and playing cards, and put them back in their proper place, only for her to throw them on the floor again, like a truculent toddler.

We carried on in this fashion for a while, then turned our attention to more complex tasks – holding cutlery, drinking from a glass, unwrapping sweets. I managed these operations fairly quickly, but already a pattern was emerging. All of these things I could do already, with my bare stumps. With the prosthetic arm they felt harder, more awkward, less secure. What's more, with my prosthetic arm on my left stump, my right stump suddenly became useless. It no longer had anything to oppose, except slippery plastic. To give an example, with my two stumps I could now fairly easily pick up and pour from my water jug. Holding the jug in my hook, however, it would slip when I tried to pour, and if I attempted to hold it between the plastic arm and my right stump, it also tended to slip.

Obviously the lack of friction in the plastic arm played a part, but the main difficulty was perception, sense of touch. The body's sense of touch plays a crucial role in the subtle art of holding and manipulating. Millions of nerve endings, just below the surface of the skin, are constantly feeding back information to the spinal cord and the brain, allowing the muscles to react instantly to each infinitesimal shift in balance and weight. As one walks through a crowded bar carrying a brimming pint glass, the fingertips are continuously monitoring and adjusting their grip on the glass, always prepared to react to the tiniest slip of the wet surface. Meanwhile the brain relays all-important information from the eye about the level of the beer, and the fingers also respond to this input, ensuring that not a drop of the precious liquid is spilt. All this while squeezing round chairs and tables, watching your feet for sleeping pub dogs, and shouting 'Excuse me!' to people's backs.

Unfortunately my prosthetic arm had no nerve endings in it, and consequently was unable to participate in this autonomic system. Hence the slips. My stumps, on the other hand, while perhaps not possessing nerve endings in the same concentration as fingertips, were still very sensitive, which was why I was enjoying such success in my efforts to relearn many quite delicate tasks.

To begin with, I put my problems with the prosthetic arm down to inexperience, and persevered with my practice, but as time passed by, I found more and more that I tended to put my arm aside while doing a difficult task. I didn't deliberately reject the arm. In fact I liked wearing it, enjoying the mechanical elegance of it, and relishing people's reactions to the bizarre-looking thing. However, constantly finding tasks harder with the arm on than without it, I gradually used it less and less, until eventually its use was confined to a few specialised tasks, such as playing chess. At Easter Anna brought me some blown eggshells to paint and I fulfilled the prophecy of the French doctor back in Bonneville by picking up the delicate shells with my hook. I preferred to hold them between my stumps though.

At first I worried about my declining interest in the prosthetic arm and felt guilty that I wasn't becoming an expert user. I had always intended to get good at using it as quickly as possible, before graduating on to the more advanced myoelectric arms. These are electrically operated arms, the signals that control the operation of their moving parts being generated in the muscles of the stump. The user learns to open and close the grip, rotate the wrist and so on, by twitching individual muscles within their residual arm. Sensors pick up the tiny electrical signals generated, which are then amplified to drive the motors.

Once I had mastered the use of myoelectric arms, I intended to get myself involved in the various research and development programmes that are continually pushing back the frontiers in the quest for better and better prosthetic devices. I would thus become the owner of the best, most hi-tech pair of electronic hands available. That was my plan.

Now, though, I found myself losing interest in this long-term goal, along with the forgotten arm, which lay gathering dust on the shelf. I asked both Helen and Malcolm what they thought. Perhaps I wasn't trying hard enough? Perhaps there was another device that would suit me better? Helen and Malcolm gave the same advice: just do what comes naturally to you, they said. No two amputees are the same. Obviously there are the physical differences, depending on the level and nature of the amputation, but mentally and socially also, every amputee has different needs and finds different ways of doing things. There are no hard and fast rules. In fact, Malcolm told me, there are many upper-limb amputees who seldom if ever wear a prosthesis. I had heard this before, but had dismissed those who chose not to benefit from the technology available as being either apathetic or foolish. Now I was beginning to understand.

I felt happier once I'd grasped the fact that I didn't have to use my artificial arm. I realised also that all the good progress I was making with my stumps wasn't simply a temporary measure before going on to greater things with prosthetic hands, but was skill that would stand me in good stead for the rest of my life. I began to take pride in all the things I could do with just my stumps. If a normal person could do something with their hands, I wanted to do it too. If I could do it without the use of an assistive device or tool, so much the better.

Helen showed me various devices in her catalogue to help the user open jam jars. All of them were complex, unwieldy things, except for one, which was simply a sheet of sticky rubber. You press the rubber onto the lid of the jar and it gives you all the grip you need to twist the lid. I found by pressing down on the lid with the flesh of my stump and twisting, I could open even the stiffest jars. Eventually I dispensed with the rubber and can now open jam jars as easily as anyone else.

Similarly with corkscrews and tin-openers, I have resisted using the electric devices available and stubbornly learnt to use the normal mechanical items found in anyone's cutlery drawer.

Throughout this period of relearning everyday tasks, I found myself re-examining the very nature of how we pick objects up and hold them. It wasn't something I had really thought about before, having just left my hands to get on with it, but now I realised that many other parts of my body could be put into service.

Obviously my stumps, as a pair, were now doing the bulk of my object-manoeuvring work. Singly also I found them to be quite useful. Once lifted, items could be conveniently held in an armpit or between stump and chest, thus freeing up the other stump. Even better, I found I could hold things in the crook of my elbow. I was delighted one evening in the Steading when someone bought me a glass of champagne and I discovered that the stem fitted neatly and securely into my elbow, allowing me to hold and drink from the glass with one arm.

My mouth was now an indispensable tool, my teeth being excellent strong grippers, and my lips very expert at manipulating small objects, just so long as they weren't too dirty. My knees too, proved useful for holding objects firmly. In fact any part of the body that can be opposed against another part, or another surface, can be useful in picking up, holding and manipulating objects. Fingers are not indispensable. They are just a luxury.

Mr MacDonald suggested that I should start spending the occasional night away from the hospital, especially at weekends when I received no treatment anyway. I couldn't go home yet, because of the stairs to my flat, but at Easter Anna and I were invited to stay with Chris Pasteur and Jane Herries in their house in Perthshire. It was my first trip out of the hospital for more than a few hours and I felt oddly nervous and excited.

Anna picked me up from the hospital on Saturday afternoon and we motored north to the sleepy village where Chris and Jane live.

Anna managed to wheel my chair right up to their front door, and from there I spent the rest of the day shuffling around on my knees. We had a superb meal and then enjoyed a fine, relaxing evening, during which I demonstrated at great length my new-found confidence with a stemmed wine glass. Then I spent my first night out of hospital in ten weeks.

After breakfast on Sunday, and the traditional Easter egg hunt, we went for a walk in the countryside and my chair wallahs had a great time wheeling me through all sorts of unsuitably muddy and rough terrain. We then visited a local bird reserve (not wheelchair friendly so I was on my knees again) and finished off with a visit to the nearby town of Dunkeld where I frightened the local children with my hook. It was so nice being out and about with my friends just doing really normal things. By the time Anna dropped me back at the hospital that evening I was utterly exhausted and I slept right through breakfast the next day.

Helen came to see me one morning with the good news that I was to be taken on a 'home visit'. She and two other community occupational therapists wanted to accompany me on a tour of my flat in order to ascertain whether I would have any special requirements.

A couple of mornings later I was picked up by the ambulance service and driven across town to my flat. The ambulance men then lifted me upstairs on a special carrying chair, where I was met by Anna and the small squad of OTs. I was supposed to go round the flat in my wheelchair, but I immediately shunned that and hopped down onto my knees.

It felt strange to be home again. Proprietorially I shuffled into each room in turn, poking into every corner in search of changes, but everything was the same. The place even smelt warmly familiar. The OTs wanted to see me open every cupboard door, flick every switch, turn on the oven, operate the taps. I felt like I was being evaluated personally and, ignoring their demands, I wasted five minutes fumbling a CD out of its box and putting it into the stereo. Anna had taken the opportunity of my homecoming to cook me a proper quality fry-up, miles apart from the hospital version, and I sat down at the kitchen table to enjoy it, leaving the OTs to discuss anti-slip mats in the bathroom.

Unfortunately the ambulance men had a schedule to stick to and all too soon I was carried away from my home and returned to the PMR where my hospital lunch was sitting growing cold.

After the success of our Perthshire trip, the word got out that Jamie was making house calls, and Anna and I received a flood of dinner invitations. It was great to get out of the hospital in the evenings and it was even better not to have to eat hospital food. Most places we ate were on the ground floor, but when we went to have dinner with Ruth and Ulric Jessop, who live in a second-floor flat, Ulric simply came out to the car, picked me up, and carried me up the stairs. Jim Hayes did the same when we went round to his flat. I felt slightly embarrassed about being lumped around like a sack of coal, but it was worth it in order to get out and about.

I wanted to spend more time at home now, but not having a pair of ambulance men at my disposal, and Anna not being of quite the same build as Ulric and Jim, the stairs were the major obstacle. Resourcefully, Anna borrowed a spare carrying chair from the mobility department of the Astley Ainsley Hospital. We then arranged for friends to be available the following Friday and Sunday evenings to help cart me up and down the two flights of stairs.

I arrived home triumphantly on Friday, feeling like royalty in my sedan chair. Anna certainly treated me like a king, spoiling me rotten with all my favourite food, and plumping up my cushions on the sofa. Obviously without further lifting assistance I was more or less interned in the flat for the weekend, but Anna made sure I wasn't short of company and invited some of our friends round for dinner on Saturday.

On the Sunday we scrounged some chair-carrying help off the neighbours, and went out to the cinema. On entering the darkened theatre of our local multiplex, there was no obvious space designated for wheelchairs, so Anna parked me at the edge of the wide central aisle and took a seat beside me. It wasn't until halfway through the film that an usher tapped Anna on the shoulder and said that she couldn't leave me in the aisle because I was an obstruction. I was furious, as was Anna, but we couldn't exactly make a fuss in the middle of the film so we allowed the woman to direct us to a space at the back of the theatre, where there was plenty of room for my chair but no seat for Anna. So Anna sat on the floor and I slipped down out of my chair to join her. We did our best to enjoy the rest of the film and saved our complaint for later.

When I was returned to my familiar hospital room that evening, I felt a little odd. I'd had an excellent weekend and was glad to be getting out of the hospital more, but I felt strangely glad to be back in my nice safe room. It felt so much more secure than the outside world. I realised I was getting institutionalised. I would have to leave hospital soon.

CHAPTER TWENTY-FIVE

The Phantom Menace

At the same time as everything else that was going on at this time, I was also being troubled by a curious phenomenon known as phantom limb sensation. It started back while I was in Chamonix Hospital, during the last week and a half of my stay there. Some days after I'd been amputated, as the numbness of the operations gradually wore off, I began to feel strange sensations in the ends of my stumps. Or to be more precise, I began to feel strange sensations *beyond* the ends of my stumps. It seemed bizarre, but in the thin air where my hands and feet used to be, I genuinely felt the presence of the missing appendages.

My hands, although I couldn't see them, were both clenched into tight hot fists, and I would occasionally feel a claustrophobic kind of panic that I couldn't unclench them. The more I strained the remaining tendons in my arms and mentally willed the invisible fingers to uncurl, the more acutely aware of their paralysis I became. I tried to force myself not to think about it.

My feet also were apparently still in their original locations. I knew this because I had pins and needles in my toes. Worse still, I would often have shooting pains, as if I'd been stabbed with a knitting needle in the feet. I could always tell exactly where on my foot I'd been stabbed – sometimes in my big toe, sometimes in another

above The long, hard slog up Ben Nevis, Scotland's highest mountain.

above right With Anna, triumphant on the summit of Ben Nevis.

Rock climbing in North Wales, on a climb called Christmas Curry at Tremadog.

Ice climbing with my prosthetic ice axes, in the grade III gully of Left Twin on Aonach Mor.

below A beautiful day in the mountains – Setting out with Manu Cauchy to climb the Cosmiques Arête on the Aiguille du Midi.

above left Downhill skiing in the mountains of Switzerland – another activity which I have reclaimed. In fact I am probably a better skier now than I was before the accident!

above right Running the London Marathon with my amputee friend Jamie Gillespie.

Anna and me, enjoying a holiday in the secluded mountains of northern Spain.

Back in the Alps again, approaching the summit of a mountain called The Mönch (4099m) in the Swiss Alps.

toe, sometimes under the arch. Always the stabbing was without warning, entirely malicious, and would send me flinching uncontrollably for a few seconds until the pain subsided.

I asked Dr Marsigny about these strange experiences. He assured me it was quite normal. Phantom pains. The severed nerves in my limbs sending confused messages back to the brain. How long would it last? I asked him. He shrugged. Perhaps for ever.

Having treated many amputees, Mr MacDonald had more experience of phantom sensations. He explained how they could take many different forms in different people. For some it was simply the clear sensation of the missing limb, floating in the space where it should have been. For others the missing hand or foot would be curiously distorted, missing fingers or toes, shrunken, or receded back into the residual limb. Some people could feel each finger or toe as real as if they were all actually there. Others felt strange sensations of hot and cold, tingling and prickling. Worse still, some people suffered regular or even constant pain – pain made worse by the fact that it has no tangible source that can be treated.

A lot of the phantom pain seems to be related to the last sensations experienced by that particular part of the body immediately prior to amputation. Hence the pre-operative painkillers, taken to prevent the pain of the operation being the last memory of the truncated nerves. There are stories of people suffering more unusual phantom sensations. The woodworker who got a splinter in his thumb one morning, and, somewhat more seriously, severed his hand on a band saw in the afternoon. For the rest of his life he could feel the splinter in his missing thumb. Or the even more unfortunate man who had to have a foot removed and thought that at least it would spell an end to his athlete's foot. He found himself condemned to endure a lifetime of unscratchable itching between his non-existent toes.

I asked Mr MacDonald if there was anything that could be done as my pains were getting worse. Lots of things had been tried, he said. Some surgeons had attempted to trim back the offending nerves, to try and remove the problem, but invariably it just shifted the trouble elsewhere. Nerve pain isn't treated effectively with normal painkillers, but there were dozens of other drugs with which sufferers had claimed successful relief of their symptoms.

However, the most important weapon in the battle against stump pain and phantom limb sensations, Mr MacDonald insisted, was the mind. While I was stuck in a hospital bed, with little else to focus my thoughts on, it was easy for the pain to grow in my head, become amplified out of proportion. Once I was up and about, though, using my limbs and thinking about other things, the pain would become less significant and perhaps disappear altogether. It's all in the mind.

All very well, I thought, but right now my mind needed the assistance of medical science. Mr MacDonald left me with a large pile of medical papers on the subject and promised to let me try any drugs I thought might help.

Over the next couple of days I avidly read through my stack of articles in the hope of coming across a miracle cure to my stump pain which was now becoming more than a mere annoyance.

The strange phantom sensations I didn't mind particularly. In fact they were often quite amusing. I would often sit on the edge of a chair and swing my legs just above the floor. This gave me the most peculiar feeling of moving my feet through solid matter. Sometimes if someone sat down on the end of my bed where I thought my feet were I would yelp with the anticipation of the pain that never arrived. It was easy to see how some poor souls, suffering similar inexplicable feelings but not daring to tell anyone about it, would silently worry that they were going mad.

Curiously my hand sensations developed in a different way, perhaps because I used my arms more. At first I imagined hands beyond the end of my stumps and would often miss when reaching for something, overestimating the length of my stump. Gradually though, the tight fists of my phantom hands receded until eventually they were actually inside my stumps, sort of shrunken into little balls. They still felt uncomfortably clenched and when I was tired or hot they would seem to swell and throb intolerably, for which there was nothing I could do except shake my stumps manically above my head in the hope that the excess blood would drain out.

However, these aches and ghostly distractions were trivial compared to the escalating pain I felt in my leg stumps. The general tingling I had originally felt grew into a more severe needling, punctuated with regular stabs of pain, especially in the left leg. I found the best way to alleviate this was to elevate the stumps and keep them moving, and I developed the peculiar habit of lying on my back and jiggling my legs about like an upturned beetle, which could be rather distracting for visitors.

I was certain the pain was mind based rather than physiological because it seemed to disappear at night when I went to sleep, but in the daytime I just couldn't seem mentally to defeat it.

I read about an interesting psychological technique for dealing with phantom hand sensations. The experimenter constructed a special box with two armholes into which the amputee inserted their good arm and their stump. The box was fitted with mirrors in such a way that when looking down into it the amputee could see their good arm on one side, and a reflection of their good arm on the other, creating the illusion of having two normal hands. By moving their two 'hands' and focusing on the mental associations between the brain and the movements of the hands, amputees found they could eventually eliminate the spurious connections that were causing their phantom sensations.

For a moment I considered trying this technique myself, until it dawned on my thick skull that I didn't have a good side with which to create the reflections. Sometimes I wondered if my brain had been damaged by frostbite as well. The other day, while lost in thought, I had spent a good half-hour thinking about people who had lost their hands and learnt to paint and write with their feet, and had wondered whether I should try that. Then I remembered that I had lost my feet also.

In the absence of a mental solution to my problems I turned to drugs. Many different things had been tried it seemed, none with any convincing success, but several seemed more commonly recommended than others. Mr MacDonald reckoned that none were likely to produce any side effects and encouraged me to experiment.

Over the next few weeks I added half a dozen different types of little tablets to my daily pile of pills. Many were drugs normally used to treat other conditions, including an anti-epilepsy drug and a drug for period pains. None of them seemed to have any effect on my stump pain.

Mr MacDonald suggested trying another commonly used treatment – electric current therapy. He brought me a TENS machine, which is a small battery-powered box with a couple of flat electrodes on wires taped to the skin. The machine generates an electric current through the surface of the skin that interrupts the signals between the nerves and the brain and can significantly relieve chronic pain. Choosing where to tape the electrodes isn't an exact science and I experimented with various areas around my lower back, before settling on taping them directly to the stump. With the electrodes taped close to the source of pain and with the current turned up high, the TENS machine genuinely eased the pain for a while, but gradually it always crept back. I began to think the pain was something I would always have to live with.

CHAPTER TWENTY-SIX

Walking Home

IN EARLY APRIL Morag made me my first leg. The pressure-casting
system Morag was using was, like the Iceross sleeves, developed by
the Össur company, and is called Icex. Making an Icex socket is
quite an entertaining business.

First Morag helped me into the Iceross. Then a stump sock went
on, for comfort, and the whole leg was wrapped in cling film. Next,
a black Lycra sleeve, which would become the socket lining, was
pulled on. Morag then carefully stuck on several cushioned pads,
making sure that all the bony and sensitive areas of my stump would
be protected from the pressure of wearing the leg. She took her time
getting everything just right, because the next stage would be irre-
versible.

The Icex itself comes vacuum packed and rolled up like a giant
black condom. Apart from the circular metal base for attaching the
foot components, it is made of a braided carbon-fibre fabric, impreg-
nated with an epoxy resin that goes off with warm water. Morag
made everything ready, double-checking it all, took a deep breath,
then plunged the Icex into the steaming basin of water. She then had
three minutes to get everything in place. She frantically unrolled the
gently fizzing braid onto my outstretched stump, smoothing out any
bumps and wrinkles with gloved hands, before hurriedly cutting off

any excess material above my knee with a large pair of scissors. Next she rolled a giant rubber balloon, rather like the PPMM Aid, over the braid. With a fancy-looking bicycle pump she furiously inflated the balloon until a dial on the pump read the correct pressure. Finally she propped my enormous leg up on a stool, and relaxed.

Inside the balloon I could feel the gentle warmth of the resin setting rock hard. Ten minutes later it was ready and Morag deflated and removed the balloon. Underneath was a perfect grey socket moulded precisely round my stump. The hard part was now to get the socket off. Despite Morag's trimmings, the top of the socket still partly came over my knee and it took a lot of huffing and puffing, from Morag and me, pulling in opposite directions, before the thing eventually came flying off, sending Morag shooting across to the other side of the room.

On that occasion we were lucky. When making Icexes on subsequent occasions, the socket has ended up so securely jammed that Morag has had to attack it with plaster saws, sheers and mole grips in order to get it off. One time I was convinced that I would have to go home with the thing on my leg.

Morag then took the leg off to the workshop to be trimmed, finished, and fitted with a foot. As she left she said, 'Oh, by the way, what shoe size are you?'

'Well you can make me any size you want,' I replied smartly.

'I could,' said Morag, 'but I presume you have several pairs of shoes at home that you don't want to have to replace?'

'Oh. Yes,' I said sheepishly. 'Size eight.'

The next day Morag arrived with my leg, shortly followed by Doreen, with the PPMM Aid. Morag had fitted a simple foot to the leg. It had no moving parts but was slightly springy at the heel and the toe. Eventually I would move on to more active feet, but these things were the best for learning on. Morag levered one of my old trainers onto the foot. She then helped me put the Iceross and the Icex on and Doreen inflated the trusty old PPMM Aid over my left leg. With the help of Morag, Doreen and the Zimmer, I cautiously stood up. Morag made a few adjustments to the alignment of the foot, and I tried shifting my weight on to the new leg. I still couldn't attempt to walk properly because of the PPMM Aid, but with my new leg on my right stump, it felt substantially more like the real thing.

I carefully transferred my weight, from side to side, between the PPMM Aid and the new leg, but found my right stump was still too tender to take all my weight for more than a second. It was still going to be a while before I walked freely on two legs.

I had another walking session with Doreen the day after. The following day, a Saturday, I tried to put the leg on to show my mum and dad, who were visiting, but I couldn't get it on. It seemed too tight. Later on in the evening it finally squeezed on. The following week I had to cancel most of my walking sessions with Doreen because I couldn't get the leg on.

Morag had explained that over at least the first twelve months, an amputee's stump or stumps gradually shrink, as the post-operative swelling subsides and the unused muscle tissue contracts. As the stump shrinks you have to wear more and more stump socks to take up the volume, until eventually it's necessary to make a new socket. Morag expected to have to make me two or three pairs of sockets in the first year.

My stump was expanding though, not shrinking. I'd only had my leg a week and already I couldn't even get it on. I felt despondent for I was impatient to learn to walk again but my progress was stalled by this setback. Morag was mystified. At first she thought it might be localised swelling caused by the pressure of wearing the leg, but as time went by my stump continued to grow until there was no hope of squeezing the leg on.

Eventually we realised it must be because of the physio I was doing. When I'd arrived in Scotland I was quite severely emaciated. The physio, while being quite light work, was slowly allowing my muscles to recover their original volume which was why my stumps were growing rather than shrinking. So it was back to square one.

A couple of weeks later, Morag decided that my stumps had stabilised enough and that I was ready for another leg. In fact, I was ready for two legs, which was very exciting. We paid another couple of visits to the casting room with our basin of warm water, the inflatable balloon, and all the other paraphernalia, and soon Morag had produced a fine-looking pair of legs. A couple of trips to the fitting room to adjust the feet and check the trim-lines, and they were ready to go.

The next day Morag wasn't available but Doreen came to help me try the new legs on. It took quite a lot of fumbling about to get the unfamiliar objects on, but immediately it was obvious that the new right leg was a lot more comfortable than the previous one had been. The left leg seemed pretty comfortable too.

I was confident enough with the Zimmer not to need to be strapped into it any more and so sat on the edge of the bed with my arms in the gutters of the Zimmer, ready to stand up. With Doreen's help I heaved myself onto my new feet and stood there swaying slightly while the blood rushed out of my head, then gently flowed back. For the first time I was standing upright on two prosthetic legs. Carefully I eased my body across to the right and allowed the right leg to bear all my weight. Then I did the same with the left leg. Good. Both were capable of supporting me. A bit sore, but bearable.

Slowly, I lifted my right leg an inch or so and brought it forward, placing the foot just in front of the other. I then lifted my left leg and brought it forward. First steps. I rattled the Zimmer forward a little and repeated it. Before I knew it I was out into the ward and the nurses were gathering to watch.

Doreen said, 'Why don't we take the Zimmer away and let you find your balance?'

'I'm not sure I'll manage,' I replied. 'I feel very high up.'

'Nonsense,' insisted Doreen. 'I'll be there to hold you,' and she took away the walking frame.

Suddenly I was standing, on my artificial legs, with no other support apart from Doreen's hand on the small of my back. I paused a few moments to accustom myself to staying in balance, and took a minuscule step forward. Then another one.

This was it. I was walking! I couldn't believe it. A big grin spread across my face from ear to ear. It was Tuesday, 27 April, three months since I'd last walked upright, ten weeks since I'd woken from a black sleep to find my hands and feet gone and thought that I'd never walk again. Sixty-one days since I'd last gone under the surgeon's knife, and here I was standing and walking on my own two feet. I couldn't believe it had happened so quickly.

I hadn't expected to walk on my prosthetic legs so soon, and I hadn't arranged for Anna to be there to see my first steps. Fortunately she arrived before I tired and was able to watch the spectacle for herself. She took a few photos before I carefully turned round and headed back for my room. By the time I reached the safety of my bed I was tired and sore having walked all of about 20 yards.

The next day I made it out of the ward and halfway down the corridor towards the canteen. That evening, Anna helped me to put the legs on again and I wore them to the pub. Although I needed help with my wallet and with carrying the beer, my friends were all very impressed, and I felt extremely proud of myself when I walked up to the bar and ordered a round of drinks. Jim said it was about time I got a round in.

On the following day, Thursday, Doreen and I ventured a little further afield, making it as far as the hospital car park where I even tried a little off-road walking on the rough grass verge. I was beginning to take more confident steps now, rather than the cautious little shuffles I had begun with and Doreen had to keep reminding me to slow down.

The next step, literally, in learning to walk again, was mastering stairs. On the way back to the ward we passed a large staircase leading up to the first floor and Doreen suggested having a go. I wasn't so sure my balance was up to it but Doreen showed me the safe way of climbing stairs. I was surprised how easy it was. Facing the rail I hooked my arms round the steel banisters and stepped sideways up the first step with both feet, before moving my arms up the banister and climbing the next step. In this way I crab-walked all the way to the top of the stairs where I had a rest on a conveniently situated chair before making my way back down again.

It was all happening so quickly I barely had time to take stock of the progress I was making. Every day when Anna arrived I was bursting with the news of fresh achievements. I felt oddly unsettled though, like I didn't know where I stood any more. Anna felt the same way too. The changing nature of my dependency on other people was forcing us constantly to readjust our relationship with one another.

That weekend I spent at home again. I couldn't wear my legs for long periods of time – no more than about two hours – but whenever we went out I put them on so I could walk down the stairs. On the few occasions when I didn't feel like wearing my legs, I climbed the stairs on my knees. We would take the wheelchair with us, and, wherever we were going, Anna would push me about in the chair for most of the time, but the main thing was we were dependent on no one else's help and that felt good for both of us.

We spent a lot of time that weekend chatting about my progress and discussing the future. I could wash, dress, feed and generally look after myself quite well by now. I couldn't cook, clean or do any household management tasks yet, but Anna could cope with all that to begin with. My stumps were all perfectly healed and I needed no regular medical care. As long as my stair-climbing progress was sustained there seemed no reason why I couldn't move back home.

Despite the fact that everything seemed to be in place, though, the thought of leaving my sheltered bedsit in the hospital scared me slightly. It was definitely time for me to make the break and go home.

On Monday I requested an audience with all the concerned parties to discuss the matter and on Tuesday morning, Mr Howie, Mr MacDonald, Helen and Doreen gathered in my room. I was nervously preparing to argue my case but they told me that they had already had a meeting to compare notes on my progress and as far as they were concerned I could go home as soon as I liked. Just like that. I could attend the limb centre as an outpatient and they would all be available to see me whenever I liked, but they saw no reason why I should continue to live at the hospital.

I hadn't thought it would be so straightforward. I realised I wasn't a prisoner in the hospital, but I had expected to have to persuade them that I was capable of looking after myself. For a minute I toyed with the idea of leaving right there and then, but I chickened out and settled for the coming Friday, just to give myself time to prepare and get used to the idea.

Over the next couple of days, preparations were made for my return home. My room was now so full of stuff that Anna had to make multiple trips to get the bulk of it home, and there were still several bagfuls to come with me on Friday.

I began saying my goodbyes to various nurses and other members of staff whose shifts meant that they wouldn't be in on Friday. I was quite sad to say goodbye to these people who had taken such good care of me over the previous months. The PMR had been my home for ten weeks and in that time I had made some good friends. My door was always open and the nurses would often drop in for a chat when things were quiet. Frequently they would seek refuge in my room to exchange ward gossip or air their grievances. I felt I had become a semi-permanent fixture of Ward 6.

On Friday morning I was summoned to the staff room for a surprise tea party. The nurses had clubbed together and bought me the present they considered most appropriate – a keg of beer. I promised to drink their health in style.

A couple of hours later the ambulance arrived to collect me and my belongings. By a miracle the ambulance was early and Anna hadn't yet arrived with the case of wine we had bought for the next ward night out, so I was on my own as the vehicle pulled out of the ambulance bay and headed down the road to my flat.

I wasn't wearing my legs and when we arrived the ambulance men started unpacking their carrying chair.

'It's all right,' I said. 'I'll manage the stairs on my knees.'

The two men looked slightly shocked. 'We were told we had to carry you up the stairs,' one of them said.

I was determined not to be carried up my own stairs again and was perhaps unnecessarily rude to them. 'Well, you can tell whoever told you that, that I don't need to be carried up the stairs,' I said curtly and set off up the stairs on my knees.

I didn't have a key and the ambulance men left me outside the front door with my bags. They offered to wait but I thanked them and sent them on their way.

Sitting on my bags I waited for Anna to return and open the door to the next chapter of our lives. I had little idea what it might contain but I was certain it would be another big adventure.

PART THREE

Life on the Outside

CHAPTER TWENTY-SEVEN

Over the Sea to Skye

THE LAST TIME Jamie and I had been together in the Cuillin Hills on the Isle of Skye was in the summer of 1997. We went to attempt the traverse of the famous Cuillin Ridge – 14 kilometres of the most rugged mountainous terrain in the British Isles, comprising well over a dozen rocky peaks, eleven of which are in the list of Scottish mountains over 3,000 feet, the Munros.

Jamie had previously completed several traverses, both in summer and winter, and I had done it a couple of times too, but this time we wanted to do it fast. Most parties take between eight and fourteen hours to complete the traverse, but the record is an incredible three hours thirty-two minutes. Jamie was modestly hoping to do it in four and a half hours. I reckoned we could do it in four.

We were both very fit, climbing well and raring to go. The only difficulty was that neither of us had brought a watch with which to time ourselves, so we spent the evening before our attempt in the Sligachan Inn asking everyone who came into the bar if we could borrow a watch. Not surprisingly we had difficulty in persuading anyone to trust us with their Rolex, but eventually a sympathetic New Zealand lad working behind the bar agreed to smuggle an alarm clock out of one of the hotel rooms.

The next morning we set off up the hill, equipped with only the lightest of running gear and a rather bulky alarm clock, and arrived on top of Sgurr nan Gillean, which is the starting point of the ridge, to find it enveloped in a light mist. The mist looked likely to clear at any moment so we elected to wait. We sat and watched as the cloud continued to boil and churn over the ridge and occasionally the pale watery disc of the sun shone weakly through. We waited and waited, shivering in our skimpy running clothes, and imploring the swirling clouds to part, but still it didn't clear. For three hours we waited on the summit of the hill but the clouds never parted and finally a light drizzle set in, putting an end to our hopes for any attempt at the ridge that day.

The rain continued for the rest of our stay on Skye and we went home empty handed. We never did make our attempt at a fast traverse of the Cuillin although I'm still certain that we could have cracked four hours.

On Wednesday, 16 June 1999, despite the fact it was mid-June, there would have been nobody attempting the ridge. A wild wind was whipping in off the sea, flogging the exposed mountains without mercy. Squally showers of heavy rain marched across the moors, soaking everything in their path.

There were twenty or so of us, close friends and family of Jamie, who had travelled up to this remote spot to pay our last respects to a very special person. The Cuillin of Skye was his favourite place in the whole world and it was where his parents had chosen to scatter his ashes.

Together we plodded along the coast, across the rugged foothills of the Cuillin, for about a kilometre, to an exposed promontory jutting out into the stormy sea. I recognised the place. We used to come here, when the mountains were hidden in cloud, and explore the rocky maze of headlands, inlets, crags and caves.

We gathered in a circle on the promontory and held our simple, informal service. Our voices were all but drowned by the crashing of the waves and the roaring of the wind, reminding us of the terrible forces of nature that had brought us there.

Holding hands in our circle we remembered Jamie in silence for a minute, then Jamie's mother Pam produced the cask and we took it in turn to throw handfuls of the ashes into the wind. I watched the stream of fine grey powder as it was carried away through the air and dissipated instantly over the sea and the land, and had difficulty in relating it to the flesh-and-blood Jamie I once knew, who was so full of laughter and kindness and all the emotions of a living human being.

I turned away and began my journey back to the road. As I struggled along the rocky undulating path, one by one the others all caught me up, walked with me for a short while, then moved effortlessly on ahead. This was the furthest I had walked across rough ground and I was finding it very difficult.

I had climbed my first hill a week after moving back home. Although it is a hill in name, Blackford Hill is not exactly one of the world's greatest mountains, but it is an attractive little prominence near to the centre of Edinburgh, not far from our flat, with great views out across the city.

Anna and I started from the car park at the Royal Observatory, built on the slopes of the hill. From there an easy-angled, grassy slope leads in a few hundred yards, with an ascent of a couple of hundred feet, to the summit viewpoint.

I wasn't yet used to walking on a slope but I found going uphill OK. With my weight on my toes and facing in to the slope, I felt reasonably stable. Anna gave me her arm for the rougher bits and although I was quite slow it wasn't far and before long we were standing at the top.

I had been on top of Blackford Hill countless times before, but on this occasion the view felt particularly special. At that moment I couldn't possibly imagine climbing anything bigger, but I promised myself this would be the first step on the climb to greater things. Anna took a couple of photos before we turned round and began our descent.

Going downhill I found much more difficult. It was awkward and tiring trying to keep control with each step. What's more, my stumps were beginning to really hurt. At one point I had to get Anna to help me down onto the ground for a rest. Then she had to haul me bodily back onto my feet again to complete the descent. Eventually I made it back to the car, with much support from Anna, thinking that perhaps this wasn't the first step to greater things after all. Perhaps I had reached my limit already. However, I didn't let myself think like that for long and took heart from my first conquered summit.

Since then I had done a couple more short off-road walks but I was finding today's walk very taxing and my stumps were already beginning to ache. By the time I was a few hundred yards from the road, most of the others were already down on the beach, miles away.

Feeling more and more miserable, I gradually slowed to a snail's pace until I just wanted to sit down and give up. I suppose the emotion of the day was making me particularly sensitive and I was feeling left behind. Fortunately Anna and Sid Tresidder stayed with me and they made sure that I carried on until I finally reached the tarmac. Then, stubbornly, I continued on down to the beach, as everyone else had, and I stood with Anna at the edge of the sea, watching the rolling surf, before turning and heading back to the small cottage where we were staying.

In the evening I talked with Jamie's older brother Mat. Mat had been a friend of mine as long as Jamie had and it was good to see him again. He and his wife Ayala were living in California now. The first time I'd seen them since the accident was on the previous Monday when they'd come round to the flat and brought with them a very important little visitor, their newborn son, JJ.

JJ was born on 14 February, two weeks after Jamie died. In honour of the uncle he would never meet, Mat and Ayala named their child Joseph Jamie – JJ for short. It must have been so hard on Mat and Ayala, going through all the intense emotion of bringing JJ into the world, so soon after losing Jamie. JJ was now a beautiful four-month-old little boy, and I could swear he had the same twinkle in his eye that his uncle did.

Stu Fisher, Jamie's younger brother Robbie and Alice also came round that Monday, and together we went through the sad business of clearing out Jamie's room. Fortunately Jamie was never very materialistic and hadn't amassed a great deal of possessions in his short life. The most precious items were his modest library of mountaineering books, and his superb collection of slides, taken throughout his rich and diverse climbing career, and we spent a nostalgic couple of hours browsing through them.

In July Anna and I returned to the Isle of Skye, on that occasion to celebrate the joint birthdays of Anna and Jane Herries. I was very excited on that trip because it was the first trial of my new pair of legs.

Morag had decided that it was time for me to move up from the simple feet I was walking on, to a more dynamic pair of carbon-fibre feet called Flexfeet. The carbon-fibre feet are 90 per cent efficient in transmitting the absorbed energy of each step through into the next step, and they allow the user a much more active lifestyle. Morag made me another pair of Icex sockets, the same as the last pair, and fitted them with a pair of Flexfeet. After a final fitting session, I left the limb centre with my new legs on the Friday morning and in the afternoon we motored north to Skye.

The next morning I was eager to try the legs out and decided to go along with a group of friends on a short walk out to a small tidal island. Things went well to begin with and it was pleasant walking across the flowering machair for a couple of kilometres. We descended a rocky path with difficulty to the shingle spit that joins the island to the mainland of Skye, and at that point I decided I'd come far enough.

Anna and I sat down to eat our lunch and watch the skylarks flitting over the heath, while the others explored the island. When they returned, we set off back the way we had come. Foolishly, I waved the others on, telling them I'd see them in the pub next to where we'd parked the cars, but as I climbed the rocky path back up to the machair, my stumps started screaming with pain. I only just made it to the top, with Anna's help, before it became too much and I had to sit down on a rock and take the legs off. I could walk no further.

Meanwhile our friends were just disappearing out of sight in the distance. We shouted but it was no use. So Anna left me where I was and set off in hot pursuit. By now the others were so far ahead that she only caught them up just as they were sitting down to their beers in the pub garden.

Kindly, three of the lads abandoned their hard-earned drinks, and jogged all the way back to where I sat, stranded on a rock in the middle of a bog. They then took it in turns to carry me across the moor, back to the pub, where Anna thoughtfully had a pint waiting for me.

I was understandably disappointed with the performance of my new legs but in retrospect I suppose I was trying to do too much too soon with them. Fortunately this first experience with the legs was definitely the worst. My progress from then on was swift and I was soon walking better than ever.

In consolation for my disappointment, that evening in the hostel where we were staying, I got someone to duct-tape a table tennis bat to my right arm and so managed to play a very credible game of table tennis. As I have discovered time and time again, simple solutions to problems are nearly always the best, although I might not have agreed with this philosophy after the game while I was having the duct tape removed from my arm.

CHAPTER TWENTY-EIGHT

Going Underground

'ALL RIGHT, MATE!' shouted Jim from the darkness. 'You can come down now!'

Ivan helped me check that my harness was properly secured while Keith attached my friction brake to the rope. Then, moving gingerly on my elbows and knees, I crawled awkwardly towards the edge of the abyss and clambered over, allowing the rope to take my weight. I was now hanging free in space, 30 feet above the bobbing light of Jim's torch. The sound of running water echoed up from somewhere in the blackness and my breath condensed in thick clouds of vapour, lit up by the beam of my torch. With my elbow I gently squeezed the release handle on the brake and began to slide slowly down the rope into the void.

It was November 1999, six months after I'd left hospital, and some of the guys from work and I had come down to Yorkshire for the weekend to go caving. We'd driven down in one of the company vans and hired the extra equipment we needed from a caving shop in Ingleton before continuing up winding lanes into the heart of Britain's finest potholing country.

I didn't fancy my chances of remaining upright on my legs on the difficult terrain underground so Keith, our expert, had chosen a cave which started only 100 yards from the road and involved a lot of

231

crawling. This meant that I could go without my legs on. The lads helped me squirm into a wetsuit, then they duct-taped on loads of knee pads and elbow wads to give me maximum protection while crawling over rocky surfaces. Entirely trussed up in neoprene, I looked and felt distinctly bizarre.

The neoprene suit and padding worked well though and I was soon crawling on my belly through weird and wonderful tunnels in the ground, carved from solid rock by the unimaginable passage of time and water. Where the roof of the cave was low and everyone was forced to crawl, I was little slower than the others, but where the roof was high enough to allow them to walk, I couldn't keep up and they were forced to stop and wait often. Eventually, after a few hundred yards, we reached a point where the tunnel dropped away beneath us and it was impossible to go any further without abseiling.

However, it wasn't the abseil that worried me. It was the climbing back up on the way out that I knew was going to be difficult. Now, as I landed gently next to Jim on a bank of pebbles beside a small, dark stream, I knew I was committed.

It was strange to think that only six months had passed since that day in May when I had sat outside our flat, waiting for Anna to let me in, feeling so insecure about the life I faced ahead of me. In actual fact, if my progress up until that point had been described as strong, it had only gone from strength to strength. After all the worrying about how I would cope with life on the outside I had never turned back, and had soon forgotten about hospital life entirely.

When I left the hospital I had been managing to wear my prosthetic legs for one, maybe two hours at a stretch, and could walk no further than 100 yards or so. Now I could wear the legs all day, from getting up till going to bed, and could quite easily walk two or three miles before my stumps became too sore. I still took the legs off when travelling, in the car or on the train, and Anna still took the wheelchair with us, in case I had a bad leg day, but in general I was becoming very mobile and the pair of us were getting out and about doing things all the time now.

I had built on the skills that Helen had helped me to learn and was now quite confident with day-to-day life in the flat. Without help I was now able to get up, put on my legs, get dressed, use all the facilities in the bathroom, negotiate the kitchen without too many breakages, operate most of the electrical equipment in the flat, use the phone, and generally cope without being a constant demand on Anna.

I was even managing a few of the household tasks, including tidying up (bending down to pick things up off the floor is an act which requires supreme balance and care), hanging up the laundry and occasionally wrestling with the vacuum cleaner. Oddly though, I could never find the same motivation for mastering these domestic chores as I could, for example, for learning to walk up a steep slope without stumbling. Housework is never-ending though, and I couldn't expect Anna to do it all forever. One day, I hoped, I might even manage washing the dishes.

We had thought, while I was in hospital, that we would have to make substantial alterations to the flat and its contents before I could live in it. However, since turning my back on the use of prosthetic arms, I had become almost zealous in my quest to find a way of doing every task with my bare stumps, keeping the amount of specialised equipment I required in my life to an absolute minimum, and I now applied this same principle to the flat.

Over the months I developed a general procedure for dealing with difficult tasks, whether encountered at home or elsewhere. This procedure is easily summarised by the term suck-it-and-see. If, for example, I found our teapot impossible to pick up and pour from without hands, I wouldn't give up on the teapot, leaving it to Anna to always pour the tea. Nor would I rush to see my friends at Rehabilitation Engineering Services and ask them to design a tipping teapot stand or some other solution to the problem. Instead I would persevere with the teapot, day after day, allowing Anna to pour after each failure, until maybe one day I would find a solution to the problem, perhaps coming up with a new way of holding the pot, or perhaps discovering that my stumps had become strong enough to grip the pot by its handle.

If I continued to have no success, it was always likely that another solution to the problem would eventually present itself. For example, a simple modification to the teapot such as the addition of some insulating material to the outside could be the answer. Or the use of a handily available 'tool' might help, such as a pair of oven gloves.

If I still couldn't cope with the problem, it was amazing how often an alternative item could be found in the shops that performed exactly the same function but was much more easily operated by me, or 'good-for-Jamie' as this quality came to be known. In the case of the teapot, Anna's father found an attractive Scandinavian design that had a large copper handle looping right over the top, easy for me to hook with one arm.

So the teapot problem was solved, as were most other difficulties, without resort to expensive and unsightly modification of the flat and everything in it. It took a long time – every single object that is normally operated or manipulated with the human hand, I had to re-examine and relearn to use. We did have to make some modifications, mostly simple things like attaching loops of string to drawer handles, and we did eventually decide to replace our bath with a shower to make life easier for me, but on the whole I learnt to live in a generally unadapted environment.

As a consequence I was soon able to cope, not only in my own home, but in any other house or hotel room that I might encounter and this made a big difference when it came to visiting friends, going on holiday and generally travelling about – activities that were very important to me as I continued to rebuild every aspect of my life.

While we were in Chamonix we had received invites to a couple of friends' weddings, and going to those weddings had been a big mental target for me. I had imagined I would go along in a wheel-chair, dressed by Anna or a carer, and had hoped I might manage to hold my own drink and eat my own food. However, by the time the weddings arrived, in July and September, eating and drinking were easy, walking was no longer a problem, and proudly wearing my kilt, I showed off my new legs and even joined in the ceilidh dancing.

We also managed to organise a short summer holiday, spending a week at Flo's parent's retreat in the Gironde region of France, eating, drinking, exploring the countryside, and generally relaxing. It was cathartic to be able to spend some time in France outside the con-fines of hospital. Perhaps it was a first step towards confronting the bad memories the country harboured for me. I was anxious not to allow those memories to lurk unchallenged.

Mr MacDonald was right about the phantom limb pains. The day I left hospital they disappeared and never came back. I was so busy doing stuff and thinking about other things that I didn't give my pains a thought. Suddenly I realised that they had vanished. I had left the PMR with a carrier bag full of bottled drugs, not a single one of which I ever took. I would still get shooting pains in my stumps when I was tired but they would never last for long and didn't bother me much.

As I got used to wearing my artificial legs I mentally projected my phantom feet into the prosthetic ones, so much so that if someone stood on my toes I would automatically wince with imagined pain. It was the strangest feeling the first time I accidentally stood in an icy pool of water while out walking. As I watched the water soak into my shoe, I swear I actually felt the cold liquid oozing between my toes.

My mini fists stayed curled up inside my stumps but eventually I got used to them being there and learnt just to ignore them. Sometimes though, I yearned to be able to stretch my fingers out and in vain I would flex the tendons in my forearms.

As soon as I left hospital I decided I wanted to go back to work straight away. When I told Anna she was wary that I was being a little hasty. 'Don't you think it's a bit soon?' she said. 'Wouldn't it be better to take it easy for a bit?'

'What would I do with myself at home, though?' I replied. 'I'd be bored stiff within two days. Gordon and Alan said they'll take me back as soon as I want, and I could always go part-time or give it up if I can't manage. They're paying me anyway so I might as well try and make myself useful.'

Anna consented and the Monday after leaving hospital I went in to the Web and began work. I say work, but I wasn't much help at first. Quite apart from my physical limitations, I was unused to working in an office, I had lost touch with what was happening in the company over the previous three months, and I had no defined job. Gradually though, I began to establish myself. I started by shadowing my boss Alan, taking a few phone calls, and generally familiarising myself with the workings of the office. Leslie, the office manager, taught me about the computer systems and I soon became competent with databases, spreadsheets and web design.

Once I had mastered the computer, got the hang of answering the phone and taking messages, and become a little better with managing paperwork and files, I discovered that I wasn't particularly handicapped for working in an office at all. I still couldn't wear my legs all day, so the hospital delivered my electric chair to the office and I was soon tearing around the large open-plan room, keeping busy, and being a regular traffic hazard to my pedestrian colleagues.

Not having been given a defined role, I started to carve myself out a niche, in the hope of making myself indispensable. It's perhaps worth explaining that the Web was not your ordinary company, and Gordon and Alan were not typical company directors. The company had been created, more or less by accident, in 1995 when Gordon Bisset and Alan Forrest, a couple of die-hard offshore rope access workers, took on a small rope access training contract. The training was a success, more contracts followed and the fledgling Web was born. Over the next few years the company grew, changing direction with the wind, employing staff more or less according to who turned up at the door, and never drifting too far from complete financial disaster.

Neither Gordon nor Alan knew the first thing about running a company, but in the growing industry of rope access they got through, relying on a mixture of charm, wit, luck and sheer audacity. By 1999 the company employed over forty people – as motley a collection of scaffolders, painters, ex-convicts, university dropouts, itinerant South Africans, drug dealers, wanabee rock stars, alcoholics, doctors of philosophy, steeplejacks, sculptors and mobsters as you could ever hope not to meet on a dark night.

For the most part, however, they were what Anna referred to as 'lovable rogues' and the Web was always an entertaining place to work, especially when, as happened every year, we blew the best part of the company's profits on the most almighty party.

The Web, therefore, was not a rigidly structured company, and in changing roles from a site worker to an office worker I was more or less free to create whatever job I wanted. The Web Agency, which was the wing of the Web that provided training and equipment supply services, had been continuing to grow under Alan's direction, but I soon discovered that the management and administration of its affairs had been falling behind, so I christened myself Training Manager and took over the running of it.

To my surprise I really enjoyed my new job. I was more used to physical work, but once I had adjusted to spending my days in an office, I found I could derive just as much satisfaction from an indoor job. The atmosphere was usually relaxed, the company amenable, and I had plenty of room to be creative.

Before long the Web Agency started to look in better shape. Business picked up, the courses ran more smoothly and profits began to improve. Certainly Gordon and Alan were pleased with the work I did and I was soon confident that my position was no longer just a charity job. In fact, when Anna decided to quit her job in order to retrain as a landscape architect, I became the main breadwinner in the household.

Being stuck in the office I missed working with the lads, many of whom were good friends, but there was always opportunity for extramural activities and when Keith organised a small caving expedition I was very keen to join in, which is how I found myself sitting on the bank of an underground stream, deep beneath the Yorkshire Dales.

One by one, the rest of the team slid down the rope to join us on the shingle bank, then we continued deeper into the cave system. Our route from there led up the water-worn bed of the stream, a smooth groove scoured into the rock. Water constantly flowed over us as we climbed against the current and on all fours I found it hard going. Eventually we reached a series of dark, still pools, flooding the chambers ahead. We waded on through the pools and when they became too deep for me to wade, Ivan and Jim carried me along between them, my legs dragging uselessly through the water.

Ahead, the way seemed to be blocked by boulders, but Keith showed us the way, clambering up through a tight gap between two great blocks, and we crawled out into a large cavern where a spectacular waterfall cascaded down from a hole in the roof.

Thankfully – I was becoming exhausted from crawling by now – this marked the end of our journey. We explored the cavern for a bit, then retreated the way we had come, through the pools and down the stream.

Descending the tumbling stream was fun but when we reached the bottom of the abseil pitch there was no alternative but to climb the rope. The guys attached the rope clamps for me and I began climbing. I was very familiar with the rope-climbing technique, having done it for years as a rope access worker, but heaving myself up with my knees and elbows was no easy matter. Painfully slowly I inched my way up the rope, moving first one clamp and then the other, while everyone else could do little else but wait and watch. Eventually, after a mammoth effort, I reached the lip of the drop and Keith, grabbing me by the scruff of the neck, hauled me over onto horizontal ground. I was very tired now. The final couple of hundred yards seemed to go on forever and my head sank lower and lower as I crawled, but finally I emerged exhausted into the sweet-smelling air of the night. Ivan and Keith carried me back to the van.

Keith calculated I had covered over a mile on my elbows and knees and I was to pay the price for this unusual exercise. For the whole of the next week, every muscle in my body ached and the length of my back was stiff as a board. But I was jubilant. It meant such a lot to me to be able to go out with my friends again and join in with the fun, even if it meant I had to crawl while they walked.

CHAPTER TWENTY-NINE

End of the Millennium

Apart from hillwalking and caving I spent a lot of time over the course of the summer and autumn of 1999 attempting all sorts of sports and activities. One activity that I wasted no time in trying was swimming. Ever since those first feverish days in Chamonix, when I'd longed to join Anna and our friends in the swimming pool, I'd dreamed of going swimming again.

The PMR had a small hydrotherapy pool which Doreen had promised to take me to, but for one reason or another it had never happened.

Now that I was out of hospital I was ready to go swimming, but I felt a little cautious and shy about going to a public pool. Fortunately Morag put me in touch with a wonderful man called John de Courcy who worked in the sports medicine department of Moray House College. In his spare time he trained for the triathlon, and used to be the Scottish Paralyimpic athletics coach. The reason I was referred to him was because on Tuesday evenings he ran a swimming club for the mentally and physically disabled.

The Tuesday swimming sessions were always complete pandemonium. There were people there with a huge range of disabilities including blindness, deafness, cerebral palsy, epilepsy, arthritis, paraplegia, Down's syndrome, and a few amputees. For the full hour of the session the pool at Moray House was a complete riot of shouting, laughing and splashing water, over which John and his helpers maintained a rudimentary control.

At one end of the pool a bunch of rowdy teenage boys would plunge in chaotic pursuit of sunken bricks and their lifesavers' award. At the other end apprehensive kids and old men splashed nervously in the shallows.

Meanwhile a blind, deaf, arthritic septuagenarian lady ploughed steadily up and down the length of the pool, not giving a hoot who or what she collided with.

And everyone had a thoroughly enjoyable time. If it wasn't for John most of them would probably never go swimming.

My first attempt at swimming didn't go quite as expected. I was currently making new achievements at a rate of knots and was perhaps becoming overconfident. I assumed that I would find swimming quite easy. As I intended to swim without my prosthetic legs on, I thought my main difficulty would be getting to the poolside and into the water. The swimming itself I supposed would be somewhat slower than it used to be but otherwise pretty similar.

I couldn't have been more wrong. John had arranged for me to be coached by a girl called Lara Ferguson, a single lower-arm amputee and a Paralympic swimmer. I got myself without problem to the edge of the pool on my knees, and plunged confidently in next to Lara. I immediately made all the motions of treading water, only to find myself pitching helplessly over onto my back and sinking up to my eyebrows.

Lara pulled me upright, spluttering. I hadn't realised quite how important the hands and feet are as paddles when manoeuvring in the water. Thrash away as I might, my stumps had no purchase in the water and were as useless as round oars. It seemed I was back to square one with swimming as well.

It didn't take long, however, with Lara's patient tuition, before I found my balance in the water once more. Then, after a lot of floundering about, I discovered that I could make my arms into rough paddles by clenching my elbows. Doggy-paddling with these I could propel myself slowly through the water. On my second session with Lara I swam a length of the pool.

I still couldn't work out what to do with my legs though, and I never really have. No matter what I do with them they don't seem to push me forward. At best they just produce a lot of fruitless splashing. At worst they propel me gently in the wrong direction. Rob and Bill had a look at the possibility of making some fins to fit on to my stumps, but it was going to be quite difficult to achieve and we shelved the project in favour of other more urgent ones.

Despite the poor performance of my legs I gradually grew more confident in the water and found it a useful way of keeping fit without hurting my legs. Eventually I was strong enough to swim in the sea, something which I love doing, although I was very embarrassed on one occasion when I got stuck in the water. It was at a beach in Cornwall and I had walked on my knees down the beach into the water, the sand sharp and very painful on my knees. I swam for fifteen or twenty minutes, playing in the light surf, then paddled back to the shore, but when I tried to stand up on my knees they were raw and painful and wouldn't bear my weight. Try as I might I just couldn't get up and I wallowed in the shallows not knowing what to do. Anna tried to get me onto her back but couldn't lift me out of the water. Eventually I had to ask a stranger, a passing beach hunk, to carry me back up the beach. I have no idea what people must think when they get such strange requests out of the blue but they always seem happy to help.

Another sport which swimming led me to was running. I always used to love running and would have given anything to be able to go for long runs in the country again. One of my most melancholy moments recently had been watching the opening scene of *Chariots of Fire* and I had so wished that I could turn back the clock, to have my hands and feet once more, and to run carefree along the sand, splashing through the water like the men in the film (in slow motion of course).

John de Courcy knew that I was interested in running and thought that I might have potential so he introduced me to a man called Peter Arnott who ran a group for disabled athletes which met once a month for a training weekend at the Don Valley Stadium in Sheffield. I had never been involved in track athletics before but was keen to learn and so went down to see what it was all about.

The first time I went down, in June 1999, I was still on my first pair of feet that weren't really suitable for running and I was still only learning to walk, but I was able to join in the fitness sessions and the pool session.

It was quite an inspiration on that occasion to watch the other athletes. There were arm amputees who ran just about as fast as mainstream athletes. There was a one-legged guy who could hop almost as fast as the runners. And of course there were the wheel-chair athletes, whose shoulders were as wide as two of me side by side.

At dinner, I chatted to a single below-knee leg amp, called Jamie Gillespie. He'd lost his leg in a motorbike accident, while serving in the army. Now he was a Paralympic athlete and he was also training to be a prosthetist.

He said to me, 'Sometimes I think that losing my leg is the best thing that ever happened to me. Before my accident I had a career in the army which would have been restricted once I left. Now, I've rep-resented my country in the Paralympic Games, I was inspired to go to university to study a profession that I love, and life's great.'

I was amazed by this positive attitude to his disability and I won-dered if I could ever feel that way about what had happened to me.

The next time I went to Sheffield, a month later, I was on my Flexfeet. I joined in with the other runners in their sprint drills, walking with exaggerated motions through the individual elements of the sprinting movement. The athletes finished their drills off with a quick sprint down the track. I set off in pursuit and to my complete surprise found myself lumbering into a slow run. It wasn't exactly Linford Christie speed, and it only lasted for a couple of dozen strides, but it was definitely a run.

I was beside myself with excitement and wanted to do it again and again, but after one more run I realised that I was already too tired and had to give it up for the day. Over the next couple of days I paid for my brief spurt of exercise with cripplingly stiff quadriceps that almost stopped me from walking entirely. If I was to make any progress with my running I needed to get fitter.

John de Courcy helped me out with an exercise programme that I could do at home – squats, lunges, leg raises, crunches, etc. – and with a bit of work I soon began to feel a little more healthy. The problem was I just didn't get nearly as much exercise as I used to.

Working in an office had me sitting on my backside most of the day, and the restraints of my artificial legs meant that I didn't get out for aerobic activity nearly as often as I used to. The swimming and the exercise programme helped, however, and I slowly improved to an acceptable level of fitness.

At the December Sheffield meet I ran in my first race. It was a mainstream event, a local club indoor 60 metres, and Peter encouraged me to put my name down. Although I had absolutely nothing to lose I was nervous as hell as my heat was called and I made my way to the start line with a tight stomach. However, when the gun went off I forgot all about the cheering crowd and the other runners and I just ran as hard and fast as I could until suddenly the finish line came rushing past me and it was all over.

I came last, of course, the other able-bodied runners easily outstripping me, but I got a massive cheer from the spectators when I crossed the line and was very happy with my time of 12.06 seconds.

Later one of the other runners in my heat approached me with typical North of England directness. 'Well done, mate. Was that your first race? It was my first race too. And d'you know what? It doesn't make any difference to me that you're disabled or whatever. I'll not treat you any different just cos you've got no legs and all that. That doesn't matter to me. Cos what matters is that I beat you. That's what counts.'

I took this slightly confused address to be a well-meaning attempt at encouragement, and congratulated the man on his victory with a slap on the back.

I was by now getting into the idea of 'reclaiming' as many of the sports, activities and games that I had ever participated in before the accident as possible. I was happy to give anything a go, be it caving, running, swimming, table tennis, darts, bowling, football or anything else, and was learning to be uninhibited about making a fool of myself in the attempt, although I did feel somewhat ridiculous the evening I spent tenpin bowling, sending bowl after bowl rolling impotently down the gutters, failing to topple even a single skittle.

Another activity I tried that summer was sailing, when Pete Jennings took me out in a Seafarer on Loch Rannoch. It was a lovely, breezy day and we cruised up and down the length of the loch. I could handle the tiller no problem at all, pushing and pulling it with my arms, and given enough time to prepare, I could wrap the jib sheets round my stumps and pull them in quite effectively, as directed by Pete. On the whole, therefore, I wasn't entirely useless as a crew member, although by the afternoon I was tired out and slept in the bottom of the boat while Pete carried on sailing back and forth.

A month or two later Anna and I were invited by our friends Ian and Susan Blackwood to join them for a weekend sailing in Ian's parents' yacht. I had been cruising off the west coast of Scotland a few times before and it was great to be afloat again, weaving in and out of the dozens of small islands off the coast from Oban, watching out for seals, whales and dolphins, and listening at night to the sound of waves lapping against the side of the boat.

There wasn't much wind that weekend and we had to motor quite a bit, but we had a great time exploring the islands and inlets, sailing in the light breeze when we could, and I made myself useful on the tiller as much as possible.

Eventually I had a go at sailing single-handed (if you'll forgive the pun). Edinburgh's local sailing school at Port Edgar had a small tri-maran called a Challenger, specifically developed so that disabled sailors could race against non-disabled. It was designed mainly with able-handed wheelchair users in mind but I found I could handle it reasonably well.

I sat in the middle hull with the tiller between my legs. All the ropes that controlled the single sail and lifted the dagger board and rudder were accessible from the same sitting position. I found operating the tiller easy. Pulling on the ropes was more difficult, especially when my stumps grew cold, and although I wasn't fast at gibing and going about, I could manoeuvre the little craft confidently back and forth across the water.

Another sport I used to dabble in and decided to have a go at doing again was orienteering. Running around in forests, parks and woodland with a map and compass looking for small orange checkpoints hidden in the undergrowth may not be everyone's cup of tea but I always thought it was a nice way to get out into the countryside for a run with a bit of an added challenge to spice it up.

The first time we went out, Anna and I simply walked round the course, Anna taking care of the map and compass while I concentrated on remaining upright on the difficult terrain. Crashing about through the countryside, over stiles and fences, through bushes and up and down steep banks proved to be excellent training for my legs and balance.

The next time we went out, I went on my own, the map, compass, and check-card all tied to me with string. Once again I walked round the course, but what I lacked in speed I made up for in careful navigation, and to my surprise I wasn't last. This became my main aim in subsequent events, not to be last, and with good route-finding and a steady plod accelerating occasionally to a brief trot, I found I invariably beat one or two of the able-bodied runners.

Soon the nights were drawing in, winter was upon us and the year was coming to an end. We spent Hogmanay peacefully with a few friends in a small cottage in a far-flung corner of the Isle of Skye, walking, drinking, playing games and eating good food.

So the millennium drew to a close. Like most people I'd often wondered where I'd be at that moment, what I'd be doing as we passed from one century to the next, and what would be happening in my life. Never in a million years could I have guessed.

What a bizarre year 1999 had been for me. Certainly it was a year of tragedy, disaster, tears and despair, but it hadn't all been bad. In fact for me a lot of it had been very positive. They say that life's a journey and it's the journey that matters, not the final destination. Well, I had certainly been on a hell of a journey that year and in many ways it was a thoroughly enriching experience. For me, climbing was always my way of testing myself, of exploring the edges of my envelope, but now, in one year, I had found out more about my physical and emotional limits than I had throughout my years of climbing. I had learnt so much about myself over the previous twelve months, and I hoped that in some ways I was a better person now than I had been a year ago.

I guess I was gradually getting used to the idea of what had happened to me. My heart no longer sank each morning when I woke up and remembered, but I would still catch myself out. Often I would go for hours at a time, blissfully unaware of the fact that I had no hands and feet. Then I would suddenly catch sight of my stumps and wake from my forgetfulness and think, Christ! I'm an amputee! I'm disabled! This is me! And it felt like a kick in the stomach every time.

Slowly, however, I was becoming accustomed to my new body and my new appearance. My stumps were all well healed now and I had become used to their various lengths, no longer underestimating when reaching out. I began to feel secure once again about who I was and what I looked like. My friends too were becoming familiar with my new appearance and mostly no longer treated me differently from anyone else.

As for Anna, who had stood by me through thick and thin, who suffered when I suffered and celebrated when I celebrated, it was also a hell of a year. In fact, in many ways, it was a lot harder for her. Everything I went through, good or bad, Anna went through it with me. She hadn't chosen this to happen in her life either, and had been forced to cope with the upheaval just the same as I was. Yet she received little of the credit that I got, none of the attention with which I was lavished and her role was often sidelined. A situation like this could easily have torn a couple apart but right now we were closer than we'd ever been.

On New Year's Day Anna and I decided to get married and I was the happiest man in the world. We could have got engaged sooner, perhaps. Maybe we would have if the events of the last year hadn't intervened, but I think we both wanted to put some time between us and those events. Time to let the mud settle and the water run clear. Time to be sure that the change in our circumstances hadn't changed the way we felt about each other. Now we were both certain.

Our friends went off to climb a hill that day, and we left them to go for a walk through the woodlands along a remote stretch of the Skye coastline. We strolled and chatted, Anna excitedly making plans, talking about guest lists, me just enjoying the moment, while it was only the two of us who knew. The year 2000, we were certain, was going to be a good one.

CHAPTER THIRTY

Return to Chamonix

I HAD PROMISED Doctor Marsigny and all the other doctors and nurses in Chamonix that I would return to their hospital one day, so that they could see how I was getting on. Now that I had made so much progress in rebuilding my life I was keen to keep my promise and show off my achievements to them all. In late March 2000 the opportunity came when Manu Cauchy, the head of the A&E department there, arranged for Anna and me to visit. He also planned to make a film of my story for French television.

For both Anna and me the trip was certain to be a difficult one. Both of us had an awful lot of emotion, much of it negative, tied up in Chamonix and Chamonix Hospital. It was important to go back though. Our short trip to France the previous summer had been the first step. Now, by returning to Chamonix, we were to have the chance to revisit the harrowing memories of the previous winter. Only by confronting those memories could we truly learn to accept what had happened and put it behind us. The alternative, burying the past, never really coming to terms with it, was sure to lead only to difficulty.

So it was with quite some trepidation that Anna and I pushed our luggage trolley out into the arrivals hall of Geneva airport late one evening. There to greet us were Manu, Anne Sauvy, John Wilkinson,

Pascale the Bond girl, the ever-bubbly Dominique, a cameraman, and a film producer. It was quite an intimidating entrance to make but on seeing the familiar faces we quickly forgot about the camera and embraced our old friends warmly. I felt very proud when everyone expressed their amazement at how well and naturally I was walking.

We had arranged to stay with John and Anne for a couple of nights so the reception party's convoy of vehicles took us up the road to their chalet on the outskirts of Chamonix where Manu, Pascale, Dominique and the film crew left us to get some rest before Manu's programme of events began in the morning.

When we arrived that night all was dark outside the chalet's large picture windows. The mountains revealed themselves only as shadows against the starry sky and high above the valley, shining like the brightest star, a single light marked the spectacular location of the Aiguille du Midi Téléférique station. It wasn't until the morning, after we had enjoyed a good night's sleep, that I saw for the first time since my accident the incredible mountains of the French Alps where my life had so dramatically changed its course just over a year ago.

Looking up at those savage peaks, still cloaked in the snows of winter despite the arrival of spring down in the valley, I felt something stir inside me and my heartbeat quickened. Of course I felt terror and horror and regret and pain. Something of all the emotions I had been through revisited me now on being faced with the mountains where the nightmare had begun. At the same time I was touched by other familiar feelings. I couldn't help feeling a surge of excitement and desire at seeing those beautiful, challenging peaks. The passion that for so long had fanned the flames of my affair with mountaineering had not disappeared. The flames had not been put out by the tragedy of last year. Trampled, suffocated and dampened perhaps, but not extinguished. Deep down I knew I was still the same person and my love of the mountains was still there.

I was itching to go back to Chamonix Hospital and see all my friends as soon as possible, but that morning Manu had another more surprising plan up his sleeve. We were to travel down to Lyon, a couple of hours' drive away, where Manu had arranged for me to meet a certain Professor Dubernard. Dubernard, it transpired, was the surgeon in charge of the team who had performed the world's first hand-transplant operation – that is transplanting a hand and forearm from a deceased donor to the arm of an amputee recipient. The recipient and his new hand had apparently made very good progress and Dubernard had recently gone on to perform the very first double hand-transplant operation on a young Frenchman, Denis Chatelier, who had lost both his hands in a fireworks accident. Dubernard and Chatelier were both available in Lyon to speak to me.

Wow. Suddenly a whole new avenue of possibility was opening up in front of me. Suddenly there appeared hope that I might one day have real hands again. What a thought.

In actual fact the thought wasn't entirely new. I was well aware of the recent developments in hand-transplant surgery. I had followed with great interest the stories in the papers of the rogue New Zealander, Clint Hallam, and the groundbreaking operation to give him a new hand, and of course I had considered the implications of this technology for me. However I realised that the technique was still highly experimental and unproven and the chance of rejection was great. The risk of secondary infection as a result of taking immuno-suppressant drugs was also high. Even if the procedure did work the waiting lists would probably be enormous. The possibility of me becoming involved was just too remote and so I hadn't ever allowed myself to build up hope that I might have functional hands once more. I stopped myself from thinking about it.

Now I was actually going to meet the man who did the operations. Just meet him, of course, but I couldn't help thinking where this might lead.

We travelled down with the film crew and on the way Manu interviewed me about how it felt to be back in France, what I thought about the hand-transplant operation, and how I had coped with the loss of my hands and feet.

I didn't know Manu that well, but he was turning out to be a surprisingly dynamic character. I knew, of course, that he was a senior doctor and also on the mountain rescue team. I also learnt that he was a qualified mountain guide and as a young man he had achieved the considerable feat of climbing to the south summit of Everest – negligibly lower than the nearby true summit – without oxygen. He was a world authority on mountain medicine and had conducted considerable research into the causes and effects of cerebral oedema. He was also an enthusiastic film-maker and had already made a television documentary about the work of the Chamonix mountain doctors. In his spare time he was converting a large property, an old schoolhouse, into a family home and three-bedroom bed and breakfast. Any remaining time he spent with his wife and two kids. All of which is why I came to know him as Manic Manu. He was a great person, had a fantastic sense of humour, and the two of us quickly became firm friends.

Soon we arrived at the hospital in Lyon, a severe building with miles of dimly lit corridors and very poor signage. Eventually we found our way to the correct department where a physiotherapist, telling us that Dubernard would see us later, took us straight in to meet Denis Chatelier.

Monsieur Chatelier was sitting at a table in the physiotherapy unit, trying to pick up a plastic cup. He reached out his right arm, positioning the outstretched fingers and thumb round the cup, and then concentrated really hard on closing the fingers. He strained and slowly the fingers made the merest flicker of movement, closing just enough to lightly grip the empty cup and raise it above the table.

When he saw that we had arrived he stood to greet us, smiling broadly, and we shook hands. I say 'shook hands' but between the two of us we didn't quite muster a firm handshake. Obviously I didn't have a hand to shake and while Denis had one he couldn't close it. So I proffered my stump and sort of pressed it into his limp palm and we made the shaking motion. I'm afraid my first thought, quite predictably I suppose, was, 'Eugh! I just touched the hand of a dead person!'

However Denis's hand was obviously not dead. It was pink, warm and clammy, and was quite securely attached to a living human being. Having said that, the two arms he carried about in front of him, somewhat ironically in the style of Frankenstein's monster, were quite obviously not his own. The skin was a different colour from his and less hairy too. Also the new sections of arm appeared to be slightly too large for Denis's light frame, although that could have been due to post-operative swelling or perhaps just an illusion caused by the inevitable conspicuousness of the two protruding limbs.

Despite the very odd appearance of Denis's arms I was very impressed with what the surgeons had done for him. The arms seemed to be strongly attached and Denis already had some movement in his fingers. It was only about two months since the operation but Denis claimed that he could actually *feel* certain sensations in his new hands, particularly hot and cold. This was the crucial issue really. It was all very well stitching hands onto a patient, fusing the bones, connecting the tendons and blood vessels, and joining muscle tissue, but if the nerves weren't connected up the hands would be next to useless. Without nerves there would be no sensation, no transfer of signals, no communication between the hands and the brain. The patient simply wouldn't be able to operate the hands. And nerve regeneration is a very slow business. It can take many years for just a centimetre or two of nerve fibre to repair itself. Denis's progress was very encouraging.

We chatted for a while, through a translator, and Denis told me how determined he was that these new limbs were going to work for him. All his hopes were pinned on them. He had never really been happy, he said, since he had lost his hands four years ago, and he had never become accustomed to being an amputee. All he wanted was to be able to hold his kids and hug them with his own arms.

I wished Denis all the best with his recovery and we left him to his physiotherapy to go and meet with Professor Dubernard. Dubernard was a large, intimidating man, who spoke very good English.

He had heard about my story, he said, and was very impressed by my determination and strength of will. These were the kinds of qualities he was looking for in his hand-transplant patients. He wanted people with the motivation and resolve to make it through what was a very difficult mental and physical challenge, and make the most of the opportunity he was offering.

I was flattered that Dubernard thought I had what he was looking for, and was taken aback by his apparent interest in me as a potential subject, but first I had some questions for him.

Assuming these hand transplants worked long term, how well could the patient expect the hands to perform? How much would he be able to do with them?

Dubernard was optimistic. He didn't see any reason, he said, why a transplanted hand shouldn't perform just as well as a patient's own hand, stitched back on after an accident. Functionality of 80 or 90 per cent could easily be attained.

What about the risk of rejection? How great was that?

Yes, there was a risk, admitted Dubernard. For the rest of the life of the patient, his body would be attempting to reject the foreign limbs. Not only that, but the limbs themselves could actually reject the host body. However, modern anti-rejection drugs were very effective, he assured me, and were constantly getting better. There was every chance that the patient could keep the limbs indefinitely.

What about those anti-rejection drugs, I asked, wasn't there a danger of side effects? Skin cancers, lymph gland cancer, increased vulnerability to illness? The patient would be taking these drugs for the rest of his life.

Dubernard was dismissive of the problems. The risk of suffering these side effects was low, he said, and most of them were easily treatable. Following a period of greater risk immediately after the operation, the danger quickly became minimal, so long as the patient remained vigilant and kept an eye out for the early warning signs.

What about the ethical issue of undertaking a very dangerous procedure to treat a completely non-life-threatening condition?

Dubernard snorted at this question. He knew what he did was controversial and had obviously had this argument up to his ears from the detractors among his profession and the press. Kidney failure was a non-life-threatening condition, he replied. Patients could live quite comfortably on dialysis, yet kidney transplants were a common procedure. This was no different. He was simply trying to improve the quality of people's lives.

Finally, I asked, what if it all goes wrong? What if the limbs are rejected and have to be removed? What happens to the patient?

Nothing, replied Dubernard. The limbs are amputated and the patient is back to where he started. He has lost nothing. Except, he added, perhaps two centimetres in length off each stump. I glanced down at my own already sadly shortened arms.

Time was marching on and Dubernard was a busy man. He concluded our short interview by repeating how impressed he was by my story and intimating that I would be an ideal candidate for one of his next operations. Think it over and get in touch, he said.

I went away, somewhat staggered, to think it over. Over the next few days I thought about the issue a great deal, and discussed it at length with Anna and various other people. It took me a long time to get my head round the idea. I had just spent over a year learning to live without hands and had made fantastic progress. Now, out of the blue, I was being offered the opportunity to have a new pair of hands. What a strange decision to have to make! Once again I was standing at a crossroads.

The whole concept of hands, or the lack of them, is a complex and difficult one. I have often been asked which is harder to live without, hands or feet. The answer is that there is no contest – hands win (hands down!). Compared to the hand, the foot is a comparatively simple organ with one main function, walking. Modern prosthetic devices, while they can never replace the real human foot, can do the job of the foot pretty effectively. That's why no one has ever attempted a foot transplant. Living without feet is really not that difficult.

Hands (on the other hand) are a different matter altogether. They are so involved, so absolutely key, to every activity that human beings carry out, that to live without them has enormous implications, many of which are not apparent at first glance.

The physical limitations of life without hands are obviously paramount. I had learnt quickly about the difficulties of this aspect of my disability while I was in hospital and had gradually come to terms with it, but it was really only after leaving hospital that I began to discover how important hands are socially. Apart from carrying out manual tasks, every day we use our hands hundreds of times, in dozens of different ways, to communicate and interact with one another.

Without my hands I found I could no longer wave, clap, give a thumbs-up, point, scratch my head, drum my fingers, beckon, knock on a door, tap a shoulder, shake a hand, thumb my nose, fold my arms, make a fist, bite my nails, give the Vs, fiddle with a fork, wag a finger, poke a rib, or indulge in any of the myriad of subtle gestures and gesticulations with which we punctuate our verbal communication. In a strange way I felt quite gagged by this handicap and it made me feel uncomfortable in social situations. I felt I couldn't hide the disability like I could hide my prosthetic legs underneath my trousers and I would feel embarrassed about going into shops or introducing myself to people.

You only have to look at our language to realise how fundamental hands are to our culture. The puns which appeared in the previous few paragraphs occurred entirely by accident and there are hundreds of other phrases in the English language which relate to hands: an old hand, a bird in the hand, second-hand, right-hand man, many hands make light work, out of one's hands, hand in glove, change hands . . . the list goes on. It's not surprising that these accidental puns are so common and I've long since lost count of the number of people who have embarrassed themselves in my company with verbal blunders.

I particularly remember one unfortunate, kindly stranger who noticed me, in my wheelchair, having difficulty reaching something in a shop. The guy came up to me and ever so politely said, 'Excuse me, can I give you a hand?' He then looked down at my arms, realised what he'd said, and immediately flushed bright crimson. 'Oh my God!' he continued. 'I'm so sorry. I've really gone and put my foot in it!' He stopped, looked down at my bandaged legs, and this time just about melted into the floor.

'It's OK,' I said, grinning at the distraught man. 'Don't feel cut up about it.'

There were other social reasons why I missed having my hands too. I was fed up with being noticed and stared at wherever I went, being treated differently all the time. I hated it when I occasionally frightened young children and made them cry if I went near them. I didn't like constantly making people feel awkward and uncomfortable, and I missed the human contact of being able to touch other people.

In all there were many, many reasons why I was tempted by Professor Dubernard's offer and I considered it very seriously.

I thought hard about the drawbacks too. The major surgery involved, the risk of failure or later rejection, the drugs, the side effects, the many months of rehabilitation that would be necessary, the uncertainty of a favourable outcome in the end, and perhaps most of all the stigma of having a dead person's hands attached to my body. At least a transplanted heart or liver is hidden, not on view for the world to see and feel revolted at. When I asked Denis, tactfully, about this issue he replied simply, 'They're not a dead person's hands, they're mine now.' So I suppose it is possible to get one's head round this tricky idea.

I think on the whole I might have been able to accept the challenges and take the risks involved in undergoing hand-transplant surgery. I don't think I was too scared, but in the end I said no. In fact, in my heart I was certain of my decision before I even met Denis Chatelier and Professor Dubernard. I kept thinking back over the previous year, all the effort I'd put in to learning how to use my new body, the progress I'd made. I thought about the words of my athlete friend Jamie Gillespie: 'Sometimes I think that losing my leg is the best thing that ever happened to me.' And I thought back to the promise I had made to myself, in those first few days in Chamonix Hospital: no regrets.

I had already made my decision, all those months ago. I had accepted the challenge I had been set and was coping extraordinarily well. There was no need for a change of direction now. When I got back to the UK I wrote Professor Dubernard a polite letter thanking him for his time and for allowing me to see his patient, but informing him that I had decided not to take his offer any further.

I have absolutely no objection to hand-transplant surgery. I think it is a miraculous technique and I have every confidence that the technology will progress from strength to strength. For many people it may turn out to be an absolute lifesaver and for those people I am grateful that it is gradually becoming a viable option. As I've said before, every amputee is different. I for one was happy the way I was. Two years later, Professor Dubernard contacted me again asking if I'd had a change of heart. I had absolutely no hesitation on that occasion in giving my reply.

CHAPTER THIRTY-ONE

More Revisitations

ARRIVING BACK AT THE CHALET from Lyon that evening, there was another surprise in store for us. Anne and John had invited some people round for dinner: Alain 'Julio' Iglesis, Philippe 'Poutsy' Pouts, Blaise Agresti, and their wives.

I was very nervous about my first proper meeting with these three big, fierce mountain rescue men who had so dramatically saved my life, but in the flesh, outside the confines of their work, they all turned out to be down-to-earth, friendly people, relaxed and sociable.

Poutsy was the loudest, always joking, fooling around and being irreverent. Blaise, despite his stern appearance, was a very kind and pleasant man, eager to please and generous. Julio (nicknamed after the famous singer) was actually quite shy and would say very little, except when the talk turned to the subject of mountaineering. Then his ears would prick up and he would launch into the conversation with enthusiasm.

I think all three were also pleased to meet me properly for the first time. Their parts in my adventure had finished the moment my frozen body had been delivered to the hospital, and they were all very interested to see for themselves what had become of me since then. I felt quite flattered that my rescue hadn't been just another job for the PGHM. As we tucked in to John and Anne's fantastic food, and drank their fine wine, we talked about the rescue, about the PGHM, about mountains and mountaineering, and the conversation went on long into the night.

Manu had arranged for Anna and me to go to Chamonix Hospital the next day so first thing in the morning he and the film crew arrived to drive us the short distance across town to the smart hospital building.

Funnily enough, despite having been there for three and a half weeks, I had seen very little of the hospital – only my own room and the ceilings of a few corridors – and so was completely unfamiliar with the building. I had never seen it from the outside and was surprised by how big it was and how stylishly it was designed.

We went in, Manu leading the way past the reception area and through the big double doors that led into the intensive care department at the rear of the hospital where I saw my first familiar sight. The big staff desk where the nurses and doctors did their paperwork when they were on duty had been visible from my bed and it was where I would call out to when I wanted assistance or more drugs. Working backwards I uncertainly picked out the door to my old room. Fortunately the room was vacant and I was able to push open the door and go in.

Inside nothing had changed. The same bed, the same bedclothes, the same bits and pieces of equipment, the sink in the corner, the tiles on the ceiling. The damaged paintwork on the walls where my pictures had been pulled off when I'd left. It was as if the room had been kept as it was, waiting for me to come back. It was so strange being there again. Even the smell of the place was shockingly familiar.

I went back out into the hall to meet the staff. I'd already met Pascale and Dominique, but soon I was hugging and kissing and shaking hands with all the doctors, nurses, surgeons, radiographers and other staff who had played such an important role in my treatment. It was thrilling to see them all again and I got so excited that I started showing off by running up and down the corridor.

Then I heard the very familiar sound of a pair of outsized leather shoes flapping along the corridor and I turned to see the unmistakable Doctor Marsigny loping up to meet us. Gaunt and bony as ever, he was the only person who turned out to be taller than I'd imagined from my bed-bound perspective, rather than shorter.

'I promised you I'd return, walk into the hospital, and shake you by the hand, and now I have,' I said proudly as we greeted one another.

He smiled and said, 'We are all very ''appy to see you here, Jamie. You are a very special patient to us.'

I half expected him to add, 'and you 'ad very serioz frozbite'.

It was then announced that we were having a '*pot*' which is a French term for nibbles and drinks, and we all abandoned the ward and went off to the common room to eat nuts, drink wine and chat about old times, new times and the future.

After the pot we went out for lunch with Marsigny and the two surgeons, Guy and Rik, both of whom were quite accustomed in continental style to drinking wine with their meals before going off to surgery in the afternoon.

Finally in the evening we had yet another meal out, this time with all the nurses and nursing assistants. Anna and I were both feeling bloated and quite exhausted by the time we staggered back to the chalet that night.

The next day Manu had yet another emotional rollercoaster ride lined up for me. We were going to visit Corrado Truchet at Chamonix Mont-Blanc Hélicoptères, or CMBH, and he was willing, if I wanted, to fly me up to Les Droites and return to the scene of last year's tragedy.

Woah! Did I want to do that? One of the main reasons why I had come back to Chamonix was to confront the memories of last year, to convince myself that I really had dealt with all the issues at stake. I didn't want Chamonix to become a place I couldn't go. If I couldn't physically revisit the scene of the accident, surely that meant that I wasn't willing to revisit somewhere in my head, storing up problems for later in life.

However, wasn't returning to Les Droites taking things a little too far? Wasn't that simply rubbing my nose in it? I don't suppose I really needed to go back up there in order to dispel my phantoms, and I wouldn't have gone if I wasn't sure I could mentally handle it; but there was a certain fascination that urged me to go, to visit one more time that tiny piece of mountainside that I never thought I'd see again, to remember those terrible days trapped in an icy hell, perhaps even to pay my respect to Jamie's ghost waiting up there forever.

Hidden up in the forest above Argentière, CMBH is an unassuming operation. A dirt track leads through the trees to a concrete landing pad, a couple of fuel tanks and a small wooden shack where Corrado was waiting to meet us. He gave us a quick tour round his helicopter, the same one that had plucked me off the mountain, pointing out its powerful engine, the lightweight body, the external winch line. Then he, Manu, the translator, the cameraman and I all squeezed into the glass bubble cockpit and in a matter of minutes we were lifting gently off the ground.

The climb up into the mountains was spectacular. Skimming just above tree level we hurtled straight into the narrow gorge that issues from the snout of the Argentière Glacier. Corrado guided the machine with ease up through the gorge, banking from side to side round its twists and turns. Higher up we passed at eye level a couple of ice climbers, inching their way up the crystal cascades that tumble down the steep gorge walls.

As we rose out of the gorge and came to the snout of the glacier, we passed into a band of cloud. Below us a fractured landscape of tumbled blocks, poised *séracs* and black fissures loomed out of the mist. Then we were coming out of the cloud again and suddenly we were over the glacier, shining white in the dazzling sunlight. Higher up stood the mountain peaks, as familiar as ever, proudly propping up a beautiful blue sky. We passed low over the Argentière Refuge where a few folk standing on the terrace waved up at us, before crossing in a few seconds over to the foot of the North Face of Les Droites.

It was quite amazing to see the whole of that long climb, which had taken Jamie and me two days, flash by so quickly. In an instant we had panned up, past the *bergshrund*, past the steep corner pitch, to the start of the ice field. As we floated past I picked out the area of rocks where we had taken our first bivouac. Then we were up into the headwall where I made out the ice smear where it had first started snowing, and the cul-de-sac over-looking the Ginat Route from where I had had to take the precarious pendulum across steep slabs. I recognised the upper runnels that had seemed to go on forever in those awful conditions, and then the final gully which had led us in darkness to the *brèche*. It all looked so different today – bright, amenable, non-threatening.

Suddenly the face ended and we were hovering in open space over the ragged knife-edge summit of Les Droites. And there below us was the *brèche*. It was funny, it looked so nondescript and insignificant now, as our helicopter circled round over it. Just a small notch in a ridge riven with small notches. One ridge on a mountain seamed with complex ridges. One mountain in a range of mountains that extended as far as the eye could see. One range of mountains in a world that is built of mountain range after mountain range.

The little notch was not a significant place. There was not even any sign of our passing. No trampled snow, abandoned equipment or frayed end of rope that commemorated the battle that had been fought there. The place appeared untouched by human hand. There wasn't even a ledge to mark the spot where we had lain, side by side for all those days, only a pristine arête of snow, wind-sculpted into a curve that smiled up at us in the sunlight.

How could I hate this place? It was so beautiful. The fault lay with us, the climbers, not with the mountain. The mountain was proud, savage, untamed and innocent of malice, as were the wind, the cloud and the snow. I was certain now that I couldn't hold a grudge against the mountains.

We circled round the *brèche* a few times, then left it, heading off along the ridge, and made a tour of all the peaks around the glacier – Les Courtes, L'Aiguille du Triolet, Mont Dolent, L'Aiguille d'Argentière, L'Aiguille du Chardonnet – stunning, every one of them, before making the stomach-lurching descent back down the glacier, hurtling through the gorge, and finally touching down gently on the landing pad where the warm sweet smell of pine was waiting to greet our nostrils.

It had been a breathtaking trip and I was quite relieved that Manu had no more traumatic experiences organised for the next couple of days. In fact Anna and I took the opportunity to explore the area a bit on our own, without the intrusion of crowds of people, film crews and helicopters.

Anna showed me some of her Chamonix, the Chamonix she had inhabited while I'd been stuck up on the mountain or in hospital. We visited the Hotel Chamonix and paid our respects to the Madame who had looked after the avalanches of mail and screeds of faxes as they had arrived for me. We walked past the apartment block where everyone had stayed and the adjacent building site, location of the great fire. We went to the Maison des Hautes Montagnes to visit Patricia and Françoise, who were delighted to see us. We checked out Anna's favourite patisserie and sampled the wares of the waffle stand at the bottom of the main street. We lunched in terrace cafés and had dinner in small, out-of-the-way restaurants. We went for walks in the surrounding countryside and explored the backstreets and markets of the town.

One afternoon we went to the Chamonix swimming pool, fulfilling the longing I'd had to go there since my days in the hospital. We were also taken by Blaise and Julio on a tour of the PGHM facilities and were wined and dined in style at the officers' dinner table.

Before we took our flight back to Edinburgh we had one last piece of fun. Much of the season's snow had melted now but Les Houches, the ski resort at the bottom end of the valley, was still open so Manu, Anna, the nurses Francine and Pascale and I went for an afternoon's snowboarding.

I had actually already had one short attempt at snowboarding on my new legs, about a month before in Scotland. I had been very keen to find a way of getting out on the snow again, not least because winter sports was something which Anna and I enjoyed doing together. Skiing is really the sport which I am more familiar with, but snowboarding looked more feasible than skiing because on a snowboard the feet are held facing rigidly in the same direction. With skis they are free to rotate independently and I was worried about my legs drifting off in the wrong directions, with catastrophic results.

I had thought a good deal about the possibility of boarding, and of various possible adaptations that could help me do it, although I had so far done nothing about it. As usual, however, it was the suck-it-and-see method of approaching the problem that produced results. One Sunday in February, we were staying with some friends in the Highlands and our friends were going out for a hillwalk too difficult for me, so Anna suggested we go up to Nevis Range and have a go at snowboarding. I didn't really think there'd be much point but I'm always up for a laugh and decided there'd be no harm in trying.

We hired the gear from a shop in Fort William. I reasoned that as my legs were already stiff and didn't need to be kept warm there was no reason to wear boots. The board dude who served us was completely unfazed when I handed him one of my legs and asked him to fit it to a board. 'Wicked,' he said, and wandered off with the leg to find a suitable board.

Up at the ski centre, we took the gondola and then the Braveheart chair up onto the bitterly windy ridge of Aonach Mor. Getting off the chairlift was the crux. Anna was carrying our one board, giving me more chance of getting up out of the moving chair. However, I have difficulty in standing up at the best of times, and on this occasion, with a moving chair and an icy, sloping landing, I made a bit of a mess of it and went sprawling. Anna, who was held back by me, had very little time to leave the swinging chair. As she did so, the chair clocked her on the side of the face, and she tumbled over, snowboard and all, into a heap in the snow beside me. Not a good start.

Once we got ourselves sorted out we walked to the edge of the slope. Anna buckled the board to my feet, and, with a great deal of heaving, pulled me upright. I stood there wobbling for a bit. Then I fell over.

Anna pulled me up again. Once more I fell over.

She pulled me up again, and this time I managed to stay upright long enough to slide down the slope for a few yards before falling over. After a few more goes I started to get the hang of it. In fact, as I gained confidence, I discovered that I felt pretty much the same on the board as I had done before the accident. Anna trotted down the slope next to me, shouting encouragement, and helping me up when I fell, although I managed to get myself onto my feet on my own a couple of times. By the time I reached the bottom of the slope, I had managed a couple of turns and I was utterly exhilarated.

However, it was icily cold up there and I didn't have particularly suitable clothes. I was also tired and sore already, so I let Anna take the board and go for a short spin. She was soon cold too so we retired early and descended to the valley to reward ourselves with a hot chocolate.

It was only later on that day, when my left foot began to behave erratically and then started rattling that I realised I'd broken it. The next day, with my tail between my legs, I hobbled into the prosthetic centre to explain to Morag what I'd been doing with my expensive legs. Fortunately it was only a broken bolt and it was a lot easier to fix than the equivalent broken bone would have been.

At the end of March, at Les Houches, the conditions were a lot more pleasant and I had a much better chance at finding my balance on the board. The weight of the equipment did put a lot of strain on my stumps, but I found as long as I kept my speed down and made my turns slowly and carefully, I could handle the board quite reasonably, and I soon became more confident.

Two problems remained: getting up after falling over, which was extraordinarily strenuous and quite painful, even with help from another person; and riding on the chairlift, where I had to get someone else to carry my board for me. Nevertheless I enjoyed myself immensely.

Neither Pascale nor Francine had tried snowboarding before, but both, curse them, proved naturally gifted and were quickly zooming gracefully down the slope. Manu, good at everything, was an expert, and would board backwards just in front of me, facing up the slope, filming me with his video camera. He did this with apparent ease, only wiping-out completely and nearly destroying the camera once. Anna stayed near me, making sure she was available each time I needed to be pulled to my feet again.

It was a lovely day and I felt absolutely thrilled to be able to do something active in the mountains again, especially in the company of some of the people who had been so involved with the very first part of my rehabilitation.

Soon it was time to leave Chamonix again, but this time our parting was a much happier one, and both Anna and I left knowing that Chamonix was no longer a place we needed to feel nervous of. We promised Manu and all our friends that we would return again.

CHAPTER THIRTY-TWO

A Big Day on the Hill

I WAS BY NOW DOING quite a lot of hillwalking and was gradually getting up bigger and bigger hills. Starting with the lowly Blackford Hill, I had progressed through the small hills of Edinburgh to the greater heights of the Pentlands and various other smallish hills in Scotland and the Lake District.

Something that helped a great deal was my pair of specially adapted walking poles. Rob took a normal pair of telescopic walker's poles, cut the handles off and fixed them to a pair of stump sockets that Malcolm made for me. It took a couple of shots to get the alignment right, but I eventually had an excellent pair of comfortable poles which make a big difference to my balance on steep ground. I also found I could walk further with the poles as I was using less energy to keep my balance and I began to manage hills of up to about 1,500 feet in ascent.

It wasn't all plain sailing though. I'll never forget one incident that occurred at the end of a long day in the hills of Glencoe. I was trudging wearily behind Anna when my way was blocked by a particularly large, evil-looking bog. In an attempt to leap across the bog, I stepped onto a firm-looking tussock in the middle but to my horror, my leg sank up to the knee in the foul black mire. My momentum carried me forward, but the leg was firmly lodged, and as I pitched forward my stump parted company with the leg, and I left it behind. With only one leg left, I had little chance of regaining my balance, and plunged headfirst into the muddy pool.

It took Anna about fifteen minutes to extricate me and my leg from the bog, and to help me put the leg back on. By the time I was upright again, we were both soaked through and black from head to toe.

Partly because of episodes like these, I was being quite cautious, never venturing too far from the road, and it might have been many more months before I was accomplishing hills of any significance were it not for a call I got from a chap called Ali Brown, a single-leg amputee.

Ali Brown was an ex-RAF serviceman who had lost his leg below the knee in a climbing accident and he had heard about me through my swimming coach, John de Courcy. Ali explained that he was involved in a mammoth RAF Mountain Rescue Association charity relay walk from Land's End to John O'Groats, taking in a whole host of hills on the way. Ali was organising a subsidiary event to encourage disabled people to get out onto the hills, and asked if I would join him on Ben Nevis in June. Ben Nevis is, of course, Britain's highest mountain, and from the nearest road there is over 4,500 feet of ascent. At that stage of my rehabilitation I could barely manage 1,500 feet, and seriously doubted whether I'd be managing much more by June, but on a whim I agreed to give it a go.

Then I pretty much put the whole thing to the back of my mind for a while, but as June approached and I continued to get fitter and fitter, Ben Nevis began to look like a feasible challenge and I got down to some serious training.

As it was to be a charity event I wanted to try and raise some money so I wrote a short email asking for sponsorship and sent it out to all my friends. Many of my friends forwarded the email to their friends, and they forwarded it to theirs, until my little note seemed to be spreading round the globe like a virus. I was soon receiving floods of replies, from all over the world, offering both money and encouragement. The size and warmth of the response I received was quite overwhelming, and I realised I was well and truly committed to climbing Ben Nevis now.

It wasn't long before the press found out. I really had no idea how much fuss they would make of the whole thing. The week before the event my phones at home and at work went red hot with pestering journalists looking for a slice of the action. Seeing as it was for charity I agreed to do one or two interviews for newspapers and television. This only served to fan the flames of media frenzy and I began to feel I was losing control of the situation.

By the Friday before Sunday's ascent I was so fed up with endless requests for interviews and photocalls that I just said to all of them, 'Look, I'll be there at nine a.m. on Sunday. You can come if you want.'

The phones went quiet for a while. Then they began to ring again: 'What do we need to bring?', 'Where do I get a map?', 'Is there a cable car up Ben Nevis?' Oh dear God!

Finally the big day arrived. Due to my typically overambitious planning, and stubborn insistence not to miss out on anything, Anna and I had driven down to Newcastle on Saturday for a friend's wedding, and driven back up that night as far as my parents' house in Glasgow.

Early on Sunday morning my dad, Anna and I drove up from Glasgow through an unpromising dawn, while nervous tension gnawed at my gut like a rat. I had still not climbed a hill even half the height of Ben Nevis and was utterly unconfident that I was going to manage. I'd arranged to meet everyone at the Milton Hotel at 9.00 a.m., although I had no idea who 'everyone' might be. By the time we drove through a drizzly, grey Fort William and pulled into the car park of the Milton I was simply dreading the whole thing.

Then there they all were. Television crews, satellite broadcast vans, photographers – the works. For the first time I realised how it must feel to be a pop star or famous football player. I was quickly ushered from camera to camera, doing several interviews in the space of a few minutes, one of which I was horrified to learn was being broadcast live.

The people from the charity, Across, were there with their Jumbulance, a full-size bus converted to take disabled and sick people on holiday which they were purchasing with the proceeds of the walk, so there were photos with them too. Between interviews a bacon roll was shoved into my stumps. The RAF was out in full force and I was taken under the wing of Al Sylvester, the leader of their Mountain Rescue Association, and bustled up the road to the start of the walk at Achintee, where another media host was waiting.

It seemed to take ages to get through the press cordon but eventually, after several more interviews, we were off, the lads of the RAF MRA setting the pace. Following on were a crowd of journalists, cameramen, sound people, presenters, photographers, charity workers, Boy Scouts, friends and family. Experienced hillwalkers and newcomers alike, some on a mission of work, some along to give me support, some along for the crack, some on the call of duty. All of creation seemed to be labouring up the hill and I hobbled along in the midst of it all, wondering why on earth I was the centre of so much attention.

The weather was still looking doubtful and a smudge of rain began to fall as the clouds hung heavily over the summit plateau. As we gained altitude, however, things began to improve. The rain stopped, the sun started to make an occasional appearance, and the clouds lifted to about summit level. The photographers and cameramen puffing alongside me flurried into activity, jostling for position. I found myself constantly being asked to wait for the crowds to pass and pause for photos at choice vantage points. My patience began to wear thin and I started to get snappy with the photographers.

Forty-five minutes into the walk and already I was starting to feel it. My thighs ached, my knees were twinging and my stumps were beginning to feel the strain. This kind of stuff used to be so easy for me. I would happily trot up and down hills like this all day and think nothing of it. I couldn't believe that it had come to this – picking my way slowly uphill step by step, almost grinding to a halt whenever the ground became at all rocky or steep, stepping aside to let old ladies and French schoolkids overtake me. To cap it all I had about a dozen journalists and photographers buzzing round me like flies, not to mention at least three film crews bothering me constantly.

I paused to catch my breath – and to get my head together. I knew this attitude didn't work. I'd been down that road before, in those grim first days after the accident, turning the whole horrific situation over and over endlessly in my head, and I'd quickly discovered that a negative attitude led to nowhere but despair. If I was going to make it up this hill I was going to have to adopt a more positive attitude.

Fortunately my support team provided plenty of entertainment and conversation to divert me along the way. Anna was never far from my side. My dad and a friend, two old men of the mountains, had plenty of tales to tell. My sister Louise and her partner Neil had come out for a rare trip into the hills. Even Geoff Allan, out of hospital now, was there, a breath of sanity waiting at every other bend in the track with refreshments and philosophical thoughts.

With the help of this fine support and views like I hadn't seen in a long time, I trudged wearily on, ignoring the circus around me, and progressed slowly up the hill.

Finally I came over a slight rise and there ahead of me was an aluminium bridge spanning a small ravine that cut the path in two. It was the landmark for which I'd been aiming for the last hour or so. It had been the target in my head, the first rung on a mental ladder stretching ahead of me to the distant summit of the hill.

Unfortunately the Ben Nevis tourist path is not the most exciting mountain climb in the world, and I found it helpful to break up the assignment into more manageable portions, but I was actually having difficulty in remembering suitable milestones with which to punctuate this walk. My ladder was woefully short of rungs, the voids in between reaching ahead into long, tedious chunks.

It's not that I hadn't been that way often enough before. In fact, I couldn't even begin to count how many times I'd trudged up there, sweating and cursing under a heavy rucksack, bound for another climbing trip on the north face. Or, travelling light, trotted up to the summit on a summer's evening to catch the last rays of sun before strolling back down in the never-ending twilight. Or stumbled down, in the depths of winter, slithering over icy rocks in the dim light of a fading head torch.

These were all memories that served me well in reflective moments, but when it came to recalling the topography of the route ahead of me, they let me down. I had never paid much attention, never had much of a thought for the boring old tourist path up the Ben.

Now my sights had changed. Since my world had been so rudely turned on its head a year past last January, everything in my life had taken on an altered significance. The mundane became a challenge. The tedious became new and exciting. Easy became difficult and difficult became impossible – almost, and the tourist track up Ben Nevis had become an aspiration.

Five and a half hours after setting out, I arrived on the familiar summit plateau that was still partially covered by lingering snow. Clouds boiling out of the icy cauldron of the north face revaporised as they blew over the warmer summit air and helicopters, courtesy of the RAF and the BBC, flew spectacularly overhead. A huge crowd was waiting to cheer my arrival, champagne corks popped, and of course, as laptops and mobile phones came out, another deluge of interviews began. I hugged Anna and posed next to the summit for the cameras, looking elated and feeling bemused and overwhelmed.

Al Sylvester told me that he had a surprise arranged for me. The RAF helicopter was going to pick me up and take me for a tour of the mountain. The wind on the summit was light and the big yellow machine was able to touch down right on the plateau, just for long enough to allow me to scramble aboard and be whisked off for a ten-minute view of Ben Nevis like I'd never seen it before.

I thought for a sneaky moment that I could now be spared the long walk down, but the RAF boys were not so unscrupulous and they set the helicopter down again in precisely the same spot to let me out.

After all the summit celebrations and shenanigans were over I suddenly realised how weary I was feeling. I had been on the go for a long time now and I hadn't even had a chance to sit down and have a rest. For the press, the event was over – the quadruple amputee had reached the summit of Ben Nevis. For me the hard part was still to come – descending 4,500 feet on my already tired and painful legs.

The descent lived up to all expectations and was a slow and exhausting grind, by the end of which I was hobbling rather than walking, leaning heavily on my sticks and wincing with every step. Eventually, after what seemed like an age, the very welcome sight of the pub at Achintee loomed out of the gathering gloom. A small crowd waited to greet me and I waved gratefully at them as I carried on past, up the steps of the bar and in to slump into the largest arm-chair I could find, where thankfully the most appreciated pint of beer ever was waiting for me.

As a footnote to the story of my Ben Nevis ascent, which raised many thousands of pounds for charity, it's worth mentioning another good thing that came out of it. By unwittingly forcing many not very fit ladies and gentlemen of the press to climb the hill with me, I helped to introduce them to the joys of hillwalking. Several of them told me afterwards that they'd had a fantastic day and wanted to go out in the hills again. Mention must be made, however, of one poor photographer, on commission for a broadsheet paper, who against his better judgement made the long journey for the all-important summit shot. This unfortunate soul suffered terribly with exhaustion, sciatica and blisters on the ascent, but he persevered valiantly. Finally he reached the summit, only to discover that I had just left and he'd missed the shot. So he turned tail and staggered back down, arriving once again some time after me. Next morning the paper ran with a photo purchased from Reuters.

A few weeks after my ascent of Ben Nevis, accompanied by Anna, Geoff and Chris Pasteur, I did the round of Cairn an Tuirc and Carn na Claise from Glenshee. Moorland birds sang in the sunny sky and we took our time as we climbed through the heather, gaz-ing northward towards the Cairngorms, eastwards over the Mounth to Lochnagar and westwards into the wild lands beyond An Socach. At one point we spotted some other walkers, in the dis-tance, enjoying their day. Ben Nevis had been fun, a once-in-a-life-time experience, but this is what I'd missed. This was the freedom which I'd had taken from me and had had to fight so hard to enjoy once more.

By most standards I was very mobile now. I had climbed Ben Nevis, which made me fitter than most, I could run about twice round a running track without stopping, and I was very rarely forced to use the wheelchair any more.

In one respect, though, I still felt handicapped and that was driving. Wherever we went Anna was the one who drove the car and I was very much reliant on her for transportation. Getting to and from work I took taxis, paid for by the Employment Service. All that changed in August, however, when I got myself a brand-new car.

When I'd first considered the problem of how I was going to manage to drive a car, I'd imagined that a fairly serious conversion would be necessary. I knew that there were special car conversions available which enabled even the most severely disabled people to drive so I was certain that it would be possible, although I couldn't quite imagine how.

When I examined the problem in greater detail, however, I discovered that the difficulty wasn't as great as I'd first thought. Sitting in the front seat of a car, I experimented with all the controls. Gear stick and handbrake I could manage OK. Indicators, lights and windscreen wipers I could handle too. The steering wheel I found difficult with just my stumps. The accelerator and footbrake I could control quite accurately with my right leg, but I couldn't really operate the clutch with my left leg.

If the car was automatic, I thought, the biggest difficulty would be the steering wheel. Malcolm came up with an off-the-shelf solution to this. He produced a steering ball that could be fixed onto any car steering wheel, and a corresponding steel cup which he laminated into a socket for my right arm. Wearing this steering arm, I pushed the cup onto the ball which produced a sort of universal joint with which I could turn the wheel.

Armed with my new equipment I went down to my local driving assessment centre where I was put through my paces driving round and round the car park. My assessor eventually gave me a clean bill of health and I was free to drive as soon as I could get an automatic car.

When my car arrived I immediately took to the streets to terrorise the neighbourhood. It felt very peculiar at first, steering with this strange contraption on my arm and accelerating and braking with my artificial foot, but I gradually got used to it and I now find driving no more difficult than I did before my accident. The best part of it is that the car I drive is almost unaltered. This both means that anyone else can drive my car (the steering ball is detachable) and I can drive any other automatic car simply by fixing on the steering ball.

One more step on the road to living a normal life.

That summer, in July, Anna and I were married at a small private ceremony near Edinburgh. The press had found out about it but fortunately they never found out where or when it was, so we were left in peace for our special day. Anna looked absolutely stunning, I did my best to look smart in my kilt, and our closest family and closest friends joined us for what was the happiest day of my life.

Then we headed down to the Lake District where we had hired the biggest marquee we could lay our hands on and threw the most extravagant party of our lives. We invited all our friends who had played such a special part in what had been a very difficult year and a half for us, and it was absolutely wonderful to see everyone in the same place at the same time. Manu and Pascale even managed to make it over, representing our new Chamonix friends. Anna and I talked and ate and drank and danced until we could keep our eyes open no longer and were forced to stumble, delirious with happiness, off to bed.

CHAPTER THIRTY-THREE

Reaching New Heights

By SPRING 2000 I was achieving so much, so many unexpected things that I could hardly keep pace with myself. Apart from leading a fairly normal life, at home and at work, I was now capable of hill-walking, snowboarding, sailing, caving, running, orienteering, and many other sports. I was enjoying life far beyond my initial expectations. However, there was still one thing missing. There was still one thing I yearned to do again and there are no prizes for guessing what. I wanted to go climbing again.

The morning after I returned home from hospital, on an impulse, Anna and I drove down to the Lake District and checked into a hotel for the night. It was our first chance to spend some proper quality time together in ages. We went for a boat trip on Derwent Water and I managed a short walk along the shore to Friar's Crag.

I remember from the lake we could see antlike rows of hillwalkers outlined against the skyline on the fells. On nearby crags we spotted the colourful dots of climbers, inching their way up sunny rock faces. I sat and watched the tiny figures for a long time. Even then I knew. 'I want to go back up there,' I said to Anna. 'I want to climb again.'

'I know you do,' said Anna, 'and I know you will.'

I suppose it was inevitable really. I wouldn't go so far as to say I couldn't live without climbing, but it was what I did. As a teenager

I used to think that climbing, with its heady blend of excitement, adventure, beauty, challenge and danger, was the only thing that gave my life meaning, and made it worth living.

As I grew older and my horizons broadened, I realised that climbing wasn't the be all and end all. It was, however, that special ingredient which made my life unique to me and helped shape my personal identity. Now that my individuality was determined by a much more physical and obvious uniqueness I no longer felt the need of climbing to define who I am. Nevertheless I still wanted to go back there. Partly I wanted to climb again to show that I hadn't been beaten. I wanted to take up the challenge, no matter how great, and prove to my friends, to the world, to myself that I wouldn't be defeated. But partly I wanted to climb again because I knew I still loved it, and if there was even the slightest possibility that I might be able to do it again then I was going to give it a shot.

I wasn't put off by the tragedy that befell Jamie and me. It certainly shook me up, but it didn't kill off the passion I had for mountains and mountaineering, and I was a 100 per cent certain that Jamie, were he alive, would have wanted me to return to the mountains, just as I was sure that he would return to the mountains himself if he was in my position.

So I made up my mind that I would do my utmost to find my way back into the mountains and onto the rock faces. I had absolutely no idea how I would go about doing it, but I felt sure I would find a way. I knew I would be more cautious this time around. I was never going to push my own limits in quite the same way, but I resolved to do my own thing, in my own way, and make the most of what talents I had left.

Gradually I formulated a plan for getting back into rock climbing. Over the course of many weeks I thought very carefully about the difficulties I faced and how I might counter them. I didn't foresee my feet as being too great an issue. They were nice and stiff and when put them into a pair of sticky rubber rock shoes I imagined I would be able to stand on small footholds quite securely. My lack of hands though was another matter. I mean, hands are fairly fundamental to the whole rock-climbing business. Without them the thought of hauling myself up a steep rock face seemed impossible.

In my head I devised some equipment that might help me get over this basic problem. Once I had figured out the exact design, I was going to ask Malcolm and Rob to make me a pair of hooks, kind of like grappling hooks, which could be attached to my arms by some sort of prosthetic socket and harness mechanism. I would first be able to try out these hooks in the secure environment of the local indoor climbing wall, and develop them into the best size, shape and alignment for hooking securely over various types of handholds. I would then be in a position to venture onto an outdoor crag where I would hopefully be able to do some simple rock climbing, providing the holds were all positive enough. Obviously my hooks were to be a temporary measure while mankind developed a proper bionic hand with which I could resume rock climbing normally, but in the meantime they would provide the means for me to achieve my goal. That was the plan.

Then the plan went out of the window one evening in March when Chris Pasteur and Jane Herries gave us a call. They were going down to Northumberland the next day for a bit of climbing and asked Anna and me if we'd like to join them.

The forecast was good, and Northumberland is a lovely place, so we thought, why not? More out of habit than anything else, I packed some climbing gear.

The strangely named Bowden Doors is a beautiful crag, the best in Northumberland. It's a mile-long escarpment, up to 45 feet in height, stretching majestically across the crest of the lonely moors west of Belford. The rock is a wonderfully compact, golden sandstone that glows the most incredible shades of yellow, orange and red in the setting sun. It's always been one of my favourite places to climb.

That day was a typically sunny day at Bowden, despite it being early in the season, and the sun soon warmed the chilly rock. Chris and Jane did a couple of routes, while Anna and I walked along the foot of the crag and I dug up old memories – all the climbs I'd done here. We passed underneath all the old favourites: Main Wall, Castle Crack, Lorraine, Tiger Wall. And the more-hard-fought conquests: the Manta, with that desperate move left into the crack; the Sting, with its horrendous rounded sandy finish; the brilliant Poseidon Adventure; and the extremely awkward Rajah. They were all climbs that occupied a part of me and my climbing history.

I stopped beneath a route called His Eminence. I never did manage that. Not for want of trying though. I'd been trying for years. Dozens of times I had made the beautiful series of sketchy moves up the bulging wall and reached that crucial set of finger pockets, like the holes in a bowling ball, only to lose contact and come flying off, tumbling onto the springy turf below, where the impacts of countless feet had carved a dusty crater.

I never got frustrated by His Eminence though, because I always assumed that one day I would manage it. One day the bowling-ball hold would provide the key and open up the secrets of the last few moves, and I would suddenly find myself standing on top, with His Eminence under my belt.

Not now though. Now it was to be added to the long list of climbs I would never do – cancelled ambitions.

We rejoined Chris and Jane who were back on the ground.

'What's it to be then, Jim Jam?' prompted Chris.

'I really don't think there's much point. It's all too steep.'

'Well, what have you got to lose?'

'Nothing, but I'll be very slow.'

'We've got all day.'

So I decided to give it a go and Chris, Jane and Anna set about getting me into a harness and levering my uncooperative feet into a rather tight-fitting pair of rock shoes. After a ten-minute struggle, the shoes snapped into place and I slipped the legs back on and stood up, ready for action.

Most of Bowden Doors is steep and uncompromising, but at the far right-hand end of the crag, a sloping ramp cuts an easy angled passage between vertical walls. Graded Moderate*, Introductory Staircase is the easiest route at Bowden Doors and seemed the obvious choice for my first attempt at climbing.

Chris swiftly led up the climb and settled himself down on the top of the crag to belay me up. As soon as he was ready, Anna tied me into the rope, checked that the soles of my shoes were clean and wished me luck.

---

*The British system of climbing grades is rather idiosyncratic. In ascending order of difficulty it begins with Easy, Moderate (Mod), Difficult (Diff), Very Difficult (VDiff), Severe, Very Severe (VS) and Hard Very Severe (HVS), followed by an open-ended Extremely Severe grade (E1, E2, E3, E4, etc).

I turned my attention to the rock. Instantly, that familiar feeling of complete focus took over me. Chris, Jane, Anna, other onlookers, my surroundings, all receded into periphery and the rock became everything, absorbing the whole of my concentration. The rock at that part of the crag runs to a lot of flat edges, and I found that the angle was relaxed enough that I could stand in balance on the flat holds. I could feel very little through my feet and I kept convincing myself that they were slowly slipping off, but every time I looked down to check they were still securely in place.

I couldn't really pull up with my arms, but where I could get them onto a good flat surface below shoulder level, I could push down effectively. Using a combination of leverage with my arms and careful footwork, I inched my way slowly upwards, taking time and great care over every single move. Eventually I was able to pull over onto the first of several large ledges that split the ramp. The next ledge was at just over head height and it took some cunning manoeuvres with my back bracing against the side wall of the ramp to gain the ledge and sprawl over onto it.

The final ledge was a good deal higher up and it took a long time, bridging between the two facets of the ramp, and searching out ways to make best use of the various handholds that presented themselves, before I reached it.

I was very surprised that up until that point I hadn't fallen off. The top was now just above me, and success seemed within reach, but the last couple of metres proved the hardest and it was another ten minutes or so, doing some very tricky and tenuous bridging, before I pulled over onto the flat top of the crag to join Chris.

'Nice one,' said Chris. 'How was that?'

'Desperate!' I replied, sprawling flat out next to him. 'It felt more like an E3 than a Mod.'

'Excellent. Want to do another one then?'

I had taken over forty minutes to climb 35 feet, my stumps were rubbed raw by the rough sandstone, and I was completely exhausted.

'Yeah, all right then.'

I made my way back down to the foot of the crag while Chris set up a rope on the second easiest route at Bowden – Second Staircase, graded Diff.

Second Staircase starts with a large, smooth, but easy-angled slab, and it took me quite a while to link together a sequence of moves to overcome it. The slab landed me on a large ledge, the frequent haunt of rooks, judging by the presence of scattered twigs and other debris. Above loomed a blocky overhang, shattered by many cracks. It was only a short obstacle but very definitely overhanging, and I didn't much fancy my chances of being able to pull over it.

I supposed I'd better give it a go though, and I began by working my way as high as I could beneath the overhang, into the sort of shallow cave where the birds roosted. Once established under the overhang, I discovered that the rightmost of the cracks that split it was nearly wide enough to wedge my body into. Pedalling my feet on the right wall, I got my head, my left arm, and my left shoulder established in the crack. I then wriggled for all I was worth, frantically trying to win some ground. My progress was painfully slow and several times I slipped back, losing preciously won inches, but eventually I got first one arm, then the other, over onto the top of the crag. All the while I was vaguely conscious of shouts of encouragement coming up from the foot of the crag. It took a further ten minutes of wriggling, my head level with Chris's knees, which were shaking with laughter, before I managed to extricate the rest of my body and land gasping on the top next to Chris.

'Harder?' asked Chris.

'Definitely E4,' I wheezed.

So that was it. I went home that night feeling absolutely elated. I was utterly shattered, every muscle in my body felt drained and sore and I was sure that my stumps, as raw as pieces of beaten meat, would never be the same again, but I didn't care because I'd been rock climbing again. Against all the odds I had realised my dream and managed to climb a near-vertical rock face. I had thought I'd come up against a lot more technical problems in learning to climb again, but in the end it was as simple as putting on a pair of rock shoes and having a go.

After Bowden Anna and I started visiting our local climbing wall regularly where I began to develop and expand upon the new techniques I had learnt in Northumberland. Over the months I got more

279

and more proficient until I was eventually climbing things that I would never had dreamed were possible when I started out.

Generally I had to use every ounce of my strength, skill, stamina and cunning to lever my way up the mainly vertical or overhanging faces of the climbing wall. I devised all sorts of ways of using my arms, elbows, shoulders, back, hips, knees, legs and feet to hold myself on and to pull and push myself up, and I came to realise that holding on and pulling up are not so much about fingers but about friction, especially friction between rock (or artificial plastic rock) and skin. Wherever I could get friction I could get purchase. And where I had purchase I had the possibility of staying in contact with the rock and even progressing up it.

My stumps soon got very tough and I learnt how to hook them over small holds, torque them into cracks, jam them into holes and crevices, lever them behind flakes, anything to get some all-important purchase on the rock. I also learnt how to handle the ropes, taking them in and paying them out using my elbows for grip.

The downside of all this rough treatment my stumps were getting was that by the end of each session they were always completely raw, red, throbbing and covered in scratches. Sometimes they were so painful that I couldn't even hold my bag and I had to get Anna to carry it home.

I persevered though, and after a few months I had managed dozens of different routes at the wall, including several which were actually overhanging.

Spurred on by my success at the climbing wall, I ventured out to the real crags more and more often. I think the day when I really satisfied myself that I had made my comeback was in August that year when Chris, Jane, Andy Hume and I made an ascent of a very well-known climb in Borrowdale, in the Lake District, called appropriately enough Little Chamonix. In fact, the last time I had done Little Chamonix was with Jamie Fisher as part of his great Classic Rock Challenge. On that occasion we had soloed the route, climbing quickly and easily while the last of the afternoon sunshine gently warmed the rock. In ten minutes we were sitting together on the top, a projecting platform of rock known as the Belvedere, our legs dangling over the void, discussing the logistics of the next few days of the Challenge, and looking out over the beautiful valley of Borrowdale.

Today Little Chamonix proved a good deal more time-consuming. Ten minutes solo climbing for a couple of fit, confident young lads, translated into three difficult and sustained roped pitches for a party of four including a quadruple amputee.

The first pitch was slabby but with small, rounded holds and it took me a long time to find the correct sequence of foot movements that led up to a series of earthy, tree-covered ledges, beyond which lay the meat of the climb.

The second pitch was a lot more fun. A slabby groove leads up to beneath a series of large overhangs which block access to the final, steep wall. Directly under the overhangs, invisible from below, a large block forms a ledge on which the climber can sit and rest, contemplating their next move.

Sitting on this block I peered nervously across at the way ahead. A difficult step off the block, down and across another slabby groove, led to a rib leading upwards and round the side of the overhang. However, the step across was awkward and without the security of a good couple of fingerholds in an obvious horizontal crack, the move was going to be extra precarious. Eventually, after dithering for an unnecessarily long period of time, cheered on by Andy and Jane above me and Chris behind me, I slithered off the block and found a purchase in the groove. A few further difficult moves and I heaved my way onto the famous 'à cheval' stance – a tiny saddle of rock perched below the spectacular final pitch.

The last pitch of Little Chamonix is steep and intimidating, and in the classic and much-photographed view from a vantage point further along the summit of the cliff, it appears considerably harder than the given grade of VDiff.

And indeed it felt considerably harder than VDiff to me, but fortunately what you can't see in the classic photo are the huge holds, like rungs of a ladder, that march up the rock, and also the partly detached rock flake that creates a sort of shallow chimney into which the body can be semi-wedged in order to give tiring arms a much-needed break.

Expecting to have to rely heavily on the rope and the strong pull of Andy, I launched up the steep wall. I didn't make fast progress, but I soon found that the holds were big enough so I could cling comfortably to the rock. The difficulty was moving from one hold to the next. Fortunately my training on the steep faces of the climbing wall paid off and I gradually worked out ways of levering my body up the face. The climbing was desperate and with each move I felt sure I was on the point of peeling off, but somehow I maintained a fragile contact with the rock. Meanwhile Chris climbed directly behind me, pointing out footholds that I couldn't see as I closely hugged the face.

When I reached the chimney flake, I jammed first my shoulders, then my hips, my knees and my feet thankfully behind it. There then followed an almighty struggle, during which my helmet got wedged completely, until I eventually emerged gasping on top of the flake. A few further moves and it was all over – I was sitting on top of the Belvedere.

While Chris, Jane and Andy fussed round congratulating me, sorting out the ropes and the equipment, I looked out at that familiar view and savoured the much-missed feeling of being at the top of a difficult climb which I had just conquered. I had completed my first 'real' multi-pitch climb. What's more I hadn't fallen off once. I had done it completely free and had needed no special equipment. I felt justified in telling the world that I was a climber once more.

CHAPTER THIRTY-FOUR

Mountain Activities

Malcolm paled visibly. 'I knew this was coming sometime,' he said quietly.

'But do you think you can do it?' I implored.

'Oh, I'm sure we could do it all right,' he replied. 'It's just that we'd have to make sure that my employer isn't going to be liable if there's an accident. Ice climbing is after all a risky activity.'

'Hazardous,' I corrected him. 'The activity is hazardous and it's the climber's job to limit the risk as far as possible. That's why I've come to see you.'

'Well OK, but we'll have to undertake a fairly serious risk assessment.'

'Does that mean you'll do it?' I asked, picking up on Malcolm's use of the future perfect tense.

Malcolm shrugged and sighed. 'Why not?' he conceded. 'But we'll have to get Rob on board too.'

Rob, when we approached him, was enthusiastic.

'We're here to facilitate your rehabilitation,' he reasoned. 'If ice climbing is what you did before your accident, and you want to go ice climbing again, then it's our job to help you do it.'

So the three of us began designing and building a pair of prosthetic ice axes.

We started in February 2001 but in March the job suddenly became more urgent when I received a call from Manu Cauchy inviting me out to Chamonix in a couple of months' time, on this occasion to attempt some climbing. If the axes were to be ready in time we were going to have to get our skates on. The NHS, despite the excellent facilities it provides, is not renowned for its speed of service, but Rob and Malcolm pulled out all the stops to get the job done in time for my departure.

I began by approaching a Scottish manufacturer of ice axes who kindly supplied the component parts of the type of axe I wanted to emulate. Rob cut the shafts of the axes down to the required length and designed an additional component that would attach the axe shaft into the top of a prosthetic stump socket.

Meanwhile Malcolm took a cast of my right arm and began laminating a socket. Using carbon fibre strengthening strips he laminated in the junction component Rob had made. The axe shaft and head were fixed to this and the first prototype was almost ready.

The difficult part, however, was holding the socket onto my arm. Malcolm had made it clear from the outset of the project that none of the standard methods of prosthetic arm suspension would be strong enough to hold my full weight when hanging from an ice axe. His socket, therefore, would rely on me providing my own method of secure suspension.

Time was now running out. If I didn't get the suspension sorted out in the next couple of weeks, the axe would be useless for my trip to Chamonix and would have to wait several more months to be tested.

With the help of some colleagues at Web, I designed a harness that secured the ice axe socket to my elbow. This harness in turn was attached to a standard climber's chest harness, guaranteeing that even if the axe slipped, it wouldn't come off my arm entirely. I got the harness made up by a friend who runs a mountaineering equipment manufacturing company and finally the prototype axe was ready to use the day before I left Edinburgh for France.

Chamonix in May 2001 was warm and foggy. Conditions the locals refer to as a *föhn* – a warm, dry wind from the Mediterranean that cools rapidly as it hits the high mountain slopes producing the characteristic fog that can last for weeks.

Manu and I skulked about in the valley for a couple of days, visiting friends and getting fat on good food and wine. I was starting to think that I might be going home without even seeing the mountains when on the third day the weather cleared.

That morning, Manu, Philippe Pouts and I took the rattly old funicular railway up to Montenvers above the snout of the great glacier, the Mer de Glace. From Montenvers it was a difficult twenty-minute walk down steep slabs and loose boulders to the surface of the glacier.

Free of the snows of winter, the glacier ice was iron hard, a dirty, bluey grey, peppered with grit ground from the bedrock over which the frozen river flowed. The sun baked down and pools of meltwater lurked in every hollow of the rippled ice surface.

Manu and Poutsy strapped my crampons to my feet. The feet were rigid and I was unlikely to be bothered if they were cold, so I had no need of mountain boots. We simply strapped the crampons over my shoes.

Crampons on, we marched on up the glacier, heading for a series of crevasses that cut through the slope and whose steep walls provide the ideal venue for an ice-climbing school. The crevasses were quite shallow with solid floors and it was possible to walk in to both the tops and the bottoms of them, making it easy to set up top ropes and practice ice climbing in complete safety.

As I only had the one axe we selected an ice wall that wasn't too steep – about 50 degrees – and while Manu went and set up the rope, Poutsy helped me into a harness and helmet and strapped me into my ice axe.

Trussed up in all my climbing equipment, I felt distinctly ungainly and dependent on the others, and with my bizarre cramponed legs and one half-arm, half-ice axe, I was certainly a strange sight to behold.

I was ready for action though, and as soon as I was tied into the end of the rope I tackled the ice wall ahead of me. The axe swung well and as the pick struck the ice it bit nicely, sinking halfway to the hilt. When I tried to pull myself up on it, however, something in the angle between the shaft and the prosthesis caused the pick to rotate out and I fell backwards, my weight toppling onto the rope.

I tried again, this time taking more care as I pulled up, and kicked my crampons one after the other into the ice. Again, the pick slipped, but I kept my balance this time, removed it carefully from the ice, and knocked it in higher up.

This was working! The axe still tended to rotate out, forcing me to lean out on it as I pulled up, rather than keeping my weight in close to the wall as I would have preferred, but nevertheless it was working and I was making progress up the wall.

As I climbed, Poutsy shouted encouragement and incomprehensible French instructions from below and Manu gave similar directions from above. Ignoring them both I concentrated on placing my axe carefully and pulling up on it without pulling it out. The wall was only 20 feet high or so and it wasn't long before I teetered my way to the top. My heart was pounding with excitement now and I lost no time in getting Poutsy to lower me back down so that I could do it again.

It was only a little crevasse, I know, but I felt extraordinarily privileged to be back in the Alps once more, climbing among those wonderful mountains.

The prototype axe obviously needed a little redesign work but the main thing was it functioned in principle and it stood me in good stead a couple of days later when my French friends and I made our ascent of the Cosmiques Arête.

Some time later, back in the UK, Malcolm, Rob and I returned to constructing the ice axes. Rob redesigned his junction component with a new angle, Malcolm made two more prosthetic sockets, one for each arm, and I made some design modifications to my suspension harnesses. I also had a mountaineering jacket specially modified to fit over the axes. Finally, just in time for the winter of 2002, both axes were ready.

This time I trialled the equipment on my home ground of Scotland. Chris Pasteur, Andy Hume and I made the most of an unpromising-looking day and took the ski gondola up Aonach Mor. Below the summit of the mountain, over the back of the ridge from the ski slopes, is a large corrie ringed with cliffs.

From the summit, we made a short abseil down the wide descent gully then traversed round the foot of the cliffs until we were below a trio of icy gullies known oddly as The Twins. Our climb was the Left Twin, a grade III ice climb, and it was positively drooling with lovely-looking ice, despite the warm conditions.

Andy, champing at the bit, quickly fired up the first pitch and before long I was tackling it myself while Chris climbed alongside me for support. The new axes were a great improvement and I found I could heave myself with confidence up the bulging ice. Without my wrists I had a good deal less flexibility about where and how I placed the axes but at least when I did get a good placement I could pull up securely on it.

My feet too, without ankles, were a lot less flexible, and it was often difficult to kick my crampons securely in. On the plus side I was spared the screaming calf muscles that are normally such a memorable feature of steep ice climbing.

Strapped into the two axes I was completely incapable of doing anything for myself apart from climb, and was totally reliant on the others for help with rope work, adjustments to clothes, eating snacks and so on, but this seemed a small price to pay for the freedom of being able to climb in the Scottish mountains again.

The climb went well and a few hours later the three of us, and a couple of other friends who caught up with us, were standing on the summit, congratulating each other, comparing notes and taking photos, in the background Ben Nevis glowing pink in the winter afternoon sunlight. As soon as we were back at the Aonach Mor ski station I phoned home to tell Anna all about it.

CHAPTER THIRTY-FIVE

A Long Run

I don't recall precisely when I decided to run the marathon. I just remember there was more and more talk about it, in the pub especially, and then suddenly one day I was committed.

Back in the summer of 1999, Anna and I, and a few other friends, had gone along to watch the Edinburgh Marathon and cheer on our mate John Irving. I recall watching those crowds of athletes flood past and finding the whole event so exciting and inspiring that I longed to be able to take part myself one day.

Now, two years later, Geoff Allan and I made a pact to run the London Marathon together. At this stage the furthest I had run was round the block – about a mile and a quarter. The prospect of running over 26 miles seemed a little daunting.

The British Red Cross were happy to provide me with a place in the marathon and at the beginning of December, with four and a half months to go, I began my training.

It all felt pretty futile to begin with. My thrice-weekly jogs around the block were broken by frequent emergency stops to sort out my legs. If I didn't stop to take off the legs, dry the sweat off the silicone liners and my stumps, and put the legs carefully back on again, they were likely to come flying off unexpectedly leaving me literally without a leg to stand on – not a prospect I relished running along a busy road.

The stops were necessary about every half a mile and I couldn't get into any sort of a rhythm. By the time I'd staggered round a mile and a half circuit I was exhausted and couldn't possibly imagine running any further. It felt like my legs were made out of lead and that I was running through treacle.

Out of pure stubbornness, however, I continued, and after a few weeks I managed to up my distance to about three miles, stopping as often as five times along the way to fix my legs.

I asked Morag if there was anything to be done about the sweat problem but she said it was a common one and there was little I could do apart from trying out various anti-perspirants. However, as I got fitter, she said, the sweating in my legs should reduce.

Then, over Christmas and New Year, things went from bad to worse. A muscle strain in my lower back kept me from running for a few days. Just as the back pain got better, I developed a nasty abscess in the flesh of my left stump, stopping me from even walking for a couple of days and putting the running training back by another two weeks.

Time was marching on and I didn't feel I was getting anywhere. As the stump sore got better I eased myself gently back into my running programme then gradually started upping the mileage. As I managed my first four-mile runs I really began to enjoy the running. It was hard work and could be horribly gruelling running for miles into a chilly headwind, but after each run, once I was back home, showered and changed, I felt a warm glow of satisfaction and achievement that lasted for the rest of the day. However, I still couldn't possibly imagine running a full 26.2 miles.

But then, one grim day at the end of January, I reached a turning point. I had been mooching about the flat trying to work up the enthusiasm to go for a run and had finally got changed into my running gear when I glanced out of the window to check the weather.

I couldn't see the other side of the street. The air was heavy with dense swirling snow and already a thick white layer was blanketing the road and pavements. My heart sank. Obviously I wasn't going out in that. Another day's training lost. As I went to get changed, however, I kept thinking to myself, Come on, Jamie. This isn't the attitude. Don't be a wimp. It's only a bit of snow. You're supposed to be able to cope with snow. You're supposed to be a hard man for God's sake.

And suddenly I made up my mind to go for it.

Once I was outside the snow didn't feel so bad at all. In fact it felt great. It kept me cool and sweat free and the inch-thick carpet beneath my feet gave me pleasantly soft running. The streets were eerily deserted and silent and when I turned down off the road onto the paths of The Hermitage the quiet was absolute. I was so happy to be out and running on such a day and I felt unstoppable. In fact, when I arrived back at the flat having completed my usual four-mile circuit I felt so good I carried on running and did it all again!

A fortnight later I managed my first half marathon, along the banks of the Water of Leith, running ten miles then walking three, and the prospect of completing a full marathon finally looked like being a real possibility.

But another week later a further setback reared its ugly head. After running 12 miles out along the Union Canal and back I developed a strange sharp pain in the end of my right leg. After a week of continued pain, training being confined to the gym, I was getting worried and made appointments to see Morag and my consultant, Mr MacDonald.

Morag and Mr Macdonald both thought the pain was caused by bursitis – an inflammation of a protective fluid-filled sack that had developed around the end of my tibia. Neither Morag nor Mr Mac-Donald could suggest any treatment apart from resting it. However, if I was going to run a marathon in five weeks' time I couldn't afford to rest it much longer. Meanwhile I continued with my low-impact training in the gym, but I found it hard to keep motivated for long training sessions in an indoor environment.

On 20 March my leg was still no better, and with only three weeks to go I was beginning to panic and seriously considered pulling out, but with a substantial amount of sponsorship money riding on me I felt under great pressure to carry on. In desperation I visited Mr MacDonald again and persuaded him to X-ray the leg. The X-ray revealed the root cause of the inflammation to be a spur of bone that had continued to grow from the end of my tibia since it was amputated. It was interesting to know the reason for the pain but little consolation as there was still nothing Mr MacDonald could do about it. He reassured me, however, that it wasn't serious and that there was no particular reason why I shouldn't run on it, so long as I could take the pain! He wished me luck.

In the corridor of the hospital I bumped into my other consultant, Mr Howie. When I explained my problem to him, Mr Howie just looked at me and shook his head.

'You're running twenty-six miles on prosthetic legs and you're complaining about having sore stumps? If you ask me, it's no bloody wonder!'

Over the following week I continued my mindless, repetitive routine in the gym, feeling more and more despondent, and was just about to pull the plug on my attempt at the marathon that year when my leg suddenly stopped hurting. Not knowing whether I would be wise to resume training on it immediately, I called Peter Arnott from my disabled training group in Sheffield.

I expected to be told that I would be foolish to attempt the marathon but Peter's advice surprised me. He said, 'Never mind the training, Jamie. It's too late for that now. Just a couple of short runs to keep yourself in shape. Then go out on the day and enjoy yourself. Remember, it's not a competitive event, it's the London Marathon and it doesn't matter how long it takes you to finish it. And if I know you like I think I know you, Jamie, you'll finish it if it's the last thing you do.'

So with bloody-minded determination, and encouraged by Peter's faith in me, I decided to go for it.

I woke at 6.30 a.m. on 14 April, Marathon Day, with butterflies in my stomach. I tried to force down a little light breakfast but I was too sick with nerves, so I kissed Anna goodbye, she wished me luck, and I walked out of our friends' flat in Islington to get the tube. Specially laid-on trains took me and my fellow competitors to the start at Blackheath Park where despite the crowds I managed to meet up with Geoff and also Jamie Gillespie, my amputee friend who was running his first marathon since losing his leg.

The incredible mass of runners pushing to get to the start and to use the rows and rows of portaloos was quite overwhelming and before long, despite having left plenty of time, I was rushing to get changed and adjust my legs, and already it was time to go. There's really nothing to compare with the feeling of being one of 32,000 runners, packed into a great big line, preparing to run the race of your life. Geoff and Jamie looked confident. I was seriously questioning what I was doing there.

Then at 9.45 the starting gun boomed, there was a roar from the crowd, and my nervous tension evaporated into the excitement of the race.

The first six or seven miles were fantastic. Carried along with the thrill of the event, the three of us jogged along, probably at too fast a pace, while all along the streets people clapped and cheered. We chatted to other runners and took plenty of water as we passed through the frequent drinks stations. All the way we were running alongside rhinoceroses, clowns, pram-pushers, supermen, super-women, twenty-year-olds, eighty-year-olds, a man carrying a canoe, and thousands upon thousands of more ordinary-looking runners.

At Mile 9 we stopped for the first time so that Jamie and I could make adjustments to our legs. The strain was beginning to show already, but we carried on at our regular pace until we'd clocked up nearly 13 miles at Tower Bridge. There was a big boost for me on the bridge when I spotted Stu Fisher, Mat Fisher and JJ in the crowd. A little further on I spotted Anna and rushed over to give her a big sweaty hug before running on.

Then we passed the halfway mark at 13.1 miles – a major landmark as both Jamie and I were starting to flag now, paying for the fast pace we had set early on.

During the leg to the Isle of Dogs we walked for long sections. The break in my training plan was starting to show. Jamie left us to run at his own pace for a while. Down in Docklands, at Mile 20, my sister Louise jumped out of the crowd. I was really suffering now and had slowed right down.

Over the next few miles various friends appeared along the route giving much-needed support. Geoff stuck with me all the way and we leap-frogged Jamie each time he stopped to readjust his leg. I was very slow now and beginning to feel demoralised. Then we were overtaken by a camel.

'That is the last straw!' I complained.

'The one that broke the camel's back?' replied Geoff in his dead-pan way, and I couldn't suppress a laugh, despite my fatigue.

I was really struggling by Mile 23 when we met Anna and friends again but I knew then that I was going to do it. Nothing was going to stop me now. The last three miles were hell. Every muscle, every bone, every joint in my body screamed for submission but I wouldn't relent – not yet.

Finally, after what seemed like a lifetime of urging ourselves on, Geoff and I came round the bend from Birdcage Walk onto The Mall and there it was – the finish. Still an elusive 200 yards away. Somehow we found the energy to put on a final spurt of speed and crossed the line with a time of 5 hours and 56 minutes, to collapse with relief into the waiting arms of our friends.

It was all over. I'd done it. For so long I had doubted myself over this and almost despaired, but I'd stuck to my guns and now I'd done it. Running a marathon is something that nobody can ever take away from you. Once you've done it, you might never run another step in your life, but you'll always have that marathon under your belt, you'll always know that you're one of that special group of people that has pulled out all the stops and run the magic distance of 26.2 miles. I am privileged to have the additional pride of being one of the first quadruple amputees, perhaps even the first, to ever achieve that feat.

While I was training for the marathon, I had the good fortune to meet someone whose bravery, determination and strength of will have been an inspiration to many, and whose tragic circumstances mean that I no longer feel alone in my situation as a quadruple amputee.

I first heard about Olivia when I was contacted through my marathon charity appeal by her very worried partner, Robin Garrett. On 14 February 2002, Olivia Giles, a young, attractive and successful Edinburgh solicitor had been going about her everyday business when she was suddenly and unexpectedly struck down by meningococcal septicaemia, a lethal form of the meningitis bug.

By the time Olivia was finally admitted to hospital and diagnosed, she was extremely ill and it was very nearly too late to save her.

However, the doctors and surgeons fought to keep her alive and eventually, after several days, the disease was beaten. By then though, the septicaemia had caused irreparable damage to the extremities of Olivia's limbs. The price Olivia paid for her life was her hands and feet, all of which had to be amputated.

At the time Robin contacted me, Olivia was still very sick, under sedation, and wasn't yet aware of what had happened to her, so there would have been little point in me visiting her, but I did go and spend some time with Robin and his mother Elizabeth and did my best to reassure them that there was hope that Olivia might once again lead a worthwhile life. During our chat in a nearby coffee shop I made a particular effort to casually demonstrate how well I could manage, parking my car outside the door and handling my coffee cup with careless ease. The pair were obviously distraught with worry about Olivia but I hope my confidence at least did a little to hearten them.

A few weeks later, just before I was due to run the marathon, I finally met Olivia herself who was now out of danger and installed in a private room in the Astley Ainsley Hospital. I have to admit that at that first meeting Olivia didn't look so great. Her frail figure, dwarfed by the electric wheelchair in which she sat, was obviously much weakened by the ravages of the disease and the septicaemia had caused scarring to areas of her skin. What was obviously normally a beautiful head of golden hair was currently dry, frizzy and unkempt. However, when I entered the room and she immediately began firing question after question at me I knew at once that this was someone who hadn't lost her fighting spirit.

Olivia's freshly amputated stumps, legs and arms, hung limply from her body, useless as yet. Having come to think of myself as physically unique, it was very strange to be confronted with another person so similar to me. I had heard of and corresponded on the Internet with another couple of quadruple amputees, both meningococcal septicaemia survivors, one in London, one in New York, but had never met them. I had become friends with a guy called Steve Ball who had lost all his fingers and thumbs, one complete foot and half the other foot in a mountaineering accident in Alaska; but

Olivia was the first full quadruple amputee I had met, and to discover that she lived less than two miles away from me made the experience doubly extraordinary.

Olivia had a hundred and one questions for me about what it was like to be a quadruple amputee, how I managed and what kind of things I could do. It was strange for me to have an audience who was genuinely interested in every detail of how I coped without hands and feet.

As well as answers to Olivia's questions I felt I had a huge amount of information and advice for her but it was obviously all too much to exchange in one sitting, particularly as she had barely come to terms with what had happened to her and had only just begun to heal after her operations. So I began visiting Olivia regularly and over the weeks and months I watched her incredible development as she strove to cope with her disability. Along the way I did my best to be encouraging and give her the benefit of my own experiences – we never had a shortage of questions and answers for each other.

Olivia's amputations are at a similar level to my own, but she was faced with a greater trial than I was due to the large amount of harm the disease has done to her body. It was only due to the skill of her plastic surgeon that her knees and elbows were saved, but all four joints have suffered damage. Skin transplants have helped to repair the damage but her stumps therefore took a lot longer to heal up than mine did, and the transplanted and scarred areas have lost sensitivity. Nevertheless Olivia persevered with learning to cope with her new body and it was amazing, each time I visited, to see how much she was achieving. She worked really hard and I was continually fascinated to watch as she was confronted with the same difficulties I had come up against only three years before and how she persistently overcame those difficulties, often in much the same way as I had, sometimes in totally new and unexpected ways.

In what seemed like no time at all Olivia was dressing, taking care of herself, walking, cooking simple meals, working on her computer, and generally proving that my own achievements weren't so unique after all. Before long she had moved back home where she carries on the ongoing task of rebuilding her life, works on behalf of meningitis awareness campaigns, and continues to catch me up in terms of functionality.

Life and Limb

At our first meeting in April 2002, when Olivia was still reeling from the horror and shock of what had happened to her, and I casually announced that I intended to run the London Marathon, I don't think she quite believed me. Nor do I think she yet believed that she would ever walk again. I was certain, of course, that she would walk again, with or without my encouragement, but I know that at that stage in my own rehabilitation it would have made an enormous difference to me to even know of the existence of another quadruple amputee. I'm basically a selfish person, and have little idea of how to go about inspiring people, so I was very happy to have the opportunity to help someone who was going through what I had already been through, simply by being there and being myself.

CHAPTER THIRTY-SIX

The Cosmiques Arête

The day is drawing on now and Manu, Julio and I are gradually approaching the top of our climb.

Manu has made a good choice for my first big mountain route since the accident. I really enjoyed our day out on the Mer de Glace a couple of days ago, testing out my new axe in the crevasses, and it was great then being back among the mountains, but the Cosmiques Arête is my first proper climb and at last it feels like I have really come home.

Clambering over rocky steps, and across narrow snow arêtes, up steep corners and round bulging pinnacles, far above the smoky haze of Chamonix on one side and the immaculate whiteness of the glacier on the other, with the sun blazing down from a clear blue sky, I know at last that I've come full circle and that I'm a mountaineer again.

In the few short years of my life I've always been a climber. I've climbed as much as I possibly could, climbed because it was the only thing that seemed to make any sense. Then, when I fell to the deepest depths, I did the only thing I ever knew how to do and climbed back up again. Now I'm back where I left off, back in the mountains where it all began, climbing onwards to their summits.

It's at moments like this that I feel I am closest to Jamie Fisher, who will never come back again, but whose spirit will always be here, free among the mountains that he loved so much.

When we stop for a break I take the chance to get out my mobile and call Anna, who is stuck back in Edinburgh, head buried in her books, preparing for her exams, and I excitedly tell her what's been happening.

She's surprised to hear where I'm calling from but relieved to know that the climb is going well. I don't suppose Anna will ever really harbour the same passion for mountaineering that I have and she often has difficulty in understanding my own drive to return to the mountains that hurt us both so badly. She accepts, however, that it is a drive that I have and that mountaineering is part of the person I am.

Anna wishes us well with the rest of the climb, asks me to ring again when we're safely at the top, then ends the call. We climb on.

A steep rock prow bars the way. On the right a horizontal snowy ledge leads to the foot of an open corner that rises back up leftwards to rejoin the crest of the ridge. Julio is sitting on the crest and I have just about made the traverse into the corner when the snow beneath my right foot unexpectedly crumbles away. My heart stops as I begin to fall towards the glacier. But before I go anywhere my weight sinks onto my axe, hooked behind a large flake. At the same time the rope comes tight and I feel Julio's relentless pull, urging me upwards. I curse my mistake, scrabble my feet back onto the ledge, then set about climbing the corner.

I know that I'm lucky I'm able to do the things I do. Things could have turned out so different. If the frostbite had taken one knee ... one elbow ... I could easily have suffered kidney failure ... I could so easily have died.

Then again, I might not have got frostbite at all ... Jamie could so easily have lived ... the whole sorry tragedy need never have happened in the first place.

However, if there's one thing I've learnt over the last few years, it's not to dwell on what might have been. We only have one reality to deal with in this life and that's difficult enough so there's no point in dreaming up others.

So rather than brooding on my bad luck and wishing that things would have been different, I rejoice in my good luck and in all the good things that happen in my life. Most of all I am grateful that my second chance has given me the opportunity to be with, and to marry, the one person in this world who means the most to me.

I often think of my friend Jamie Gillespie and his assertion that losing his leg was the best thing that ever happened in his life and I ask myself whether I might ever make a similarly bold statement. Well, I don't suppose that I'll ever claim that losing all of my hands and feet was the most wonderful thing that ever happened to me, but on the other hand, since the accident I have enjoyed a fantastic life and I am totally positive that my future continues to be bright. My accident and its aftermath have generated all sorts of unexpected prospects for me, opened countless doors, and utterly changed my outlook on life, although many of my friends would tell you that I haven't changed a bit.

On balance I can't complain that the amputation of my limbs has had a negative effect on me. I no longer wake each morning, or from every carefree daydream, only to sink immediately into despair as I recall that I have no hands and feet – I've long since come to terms with my situation. Instead I view what happened to me as a landmark in my life. A defining moment – a punctuation mark. It is the full stop that denotes the end of one chapter in my life and the beginning of another – neither good nor bad.

I reach the top of the corner, Manu hard on my heels, and we move leftwards into a series of icy grooves running up the side of the final imposing rock buttress. Julio disappears out of sight, then the familiar pull on the rope comes. The icy grooves are difficult – as hard as anything on the climb yet, and I'm tiring now.

Julio's pulling doesn't help as it off-balances me, but I struggle on, and as I pull over the top of the steepest section, the summit of the Aigulle du Midi and the *téléférique* station come into view, less than 100 metres away. A joyful sight. Manu joins us on the level platform at the top of the buttress and the three of us continue together along the final narrow ridge until we reach the railings of the *téléférique* station and the top of our climb.

I said that I'd come here asking questions. Questions about why what had happened, happened. Questions about how it might have been prevented. Questions of the meaning of life, death and fate. Well, I know that I'll never find answers to those questions – not in this life anyway – but perhaps it's important to ask the questions nevertheless. By asking myself those fundamental questions, and in realising that they cannot be answered, I learn something about myself, learn how truly remarkable and mysterious this world is, and how incredibly lucky I am to be alive and able to experience it.

Safely installed on the terrace of the *'frique* station, Manu, Julio and I hug and shake hands and congratulate each other with beaming smiles. I strip off my hot, sweaty climbing equipment while Manu takes photos with his little camera. In the background, the great white dome of Mont Blanc, the highest mountain in Western Europe, rises majestically above all the surrounding peaks.

'Next year,' says Manu, 'next year you must return for a belle ascent of the Mont Blanc!'

'OK, Manu,' I reply, 'next year.'

Index

Index

Index

Index